GEOMETRIC KNIT BLANKETS

Date: 4/6/21

GEOMETRIC KNIT BLANKETS

MARGARET HOLZMANN

STACKPOLE
BOOKS

Guilford, Connecticut

Published by Stackpole Books
An imprint of The Rowman & Littlefield Publishing Group, Inc.
4501 Forbes Blvd., Ste. 200
Lanham, MD 20706
www.stackpolebooks.com

Distributed by NATIONAL BOOK NETWORK
800-462-6420

British Library Cataloguing in Publication Information available

Library of Congress Cataloging-in-Publication Data available
Names: Holzmann, Margaret, author.
Title: Geometric knit blankets / Margaret Holzmann.
Description: Guilford, Connecticut : Stackpole Books, [2021] | Summary:
  "Tired of those same old ripple afghans, cable and lace blankets? The
  patterns in this book are inspired by quilts, tile, and other geometric
  designs. Every blanket is a unique statement of your style or focal
  point for your room, and all are for the intermediate knitter or
  confident beginner"— Provided by publisher.
Identifiers: LCCN 2020033361 (print) | LCCN 2020033362 (ebook) | ISBN
  9780811738682 (paperback) | ISBN 9780811768665 (epub)
Subjects: LCSH: Knitting—Patterns. | Blankets. | Afghans (Coverlets) |
  Repetitive patterns (Decorative arts)
Classification: LCC TT825 .H64 2021 (print) | LCC TT825 (ebook) | DDC
  746.43/2041—dc23
LC record available at https://lccn.loc.gov/2020033361
LC ebook record available at https://lccn.loc.gov/2020033362

♾™ The paper used in this publication meets the minimum requirements of American National
Standard for Information Sciences—Permanence of Paper for Printed Library Materials, ANSI/
NISO Z39.48-1992.

First Edition

CONTENTS

Patterns

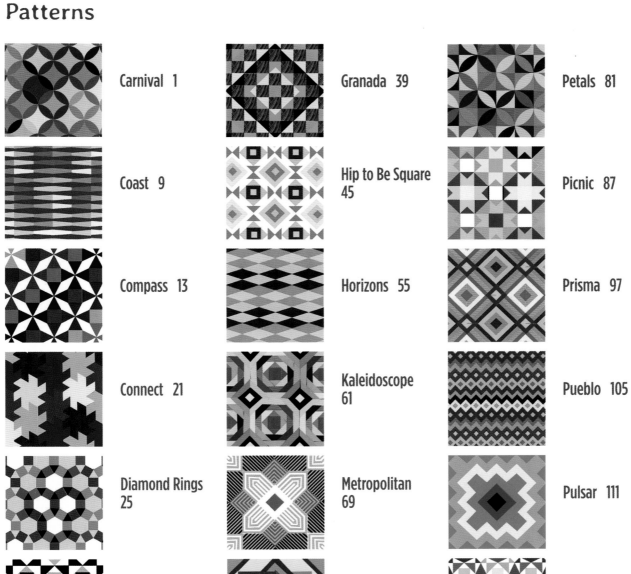

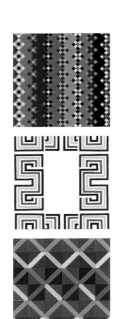
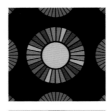
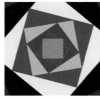

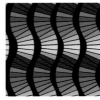
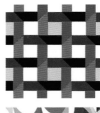

GENERAL NOTES FOR ALL PATTERNS

1. Symbols are used on construction figures and at the beginning of each pattern to indicate which techniques are used. The technique symbol key is shown below.

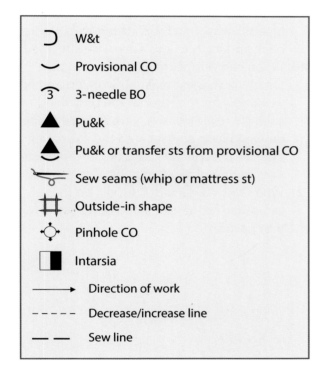

⊃	W&t
⌣	Provisional CO
3	3-needle BO
▲	Pu&k
◮	Pu&k or transfer sts from provisional CO
⟋	Sew seams (whip or mattress st)
⊞	Outside-in shape
◇	Pinhole CO
◧	Intarsia
⟶	Direction of work
- - - -	Decrease/increase line
——	Sew line

2. Some blankets have multiple construction options. The techniques used by a construction method are listed next to its name in the pattern and are shown in the key above.

3. Because skills needed are specified for each blanket, no skill levels have been included.

4. Most blankets require a 40"/100 cm circular needle (but longer is also fine) to work a garter stitch border picked up on each edge of the completed blanket face. Many blankets have smaller knitted components that may be knitted on shorter circular or straight needles, if desired.

5. Some blankets require a square that is worked outside-in or inside-out. Where double-pointed needles (dpns) are called for, the magic loop method or two circular needles may be substituted, with markers placed where stitches would have been divided between dpns.

6. When markers (m) are used, slip them when they are encountered unless directions say to remove and/or replace. Directions do not explicitly say when to slip markers.

7. When picking up stitches on the edges of completed pieces, a crochet hook of the same size as the knitting needle may be used. Always insert needle through two loops on the edge.

8. Blanket instructions may refer to a "garter st ridge," which is created by working two consecutive knit rows. One ridge equals two rows.

9. Blankets that are sewn together may call for "whip stitch" or "mattress stitch." See "Glossary" for how to work these stitches to seam together garter stitch pieces.

10. On blankets that use the wrap & turn technique, when knitting a wrapped stitch, knit only the stitch on the needle. Do not knit wraps and wrapped stitches together.

11. On blankets that specify a garter stitch border, an I-cord or Sawtooth border can be substituted if desired. Instructions for these alternate borders are found at the end of the book.

12. A gauge has been specified for all patterns. Check gauge before starting, and change needle size if needed to obtain gauge. Block gauge swatch if using a natural fiber yarn. Yarn requirements are based on the given gauge; if gauge is different, more or less

yarn may be required. Gauge may differ from yarn label because it is calculated over garter stitch, whereas yarn labels generally use stockinette stitch.

13. Yarn weight has been specified in the materials to aid in substitutions. Changing to a different yarn weight and needle size will result in a larger or smaller blanket. If using a heavier weight yarn than called for in the pattern, add 5 percent to yarn requirements for each 0.5 stitch per inch decrease between pattern gauge and gauge of substitute yarn. If using a lighter weight yarn than called for in the pattern, decrease yarn requirements by 5 percent for each 0.5 stitch per inch increase between pattern gauge and gauge of substitute yarn.

14. Blocking is not recommended for blankets worked in 100 percent acrylic yarn and will not yield any improvements. For blankets worked in other fibers, follow manufacturer's laundering instructions, lay blanket on a flat surface and shape to final measurements, or steam block to final measurements.

15. If a pattern says to "leave a long tail" when cutting yarn but does not specify a length, leave a tail three times the length of the seam to be sewn.

16. On bind-offs, when knitting the last stitch of the row, lift the stitch below up onto the needle and knit both stitches together, and then fasten off.

17. Use a knitted cast-on (CO) for all cast-ons unless otherwise specified. If a CO edge will later have stitches picked up on it, a provisional CO may be substituted.

18. For blankets worked as one piece, or on shapes with a small number of stitches, it may be convenient to purl backward on rows with a small number of stitches to avoid having to turn the work frequently (see "Glossary").

19. Pattern stitches/shapes (illustrated in light blue boxes within the patterns) are worked back and forth unless otherwise specified.

20. When carrying yarn between uses, patterns will suggest twisting working and non-working yarn together at the beginning of each RS row. However, yarn may be draped between uses and secured by alternately inserting needle over and under the draped yarn during pick up and knit along the edge.

21. When dpns are used, they will be the same size as the circular needles listed for that pattern.

TECHNIQUES USED IN BLANKETS

Knitters have favorite techniques and those they like to avoid. One person may dislike working in the round, and another may avoid intarsia at all costs. To help you figure out which blankets are best suited to your knitting preferences, the following diagram provides a quick reference. A list of technique symbols is also included at the beginning of each pattern.

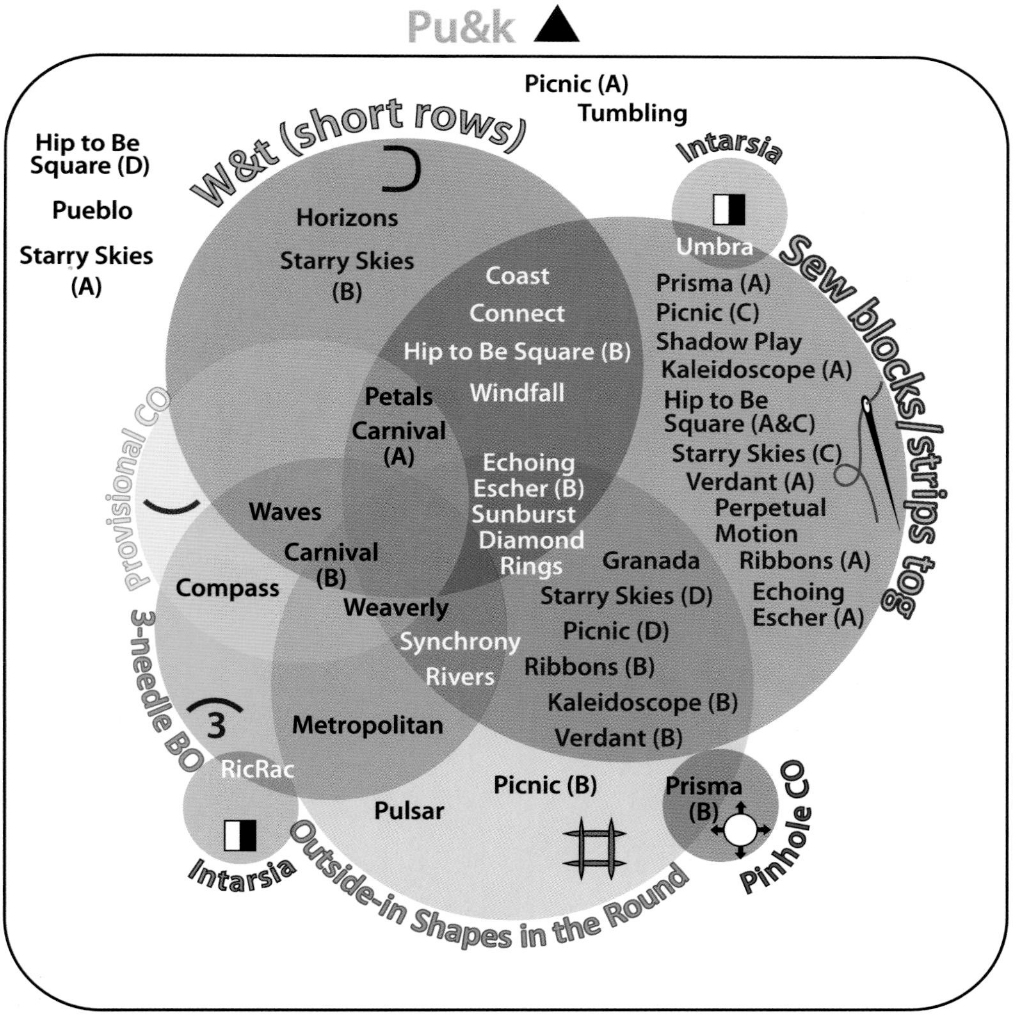

Pu&k
Picnic (A)
Tumbling
Hip to Be Square (D)
Pueblo
Starry Skies (A)
W&t (short rows)
Intarsia
Horizons
Starry Skies (B)
Umbra
Sew blocks/strips tog
Coast
Connect
Hip to Be Square (B)
Windfall
Prisma (A)
Picnic (C)
Shadow Play
Kaleidoscope (A)
Hip to Be Square (A&C)
Starry Skies (C)
Verdant (A)
Perpetual Motion
Ribbons (A)
Echoing Escher (A)
Petals
Carnival (A)
Echoing Escher (B)
Sunburst
Diamond Rings
Provisional CO
Waves
Carnival (B)
Compass
Weaverly
Granada
Starry Skies (D)
Picnic (D)
Synchrony
Rivers
Ribbons (B)
Kaleidoscope (B)
Verdant (B)
3-needle BO
3
Metropolitan
RicRac
Pulsar
Picnic (B)
Prisma (B)
Pinhole CO
Intarsia
Outside-in Shapes in the Round

Carnival

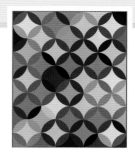

Colorful circles evoke the excitement and fun of a summer carnival.

. . . .

Techniques

Method A: ▲ ⊃ ⌣ 🛩

Method B: ▲ ⊃ ⌣ ↷ ♯

Size

54 x 66"/137 x 168 cm

Yarn

Sugarbush Bold, worsted (100% extra fine superwash merino; 190 yd./174 m; 3.5 oz./100 g):

A: 2 balls Clover (chartreuse)
B: 2 balls Fir (olive green)
C: 2 balls Pine Pass (light olive green)
D: 4 balls Bisque (light yellow)
E: 1 ball Fleur de Rose (bright magenta)
F: 2 balls Copper Mine (bright orange)
G: 1 ball Plumtastic (plum)
H: 1 ball Prairie Gold (gold)
I: 1 ball Trinity Bay Blue (cobalt blue)
J: 2 balls Cabot Blue (baby blue)
K: 1 ball Rusty Road (rust)
L: 2 balls Dover's Sand (ecru)
M: 5 balls Spruce Grove (green-gray)
N: 2 balls Silver Islet (silver-gray)
O: 1 ball Maritime Mauve (dark purple)
P: 2 balls Baffin Blue (Wedgewood blue)
Q: 1 ball Deep Blue Superior (navy)
R: 1 ball Truro Teal (medium green)
S: 1 ball Mossy Teal (dark teal)

Needles

US Size 8/5 mm, 40"/100 cm circular needles, US Size 8/5 mm dpns (Method B)

Notions

US Size 7/4.5 mm crochet hook, tapestry needle, stitch markers, stitch holders

Gauge

17 sts and 34 rows = 4"/10 cm in garter st

Notes

• There are two methods, A and B, for constructing the blanket face (see Figure 1). Method A is worked in blocks that have crocheted edges and are sewn together. Method B starts by working the Lens shapes that are arranged in groups and connected with a 4-Point Star.

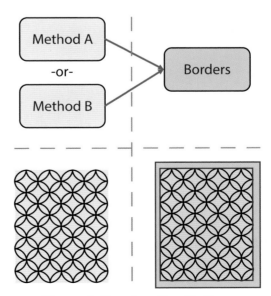

Figure 1: *Construction Options*

- In Method A as well as Method B, the Lens shapes are worked using a wrap & turn technique (see "Glossary"). In Method B, the 4-Point Stars between the Lenses are worked in the round, outside-in, using 3-needle BO to create the angled points.
- The borders are picked up and knit the same in both methods.
- This blanket uses the same shapes and general design as the Petals blanket on page 81 but is worked in a different gauge and colors.
- Long tails of 100"/254 cm are used for crochet edge around blocks, and 25"/60 cm tails are used for sewing blocks together.

Blanket Instructions

METHOD A

Block
Make 80 Blocks using the color and construction chart in Figure 2 and color combinations in Figure 3. A Block consists of a Lens and two Triangles (T1, T2) and is finished with a single-crochet edging.

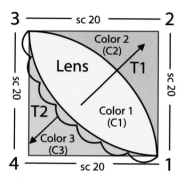

Figure 2: *Color and Construction Chart for Block – Method A*

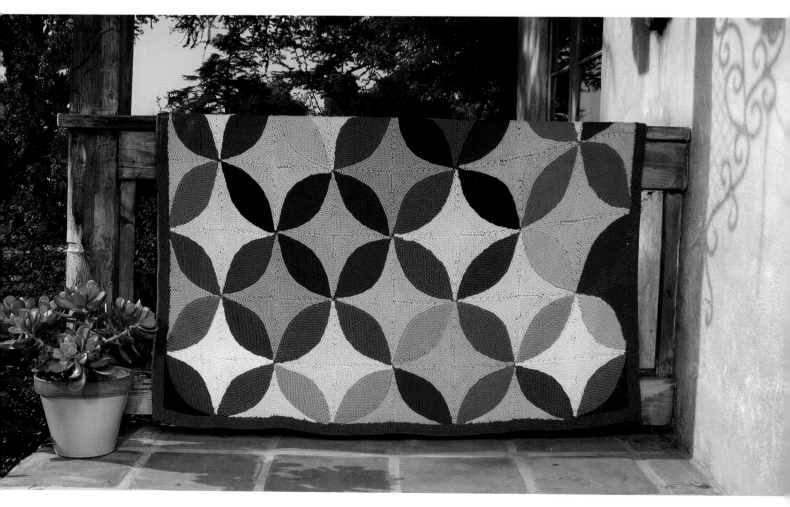

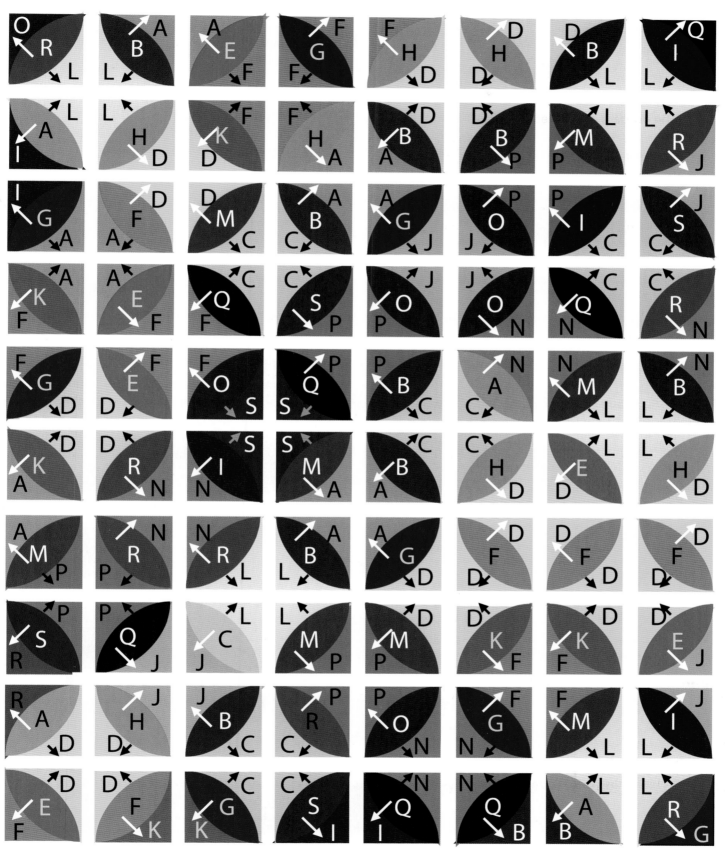

Figure 3: *Color Chart for Blocks – Method A*

Lens

With Color 1 (C1), provisionally CO 38 sts. Work [Lens]. Cut C1.

Lens – Both Methods—38 sts

Row 1 (RS): K22, w&t.
Row 2 (WS): K6, w&t.
Rows 3 & 4: Knit to 3 sts past wrap, w&t.
Rows 5 & 6: Knit to 2 sts past wrap, w&t.
Rows 7–12: Knit to 1 st past wrap, k1, w&t.
Rows 13–16: Knit to wrap, w&t.
Rows 17–20: Knit to 1 st bef wrap, w&t.
Rows 21–26: Knit to 2 sts bef wrap, w&t.
Row 27: Knit to 3 sts bef wrap, w&t.
Row 28: Knit to 5 sts bef wrap, w&t.
Row 29: Knit to 4 sts bef wrap, w&t.
Row 30: K4.

Note: *Row 30 ends in the middle of the row.*

Triangle 1 (T1)

On RS, attach Color 2 (C2) at beg of row, leaving a 100"/254 cm tail.

Tip: Wind tail into a ball or hank and secure with m or safety pin so that it stays wound while the block is worked.

Work [T]. Cut yarn, leaving a 25"/65 cm tail, and fasten off.

Triangle (T) – Both Methods—38 sts, increasing to 42 sts, decreasing to 1 st

Setup row (RS): K8, (bli, k7) 3 times, bli, knit to end—4 sts inc'd; 42 sts.
Row 1 (WS): Knit.
Row 2 (RS): BO 3, knit to end—3 sts dec'd; 39 sts.
Rows 3–7: Rep [Row 2]—15 sts dec'd; 24 sts.
Rows 8–13: BO 2, knit to end—12 sts dec'd; 12 sts.
Rows 14–24: K2tog, knit to end—11 sts dec'd; 1 st.

Triangle 2 (T2)

Transfer 38 provisional sts to needle. On RS, attach Color 3 (C3), leaving a 100"/254 cm tail. See previous Tip.
Work [T] as for T1.

Crochet Edges

At corners 1 and 3 in Figure 2, with the long C2/C3 CO tails, use a tapestry needle to take a st in the corner of the adjacent T and fasten securely.

With long tail of C2, working on RS and starting at corner 1 in Figure 2, *sc20 sts to next corner (1 st for each BO st), sc2 to turn corner, sc20 sts to next corner, slip st in corner*. Cut yarn and fasten off.

With long tail of C3, working on RS, starting at corner 3 in Figure 2, rep bet * and *. Fasten off, leaving extra yarn for sewing blocks.

Assembly

Lay out blocks as shown in Figure 3, orienting them according to the long and short arrows in Figure 2. Using long tails of matching yarn and whip st, sew tog blocks into vertical strips and then sew vertical strips tog, matching corners of blocks.

Continue at **Borders**.

METHOD B

Lens

Make 80 Lenses in the colors specified in Table 1. Place sts on holder and do not BO.

Color	Qty	Color	Qty	Color	Qty	Color	Qty
A	4	F	5	K	5	R	8
B	10	G	7	M	8	S	4
C	1	H	7	O	5		
E	6	I	4	Q	6		

Table 1: *Lens Color – Quantities*

Tip: If all 80 Lenses are worked first, use scrap yarn as st holders. Alternatively, work adjacent Lenses and then work the 4-Point Star to connect them; rep to form small modules that are joined with additional 4-Point Stars.

Assembly

4-Point Stars (4PS)

Lay out Lenses as in Figure 5, orienting them according to the arrow in Figure 4.

On RS, in the 12 star-shaped openings between sets of 4 Lenses in Figure 5, working clockwise around the opening, transfer 38 sts per Lens from holder or provisional CO to circular needle—152 sts. Attach yarn in color specified and work [4PS], changing to dpns when necessary to accommodate sts.

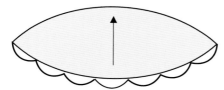

Figure 4: *Lens Construction and Orientation – Method B*

4-Point Stars (4PS) – Method B—152 sts, increasing to 168 sts, decreasing to 8 sts

Worked in the round. Pm bet each set of Lens sts.

Note: *When performing 3-needle BOs on odd-numbered Rnds 1–11, the BO crosses the BOR, using the last sts of the current rnd and the first sts of the next rnd. The last m is replaced at the new BOR.*

Setup rnd: *K8, (bli, k7) 3 times, bli, knit to m, sm; rep from * 3 times—16 sts inc'd; 168 sts.

Rnd 1: *Purl to m, rm, 3-needle BO 3 times, sl rem 1 st from 3rd needle to R needle, pm; rep from * 3 more times—20 sts dec'd; 148 sts.

Rnd 2: *Knit to 2 sts bef m, k2togtbl, sm; rep from * 3 more times—4 sts dec'd; 144 sts.

Rnds 3–6: Rep [Rnds 1 & 2] twice—48 sts dec'd; 96 sts.

Rnd 7: *Purl to m, rm, 3-needle BO 2 times, sl rem 1 st from 3rd needle to R needle, pm; rep from * 3 more times—12 sts dec'd; 84 sts.

Rnd 8: Rep [Rnd 2]—4 sts dec'd; 80 sts.

Rnds 9–12: Rep [Rnds 7 & 8] twice—32 sts dec'd; 48 sts.

Rnd 13: Purl.

Rnd 14: *Sm, k2tog, knit to 2 sts bef next m, ssk; rep from * 3 more times—8 sts dec'd; 40 sts.

Rnds 15–22: Rep [Rnds 13–14] 4 times—32 st dec'd; 8 sts.

Cut yarn, leaving a 10"/25 cm tail. Thread tail through tapestry needle. Insert needle through all rem sts on needle. Pull to tighten and fasten off securely.

2-Point Stars (2PS)

On RS, along edges of blanket, at each of the triangular-shaped openings between pairs of Lenses in Figure 6, retrieve 38 sts from provisional CO of each Lens—76 sts. Work [2PS].

2-Point Stars (2PS) – Method B—76 sts, decreasing to 4 sts

Pm bet the two sets of Lens sts.

Row 1: BO3, k8, (bli, k5) 4 times, knit to m, rm, 3-needle BO 3 times, sl rem 1 st from 3rd needle to R needle, pm; k8, (bli, k5) 4 times, knit to end—76 sts.

Row 2: BO3, knit to 1 st bef m, rm, k2togtbl, pm; knit to end—4 sts dec'd; 72 sts.

Row 3: BO3, knit to m, rm, 3-needle BO 3 times, sl rem 1 st from 3rd needle to R needle, pm; knit to end—8 sts dec'd; 64 sts.

Row 4: Rep [Row 2]—4 sts dec'd; 60 sts.

Rows 5 & 6: Rep [Rows 3 & 4]—12 sts dec'd; 48 sts.

Row 7: BO2, knit to m, rm, 3-needle BO 2 times, sl rem 1 st from 3rd needle to R needle, pm; knit to end—5 sts dec'd; 43 sts.

Row 8: BO2, knit to 1 st bef m, rm, k2togtbl, pm, knit to end—3 sts dec'd; 40 sts.

Rows 9–12: Rep [Rows 7 & 8] twice—16 sts dec'd; 24 sts.

Row 13: Knit.

Row 14: K2tog, knit to 2 sts bef m, ssk, k2tog, knit to last 2 sts, ssk—4 sts dec'd; 20 sts.

Rows 15–22: Rep [Rows 13 & 14] 4 times—16 sts dec'd; 4 sts.

Cut yarn, leaving a 10"/25 cm tail. Thread tail through tapestry needle. Insert needle through all rem sts on needle. Pull to tighten and fasten off securely.

Figure 5: *4-Point-Stars – Method B*

Corner Triangles

On RS, at each of the 4 corners of blanket in Figure 6, attach yarn in color specified, retrieve 38 sts from provisional CO of Lens and work [T].

Continue at **Borders**.

BORDERS – BOTH METHODS

Top Border

On RS, attach M to top-right corner of blanket. Pu&k 27 sts per T edge (54 per 2PS edge)—216 sts. Knit 11 rows. BO loosely.

Bottom Border

On RS, attach M to bottom-left corner of blanket. Rep as for Top Border.

Right Border

On RS, on right edge of blanket, attach M to the bottom-right corner of the Bottom Border. Pu&k 6 sts (one per garter st ridge) on the Bottom Border edge, 27 per T edge (54 per 2PS edge), and 6 sts on the Top Border—282 sts. Knit 11 rows. BO loosely.

Left Border

On RS, on left edge of blanket, attach M to the top-left corner of the Top Border. Rep as for Right Border.

FINISHING

Block to measurements. Weave in ends.

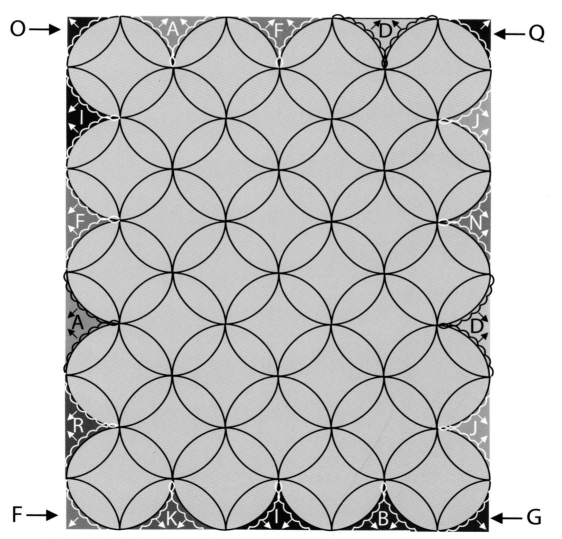

Figure 6: *2-Point Stars and Corners from Provisionally CO Sts – Method B*

Coast

Ocean breezes, waves, and sand dunes inspired this undulating striped blanket.

Techniques

▲ 🪡 ⊃

Size
53 x 73"/135 x 185 cm

Yarn
Premier Anti-Pilling Bamboo, chunky (80% anti-pilling acrylic/20% rayon from bamboo; 131 yd./120 m; 3.5 oz./100 g):

A: 19 skeins Blueberry Pie (blue-purple) #1085-13
C: 2 skeins Earl Grey (light gray) #1085-04

Premier, Puzzle Bulky (100% acrylic; 328 yd./300 m; 7 oz./200 g):

B: 7 skeins Riddle (self-striping blue, beige, and gray) #1050-07

Needles
US Size 9/5.5 mm, 40"/100 cm circular needles

Notions
Stitch holders, tapestry needle

Gauge
15 sts and 30 rows = 4"/10 cm in garter st

Notes
- This blanket is worked in strips, composed of alternating wedges that are made from short-row knitting. The strips are sewn together, and borders are added by picking up stitches from edges of the completed blanket face.
- To eliminate sewing strips together, use the join-as-you-go technique (see "Glossary") to attach the current strip to the previously completed strip during knitting.
- Pattern shapes begin on a RS row.

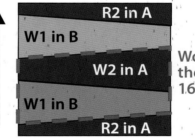

Work once, then rep 16 times

Strip 1

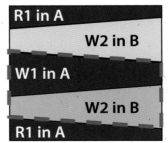

Work once, then rep 16 times

Strip 2

Figure 1: *Construction of Strips 1 and 2*

Blanket Instructions

See Figure 1 for construction of Strips 1 and 2.

Note: *If using the join-as-you-go method, alternate working Strip 1 and Strip 2, joining each subsequent strip to the last one worked (see Figure 2). When all 8 strips are complete, proceed to Border instructions.*

STRIPS

Do not cut yarn between uses. Carry non-working yarn alongside and twist with working yarn at the beg of each RS row.

Strip 1 – Make 4

With A, CO 22 sts, work [R2], *with B work [W1], with A work [W2], rep from * 16 more times, with B work [W1], with A work [R2]. Place sts on holder.

Wedge 1 (W1)—22 sts

Rows 1–3: Knit.
Row 4 (WS): K4, w&t.
Row 5 and all odd rows to 19: Knit.
Row 6: K11, w&t.
Row 8: K18, w&t.
Row 10: Knit
Row 12: K18, w&t.
Row 14: K11, w&t.
Row 16: K4, w&t.
Rows 18 & 20: Knit.

Wedge 2 (W2)—22 sts

Rows 1–4: Knit.
Row 5 (RS): K4, w&t.
Row 6 and all even rows to 20: Knit.
Row 7: K11, w&t.
Row 9: K18, w&t.
Row 11: Knit.
Row 13: K18, w&t.
Row 15: K11, w&t.
Row 17: K4, w&t.
Rows 19: Knit.

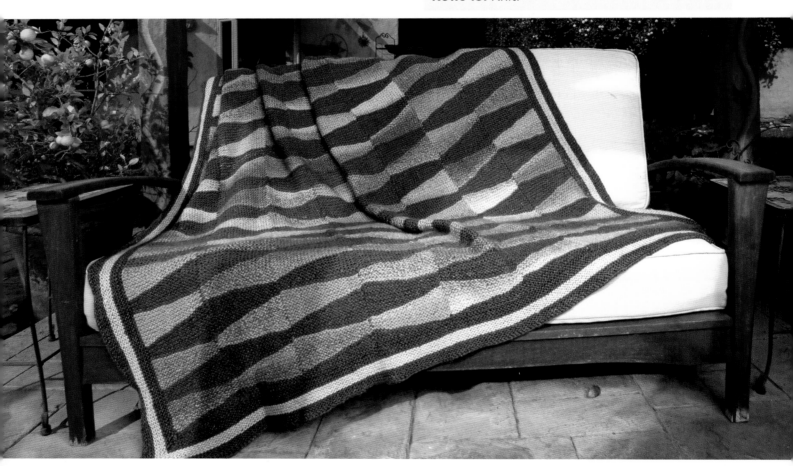

Ridge 1 (R1)—22 sts

Work [W1, Rows 11–20].

Ridge 2 (R2)—22 sts

Work [W2, Rows 11–20].

Strip 2 – Make 4

With A, CO 22 sts, work [R1], *with B work [W2], with A work [W1], rep from * 16 more times, with B work [W2], with A work [R1]. Place sts on holder.

ASSEMBLY

Lay out strips as shown in Figure 2. Using whip stitch and yarn color specified in Figure 2, sew strips tog.

BORDERS

Top Border

Transfer all Strip sts on holders to circular needle—22 sts per Strip; 176 sts. On RS, attach A to top-right corner of blanket.

Setup row (RS): Knit.

Row 1 (WS): Knit.

Row 2: Kf&b, knit to last st, kf&b—2 sts inc'd.

Row 3: Knit.

Rows 4–7: Rep [Rows 2 & 3] 2 times—4 sts inc'd. Cut A, leaving a 10"/25 cm tail.

Rows 8–15: With C, rep [Rows 2 & 3] 4 times—8 sts inc'd. Cut C, leaving a 10"/25 cm tail.

Rows 16–23: With A, rep [Rows 2 & 3] 4 times—8 sts inc'd; 198 sts. BO loosely. Cut A, leaving a 10"/25 cm tail.

Bottom Border

On RS, attach A to bottom-left corner of blanket, pu&k 176 sts along bottom edge (22 sts per strip). Rep from Row 1 of Top Border.

Right Border

On RS, attach A to bottom-right corner of blanket. Pu&k 252 sts (4 sts on the edge of each W1, 10 on the edge of each W2, and 2 on the edge of each R2). Work as for Top Border from Row 1, ending with 274 sts.

Left Border

On RS, attach A to top-left corner of blanket. Rep as for Right Border, picking up 4 sts on the edge of each W2, 10 on the edge of each W1, and 2 on the edge of each R1.

Using long tails of matching color, and whip st, sew tog the border corners.

FINISHING

Weave in ends.

Figure 2:
Assembly Diagram

Strip 1   Strip 2   Strip 1   Strip 2   Strip 1   Strip 2   Strip 1   Strip 2

Compass

Find your way home to the warmth and comfort of this colorful blanket.

. . . .

Techniques

Size

60.5 x 76.5"/154 x 194 cm

Yarn

Jaggerspun Yarns Mousam Falls, aran (100% superwash wool; 185 yd./169 m; 3.5 oz./100 g):
A: 2 hanks French Blue (medium blue)
B: 1 hank Artichoke (yellow-green)
C: 2 hanks Tourmaline (teal)
D: 3 hanks Lilac (light purple)
E: 3 hanks Bottle Green (true green)
F: 4 hanks Thistle (medium purple)
G: 3 hanks Plum (red-purple)
H: 2 hanks Lapis (dark purple)
I: 11 hanks Ecru (off-white)

Needles

2 US Size 7/4.5 mm, 40"/100 cm circular needles

Notions

Stitch holders or waste yarn, stitch markers, tapestry needle

Gauge

16 sts and 32 rows = 4"/10 cm in garter st

Notes

• Blanket begins with Compasses worked individually and assembled into strips by working a wedge on each Compass and joining wedges with a 3-needle bind-off. Strips are joined by working wedges on edges of strips and joining wedges with a 3-needle bind-off. Wedges are worked to fill in spaces on the edge of the blanket. Borders are worked from a combination of stitches on holders and stitches picked up on edges.
• Since many holders are needed, use of waste yarn is recommended.

Blanket Instructions

COMPASSES

The blanket has 4-, 3-, and 2-Point Compasses. 4-Point Compasses are used in the interior of the blanket, 3-Point Compasses make up the edges, and 2-Point Compasses form the blanket corners.

Make Compasses in colors and quantities specified in Table 1. An empty, gray cell indicates that the Point should not be worked for that Compass. For example, BA in the first row of the table is a 2-Point Compass; the Square is made in color B, South and East Points are worked in color A; there are no North or West Points.

Strip #	Name	Make	Color for:				
			Square	North Point	West Point	South Point	East Point
1	BA	1	B			A	A
2	CAD1	1	C	A	A	D	D
	CAD2	1	C	A		D	
	CAD3	1	C		A	D	D
3	EDF1	3	E	D	D	F	F
	EDF2	1	E	D		F	F
	EDF3	1	E		D	F	F
4	HFG1	5	H	F	F	G	G
	HFG2	1	H	F		G	G
	HFG3	1	H		F	G	
5	FGE1	5	F	G	G	E	E
	FGE2	1	F	G			E
	FGE3	1	F	G	G	E	
6	DEC1	3	D	E	E	C	C
	DEC2	1	D	E	E		C
	DEC3	1	D	E	E	C	
7	ACB1	1	A	C	C	B	B
	ACB2	1	A	C	C		B
	ACB3	1	A	C	C	B	
8	AB	1	A	B	B		

Table 1: *Color Schemes and Quantities for Compasses*

See Figure 1 for construction. When working Points, work only those needed, as indicated in Table 1.

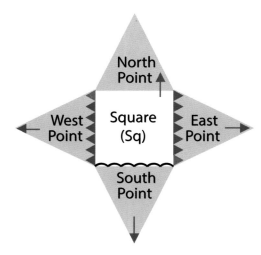

Figure 1: *Compass Construction*

Square (Sq)

In color specified in Table 1, work [Sq].

> **Square (Sq)—24 sts**
>
> Provisionally CO 24 sts.
> Knit 48 rows. Cut yarn but do not BO.

Points

North Point

Attach yarn color for North Point. Knit 1 row and then work [Pt].

> **Point (Pt)—24 sts dec'ing to 1 st**
>
> **Rows 1 & 3 (WS):** Knit.
> **Row 2 (RS):** Knit.
> **Row 4:** K2tog, knit to 2 sts bef end, ssk—2 sts dec'd; 22 sts.
> **Rows 5-7:** Knit.
> **Rows 8-47:** Rep [Rows 4-7] 10 times—20 sts dec'd; 2 sts.
> **Row 48:** K2tog—1 st dec'd; 1 st.
> Cut yarn and fasten off.

West Point

Attach yarn color for West Point at the red triangle on the left edge of Sq in Figure 1; pu&k 24 sts on left edge of Sq (one per garter st ridge) and work [Pt].

South Point

On RS, transfer 24 provisionally CO sts to needle, attach yarn color for South Point. Knit 1 row and then work [Pt].

East Point

Attach yarn color for East Point at the red triangle on the right edge of Sq in Figure 1; pu&k 24 sts to corner on the right edge of Sq (one per garter st ridge) and work [Pt].

CONSTRUCTING STRIPS

Lay out Compasses as shown in Figure 2.

Northwest Diamonds

See Figure 3 for construction.

Lower Wedges (LW)

In each of the 24 diamond-shaped openings in Strips 2–7, attach I at red triangle at the tip of the East Point. *Pu&k 24 sts evenly on edge (1 st per garter st ridge), 1 st in the corner of Sq, pm, and 24 sts to the next corner—49 sts. Work [Wd]* and then transfer sts to holder and cut yarn.

> **Wedge (Wd)**—49 sts inc'ing to 53 sts, dec'ing to 47 sts
>
> **Row 1 (WS):** K8, bli, k8, bli, knit to 16 sts bef end, bli, k8, bli, knit to 3 sts bef end, w&t—53 sts; 50 sts bet wraps.
>
> **Row 2 (RS):** Knit to 2 sts bef m, rm, cdd, pm, knit to 3 sts bef end, w&t—2 sts dec'd, 51 sts; 45 sts bet wraps.

Row 3: Knit to 3 sts bef wrap, w&t—42 sts bet wraps.

Rows 4–7: Rep [Row 3] 4 times—30 sts bet wraps.

Row 8: Knit to 2 sts bef m, rm, cdd, pm, knit to 3 sts bef wrap, w&t—2 sts dec'd, 49 sts; 25 sts bet wraps.

Rows 9–13: Rep [Row 3] 5 times—10 sts bet wraps.

Row 14: Rep [Row 8]—2 sts dec'd; 47 sts; 5 sts bet wraps.

Row 15: Knit to end.

Upper Wedges (UW)

On the adjacent Compasses, attach I at red triangle at the tip of the West Point. Work as for Lower Wedge bet * and *, and do not cut yarn.

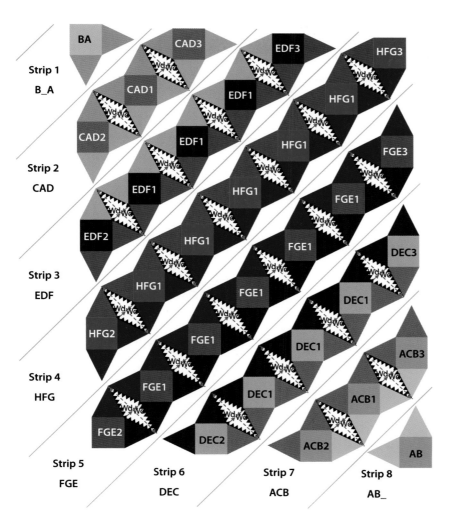

Figure 2:
Constructing Strips from Compasses for Northwest Diamond

Joining Wedges

Transfer the sts of Lower Wedge from holder to needle so that work is ready to beg on RS. With RS of Upper Wedge and Lower Wedge tog, 3-needle BO across the 47 sts on each needle. Tie end yarns tog to close Points on either end of Diamond. Do not weave in ends until Finishing.

ASSEMBLING STRIPS

Arrange Strips as shown in Figure 4.

Northeast Diamonds

Lower Wedges (LW)

In each of the 24 diamond-shaped openings bet strips, attach I at red triangle and work as for Northwest Lower Wedge, picking up sts on North and West Point edges.

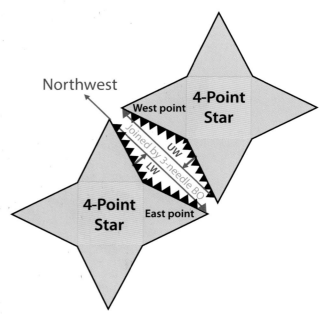

Figure 3: *Construction of Northwest Diamond*

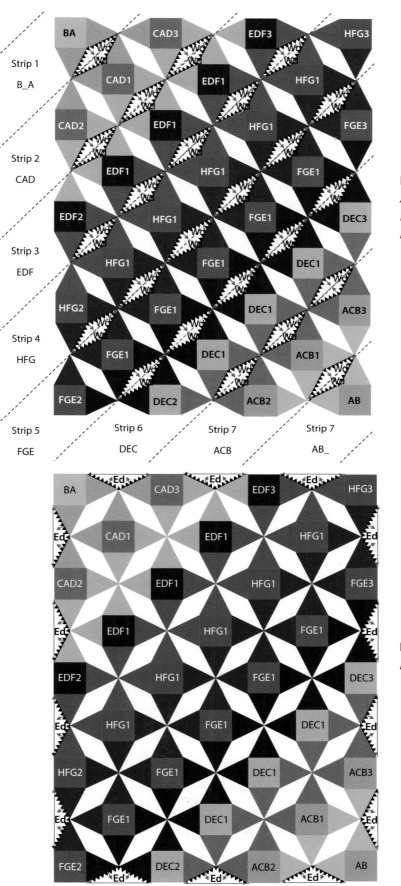

Figure 4:
Assembling Strips for Northeast Diamonds

Figure 5:
Edges

Upper Wedges (UW)

On adjacent Compasses, attach I and work as for Northwest Upper Wedge, picking up sts on South and East Point edges. Transfer sts to holder and cut yarn.

Joining Wedges and Strips

When all Wedges along the dashed lines are complete, transfer all sts from holder(s) for one strip to circular needle so that RS is ready to work. Transfer all sts from holders for adjacent strip to a 2nd circular needle so that RS sts are ready to work. With RS of Upper and Lower Wedges tog, attach I and perform 3-needle BO across all sts. Cut yarn and fasten off.

Where 4 Points come tog, close the gaps by threading the yarn tail of a Wedge onto a tapestry needle. Working around the opening, insert needle into each consecutive Wedge and Point, and then pull tight and tie off securely.

Edges

At each of the 14 white spaces marked "Ed" in Figure 5, attach I at red triangle. Pu&k 24 sts evenly along edge (1 st per garter st ridge), 1 st bet Points, pm, and 24 sts to tip of next Point—49 sts. Work [Ed]. Transfer sts to holder.

> **Edge (Ed)**—49 sts inc'ing to 53 sts dec'ing to 43 sts
>
> **Row 1 (WS):** K8, bli, k8, bli, knit to 16 sts bef end, bli, k8, bli, knit to 2 sts bef end, w&t—53 sts; 51 sts bet wraps.
>
> **Row 2 (RS):** Knit to 2 sts bef m, rm, cdd, pm, knit to 2 sts bef end, w&t—2 sts dec'd; 51 sts; 47 sts bet wraps.
>
> **Row 3:** Knit to 2 sts bef wrap, w&t—45 sts bet wraps.
>
> **Rows 4–5:** Rep [Row 3] 2 times—41 sts bet wraps.
>
> **Row 6:** Knit to 2 sts bef m, rm, cdd, pm, knit to 2 sts bef wrap, w&t—2 sts dec'd; 49 sts; 37 sts bet wraps.
>
> **Rows 7–9:** Rep [Row 3] 3 times—31 sts bet wraps.
>
> **Rows 10–17:** Rep [Rows 6–9] 2 times—4 sts dec'd; 45 sts; 11 sts bet wraps.
>
> **Rows 18–20:** Rep [Rows 6–8] once—2 sts dec'd; 43 sts; 3 sts bet wraps.
>
> **Row 21:** Knit to end.

BORDERS

Right Border

On RS, attach I at bottom-right corner of blanket. Pu&k 24 sts on edge of each Sq and knit across 43 sts of each Ed from holders—292 sts.
Knit 13 rows. BO loosely.

Left Border

Attach I at top-left corner of blanket, and rep as for Right Border.

Top Border

On RS, attach I at top-right edge of Right Border. Pu&k 7 sts on edge of Right Border, 1 st bet border and blanket body, knit across 24 sts of each Sq and 43 sts of each Ed from holders, pu&k 1 st bet border and blanket body, and 7 sts on edge of Left Border—241 sts. Knit 13 rows. BO loosely.

Bottom Border

Attach I at bottom-left edge of Left Border. Work as for Top Border.

FINISHING

Weave in ends.

Connect

Interconnecting whirling disks in subdued colors create the illusion of motion on this small rectangular blanket.

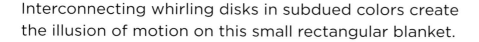

Techniques

Size
46 x 58.5"/117 x 149 cm

Yarn
Erika Knight Wild Wool, aran (85% wool/15% nettle; 186 yd./170 m; 3.5 oz./100 g):
A: 4 hanks Mooch (purple)
B: 3 hanks Pootle (gold)
C: 2 hanks Traipse (gray)
D: 2 hanks Wander (blue)
E: 2 hanks Brisk (green)
F: 2 hanks Dawdle (pink)
G: 2 hanks Meander (light blue)

Needles
US Size 8/5 mm, 40"/100 cm circular needles

Notions
Stitch holder, tapestry needle

Gauge
15 sts and 30 rows = 4"/10 cm in garter st

Note
• This blanket is worked in strips composed of triangles and rectangles. The strips can be sewn together or joined as they are knitted.

Blanket Instructions

For all shapes, except those in Strip 16, leave a tail 4 times the length of the edge of the shape to be sewn (the length along the strip edge from the point where the yarn color was joined).

The abbreviation "cc" means change color. Refer to Figure 1 for shape key and to Figure 2 for construction and color changes. After completing a strip, add sts to circular needle or long piece of scrap yarn.

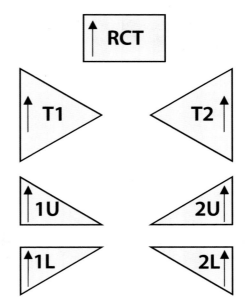

Figure 1: *Shape Key*

Note: *On Strips 8, 9, and 16, there is no final cc; continue with A for the subsequent shapes.*

Track progress by making a checkmark next to each shape in Figure 1 as it is completed.

Strip 1: CO 10 sts. Work: [Rct] 2 times, *[2U], cc [1L], [Rct], [2U], cc [T1], cc [T2], cc [1L], [Rct]; rep from * 5 times, [Rct] 3 times.

Strip 2: CO 10 sts. *Work: [1U], cc [2L], [Rct] 5 times; rep from * 5 times, [1U], cc [2L], [Rct] 4 times.

Strip 3: CO 10 sts. Work: [Rct], *[1U], cc [2L], [Rct] 5 times; rep from * 5 times, [1U], cc [2L], [Rct] 3 times.

Strip 4: CO 10 sts. * Work: [Rct], [2U], cc [T1], cc [T2], cc [1L], [Rct], [2U], cc [1L]; rep from * 5 times, [Rct], [2U], cc [T1], cc [T2], cc [1L], [Rct].

Strip 5: CO 10 sts. Work: [Rct] 3 times, *[1U], cc [2L], [Rct] 5 times; rep from * 5 times, [1U], cc [2L], [Rct].

Strip 6: CO 10 sts. Work: [Rct] 4 times, *[1U], cc [2L], [Rct] 5 times; rep from * 5 times, [1U], cc [2L].

Strip 7: CO 10 sts. Work: [Rct] 2 times, *[2U], cc [1L], Rct, [2U], cc [T1] cc [T2], cc [1L], [Rct]; rep from * 5 times, [2U], cc [1L], [Rct] 2 times.

Strips 8–13: Rep Strips 2–7.

Strips 14–16: Rep Strips 2–4.

Rectangle (Rct)—10 sts

Knit 10 rows.

Triangle 1 (T1)—10 sts

Row 1 and all RS rows to 19: Knit.
Row 2 (WS): K1, w&t.
Rows 4, 6, 8, 10: Knit 1 st past wrap, w&t.
Rows 12, 14, 16, 18: Knit to 2 sts bef wrap, w&t.
Row 20: Knit.

Triangle 2 (T2)—10 sts

Row 1 (RS): K1, w&t.
Row 2 and all WS rows to 20: Knit.
Rows 3, 5, 7, 9: Knit to 1 st past wrap, w&t.
Rows 11, 13, 15, 17: Knit to 2 sts bef wrap, w&t.
Row 19: Knit.

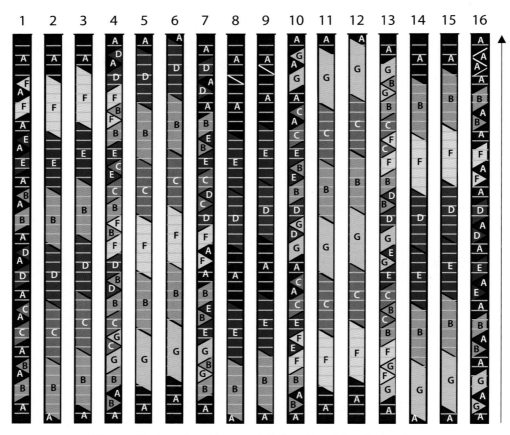

Figure 2: *Construction and Color Chart for Strips 1–16*

Triangle 1L (1L)—10 sts

Row 1 and all RS rows to 9: Knit.
Row 2 (WS): K1, w&t.
Rows 4, 6, 8, 10: Knit to 1 st past wrap, w&t.

Triangle 1U (1U)—10 sts

Row 1 and all RS rows to 9: Knit.
Row 2 (WS): Knit to last st, w&t.
Rows 4, 6, 8, 10: Knit to 2 sts bef wrap, w&t.

Triangle 2L (2L)—10 sts

Row 1 (RS): K1, w&t.
Row 2 and all WS rows to 10: Knit.
Rows 3, 5, 7, 9: Knit to 1 st past wrap, w&t.

Triangle 2U (2U)—10 sts

Row 1 (RS): Knit to last st, w&t.
Row 2 and all WS rows to 10: Knit.
Rows 3, 5, 7, 9: Knit to 2 sts bef wrap, w&t.

ASSEMBLY

Lay out strips as shown in Figure 2. Pm after every fifth garter st ridge in areas of strips that have multiple reps of Rct to help align the shapes. Sew all strips tog using whip st and long tails.

BORDERS

Top Border

With 160 sts accumulated on circular needle or scrap yarn, attach A on RS and knit 12 rows. BO loosely.

Bottom Border

Starting on the bottom-left corner of the RS, attach A, pu&k 10 sts per strip—160 sts. Knit 11 rows. BO loosely.

Right Border

Starting on the bottom-right corner of the RS, attach A, pu&k 7 sts on the edge of the Bottom Border, 205 sts evenly along the edge of strip (1 per garter st ridge) and 7 sts on the Top Border edge—219 sts. Knit 11 rows. BO loosely.

Left Border

Starting at the top-left corner, attach A and rep as for Right Border.

FINISHING

Weave in ends. Block to measurements.

Diamond Rings

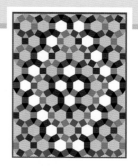

Interconnected rings in a myriad of blues and mauve remind us of family bonds and promises kept.

Techniques

Size
54 x 71"/137 x 180 cm

Yarn
Anzula For Better or Worsted (80% superwash merino/10% cashmere/10% nylon; 200 yd./182 m; 4 oz./115 g):
A: 5 hanks Lapis (gray-blue)
B: 2 hanks Ballerina (pink)
C: 2 hanks Birdie (bright, medium blue)
D: 2 hanks Aqua (teal)
E: 2 hanks Chiva (royal blue)
F: 8 hanks Seabreeze (light teal)
G: 2 hanks Blueberry (purple-blue)
H: 2 hanks Black (black)
I: 4 hanks Au Natural (off-white)

Needles
US Size 7/4.5 mm, 40"/100 cm circular needles and dpns

Notions
Stitch holders, stitch markers, tapestry needle

Gauge
18 sts and 36 rows = 4"/10 cm in garter st

Notes
- This blanket is worked in diagonal strips that are sewn together. Edge inserts and corners are worked to complete the rectangular shape.
- The blanket is worked in garter stitch; if preferred, WS rows may be worked by purling backward to avoid turning work (see "Glossary" for more information).
- Garter stitch borders are added last.
- Markers referred to in pattern stitches are placed in the written instructions.
- On Figures, the location to begin pu&k is marked with a red triangle.

Blanket Instructions

For all Strips, refer to Figure 1 for yarn colors. On the final shape worked for each strip, cut yarn, leaving a tail 3 times the length of the strip seam to be sewn.

Strip 1: CO 14 sts. Work ([S], [T]) 3 times, work [S], BO.

Square (S)—14 sts

Rows 1 (RS)–28 (WS): Knit.

Note: *When starting an S after a pu&k, beg on Row 2.*

Triangle (T)—14 sts

Row 1 (WS): K1, w&t next st.
Row 2: Knit.
Row 3: Knit to 1 st after wrap, w&t.
Rows 4–13: Rep [Rows 2 & 3] 5 times.
Rows 14, 16 & 18: Knit.
Row 15: Knit to 2 sts bef wrap, w&t.
Rows 17–26: Rep [Rows 15 & 16] 5 times.
Row 27: Knit.

Hexagon Insert: Using dpns, CO 28 sts on first dpn, pu&k 14 sts on inner edge of each of squares 1 and 2 and place on second dpn, pu&k 14 sts on the inner edge of each edge of completed squares 3 and 4 and place on third dpn (see Figure 2). Pm's at each 14th interval in the middle of each dpn. Join in a circle, untwisting sts—84 sts. Work [H].

Hexagon (H)—84 st dec'ing to 12 sts

Worked in the round.
Rnd 1 and all odd rows (WS): Purl.
Rnd 2: *K2tog, knit to 2 sts bef end of dpn or m, ssk; rep from * 5 times—12 sts dec'd; 72 sts.
Rnd 4: Knit.
Rnds 5–24: Rep [Rnds 1–4] 5 times—60 sts dec'd; 12 sts.
Cut yarn, leaving a 8"/20 cm tail. Thread yarn on needle and draw through all sts on needle. Tighten and fasten off.

Strip 2: Work as for Strip 1. *Pu&k 14 sts on the left edge of the 3rd triangle (see Figure 3 for attachment point for next hexagon). Work ([S], [T]) twice, work [S]. BO. Work [H] insert in hexagon frame.* Rep bet * and * once.

Strip 3: Work as for Strip 2, rep bet * and * 3 times.

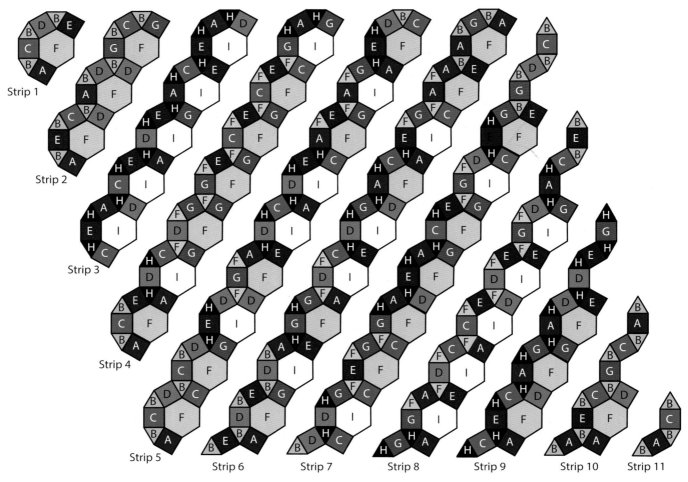

Figure 1: *Color Chart*

Strip 4: Work as for Strip 2, rep bet * and * 5 times.

Strip 5: Work as for Strip 2, rep bet * and * 7 times.

Strip 6: CO 14 sts, work [T, S] twice. BO. *Pu&k 14 sts on the left edge of the 2nd triangle as shown in Figure 4. Work ([S], [T]) twice, work [S]. BO. Work [H] insert in hexagon frame, as for Strip 1.* Rep bet * and * 8 times.

Strip 7: Work as for Strip 6, rep bet * and * 6 times.

On left side of the 2nd triangle of last rep pu&k 14 sts as shown in Figure 5. Work ([S], [T]) twice. BO. On the left edge of last triangle, pu&k 14 sts, work [S], [T]. Cut and fasten off. Work [H] Insert in each hexagon frame, as for Strip 1.

Strip 8: Work as for Strip 7, rep bet * and * 4 times.

Strip 9: Work as for Strip 7, rep bet * and * 2 times.

Strip 10: Work as for Strip 7, rep bet * and * 0 times.

Strip 11: Work [T], [S], [T] BO. On left edge of second T, pu&k 14 sts as shown in Figure 6, work [S, T]. BO.

ASSEMBLY

Align strips as shown in Figure 1 and sew with mattress st, using long tails of matching color and matching seams. Figure 7 shows the blanket face highlighting the locations of Corners, Side Wedges/Dishes, and Top/Bottom Wedges.

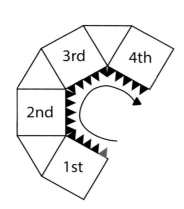

Figure 2: *Pick Up and Knit Sts for Hexagon*

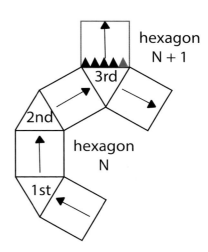

Figure 3: *Attachment Point for Next Hexagon*

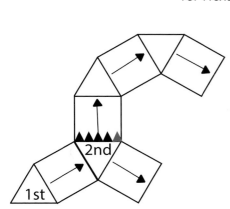

Figure 4:
Beginning of Strips 6–10

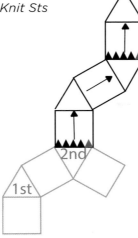

Figure 5:
End of Strips 7–10

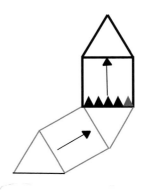

Figure 6:
Construction of Strip 11

Green – Top/Bottom Wedges

Red – Side Half Hexagons and Dishes

Blue – Corners

Figure 7: *Assembled Blanket Showing Location of Wedges, Dishes, and Corners*

EDGE SHAPES AND BORDERS

Corners

Working on the RS, starting on the top-right corner of blanket, attach F at red triangle on edge 1 in Figure 8. *Pu&k 14 sts to next corner, pm, 14 sts to next corner on edge 2—28 sts.

Work [CR]—36 sts. Cut and fasten off, transferring sts to holder.*

Rep bet * and * on edges 3 & 4, 5 & 6, and 7 & 8.

Corner (CR)—28 sts inc'ing to 36 sts

Row 1 (WS): Knit to 1 st bef m, bli, k1, k1, bli, knit to 2 st bef end of row, w&t—2 sts inc'd; 30 sts.

Row 2: Knit to 2 sts bef end of row, w&t.

Row 3: Knit to 2 sts bef wrap, w&t.

Row 4: Rep [Row 3].

Row 5: Knit to 1 st bef m, bli, k1, k1, bli, knit to 2 sts bef wrap, w&t—2 sts inc'd; 32 sts.

Rows 6–8: Rep [Row 3] 3 times.

Row 9: Rep [Row 5]—2 sts inc'd; 34 sts.

Rows 10–13: Rep [Rows 6–9]—2 sts inc'd; 36 sts.

Rows 14–16: Rep [Rows 6–8].

Row 17: Knit.

Note: *Illustration does not show all blanket repeats.*

Top Wedges

Starting on the top-right corner of blanket, on the RS of the inset shape shown in Figure 9, attach F and pu&k 14 sts on edge 1, pm, and 14 sts on edge 2—28 sts.

Work [W]—22 sts. Cut and fasten off, transferring sts to holder. Rep for other 4 inset shapes on top edge of blanket.

Wedge (W)—28 sts dec'ing to 22 sts

Row 1 (WS): Knit to 2 sts bef m, k2tog, ssk, knit to 2 sts from end, w&t—2 sts dec'd; 26 sts.

Row 2: Knit to 2 sts from end, w&t.

Row 3: Knit to 2 sts bef wrap, w&t.

Row 4: Rep [Row 3].

Row 5: Knit to 2 sts bef m, k2tog, ssk, knit to 2 sts bef wrap, w&t—2 sts dec'd; 24 sts.

Rows 6–8: Rep [Row 3] 3 times.

Row 9: Rep [Row 5]—2 sts dec'd; 22 sts.

Row 10: Rep [Row 3].

Row 11: Knit.

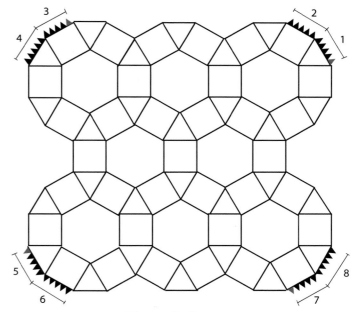

Figure 8: *Corners*

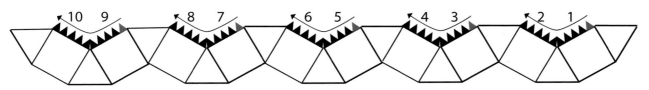

Figure 9: *Top and Bottom Wedges*

Top Border

On RS, starting at the top-right corner, attach A and knit 18 sts after corner marker from Corner sts on holder, *pu&k 14 sts along edge of adjoining triangle, knit 22 sts from Wedge sts on holder; rep from * 4 times, pu&k 14 sts along last T, knit 18 sts to corner marker from Corner sts on holder—230 sts. Knit 11 rows.
BO loosely. Cut and fasten off.

Bottom Wedges and Border

Rep instructions for Top Wedges and Border on bottom edge of blanket.

Right Side Inserts

Step 1: Half Hexagon

On RS, starting on the bottom-right of blanket, attach F and pu&k 14 sts on each of the 3 edges 1, 2, and 3 in Figure 10; pm bet each pair of edges—42 sts.
Work [HH]—6 sts. Cut and fasten off.

Half Hexagon (HH)—42 sts dec'ing to 6 sts

Row 1: Knit

Row 2: *K2tog, knit to 2 sts bef m, ssk; rep from * once, k2tog, knit to 2 sts bef end, ssk—6 sts dec'd; 36 sts.

Rows 3–4: Knit.

Rows 5–24: Rep [Rows 1–4] 5 times—30 sts dec'd; 6 sts.

Cut yarn, leaving a 10"/25 cm tail. Thread yarn on needle and draw through all sts on needle. Tighten and fasten off.

Step 2: Dish

Starting at the right edge of the shape shown in Step 2 of Figure 10, attach F and pu&k 14 sts along edge 4, pm, 28 sts along edge 5, pm, and 14 sts along edge 6—56 sts.
Work [D]—50 sts.

Dish (D)—56 sts dec'ing to 50 sts

Row 1 (WS): Knit to m, sm, k2tog, knit to 2 sts bef next m, ssk, knit to 2 sts from end, w&t—2 sts dec'd; 54 sts.

Row 2: Knit to 2 sts from end, w&t.

Row 3: Knit to 2 sts bef wrap, w&t.

Row 4: Rep [Row 3].

Row 5: Knit to m, k2tog, knit to 2 sts bef next m, ssk, knit to 2 sts bef wrap, w&t—2 sts dec'd; 52 sts.

Rows 6–9: Rep [Rows 2–5]—2 sts dec'd; 50 sts.

Row 10: Rep [Row 3].

Row 11: Knit.

Cut and fasten off, transferring sts to holder.
Rep Steps 1 and 2 to make 3 more Right Side Inserts.

Right Border

On RS, starting at the bottom-right corner, attach A and pu&k 7 sts on the edge of Bottom Border, knit rem 18 sts from bottom-right Corner sts on holder, *pu&k 14 sts on adjacent square, knit 50 sts from Dish sts on holder; rep from * 3 times, pu&k 14 st on adjacent square, knit rem 18 sts from top-right Corner sts on holder, pu&k 7 sts on edge of Top Border—320 sts. With A, knit 11 rows.
BO loosely. Cut and fasten off.

Left Side Inserts and Border

Rep instructions for Right Side Inserts and Right Border.

FINISHING

Weave in ends.

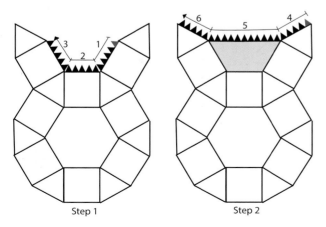

Step 1   Step 2

Figure 10: *Side Inserts*

Echoing Escher

Monochrome blocks in alternating colors create
a visual illusion of two different designs.

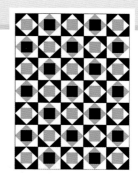

. . . .

Techniques

Method A: ▲ 🛒

Method B: ▲ 🛒 ⊃ ♯

Size

53 x 73.5"/135 x 187 cm

Yarn

Cascade 220 Superwash, aran (100% superwash
  merino wool; 150 yd./137.5 m; 3.5 oz./100 g):
A: 11 hanks Silver Grey #1946
B: 11 hanks White #871
C: 11 hanks Black #815

Needles

US Size 7/4.5 mm, 40"/100 cm circular needles,
  US Size 7/4.5 mm dpns (Method B)

Notions

Stitch holders, stitch markers, tapestry needle

Gauge

19 sts and 38 rows = 4"/10 cm in garter st

Notes

• This blanket is worked in blocks that are sewn
  together. There are two different construction
  options for blocks: A and B, as shown in
  Figure 1.

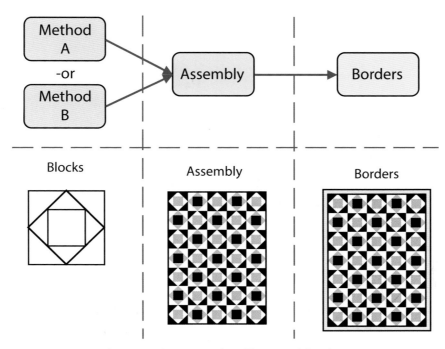

Figure 1: *Construction Flow and Options*

- Method A: Blocks begin with the center square worked in garter stitch, followed by the first small triangle. Stitches are picked up and knit from the 3 remaining sides of the square and additional small triangles are worked. Finally, stitches are picked up on the edges of the small triangles to work the larger triangles.
- Method B: The order of the block construction is reversed. The large triangles are worked sideways; then stitches for the small triangles are picked up on the edges of the large triangles. Small triangles are worked using wrap & turn. The center square is knit outside-in in the round, beginning from the stitches of the completed small triangles. This method results in fewer ends to weave in per block.
- Assembly and borders are worked the same for both methods.

Color Scheme 1 (CS1)

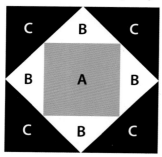

Color Scheme 2 (CS2)

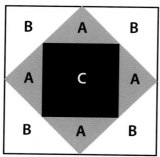

Figure 2: *Block Color Schemes*

Blanket Instructions

METHOD A

Blocks – Make 35: 18 in CS1 and 17 in CS2
See Figure 2 for color schemes and Figure 3 for construction.

Square (AS)

With yarn color specified in Figure 2, work [AS]. Cut yarn.

A Square (AS) – Method A—24 sts
CO 24 sts. Knit 48 rows. Leave sts on needle and cut yarn.

Inner Triangles (A1a–A1d)

A1a

Attach yarn color for A1s specified in Figure 2; knit 1 row (RS). Work [AI].

A Inner Triangle (AI) – Method A—24 sts dec'ing to 1 st

Note: *Mark A1a for assembly later.*

Row 1 (WS): Knit.
Row 2 (RS): K2tog, knit to last 2 sts, ssk—2 sts dec'd; 22 sts.
Rows 3–22: Rep [Rows 1 & 2] 10 times—20 sts dec'd; 2 sts.
Row 23: K2tog—1 st dec'd; 1 st.
Cut yarn and fasten off.

A1b to A1d

In spaces labeled "A1b," "A1c," and "A1d" in Figure 3, attach yarn at red triangle on corner of AS and pu&k 24 sts (1 st per garter st ridge) to corner. Work [AI].

Outer Triangles (AO)

In each of the four spaces labeled "AOT" in Figure 3, *attach yarn color specified in Figure 2. Working counterclockwise, pu&k 16 sts evenly on edge of AI to corner of AS, 1 st on corner of AS, and 16 sts on the edge of next AI—33 sts. (Pick up in all garter st bumps and in the legs bet bumps 3 & 4, 5 & 6, 7 & 8, and 9 & 10.) Work [AOT].

A Outer Triangle (AOT) - Method A—33 sts dec'ing to 1 st

Row 1 (WS): Knit.

Row 2 (RS): K2tog, knit to last 2 sts, ssk—2 sts dec'd; 31 sts.

Rows 3–30: Rep [Rows 1 & 2] 14 times—28 sts dec'd; 3 sts.

Row 31: Knit.

Row 32: Cdd—2 sts dec'd; 1 st.

Cut yarn and fasten off.

Continue at **Assembly**.

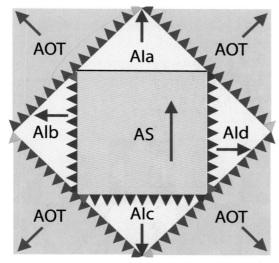

Figure 3: *Method A Block Construction*

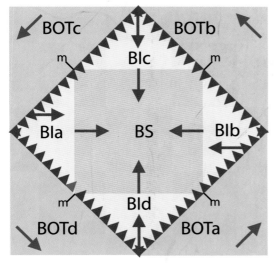

Figure 4: *Method B Block Construction*

METHOD B

Blocks – Make 35: 18 in CS1 and 17 in CS2

See Figure 2 for color schemes, and Figure 4 for construction.

Outer Triangles (BOTa–BOTd)

With yarn specified in Figure 2, CO 1 st.

Work [BOT] 4 times without cutting yarn bet triangles. Cut yarn and fasten off.

B Outer Triangle (BOT) - Method B—1 st inc'ing to 17 sts, dec'ing to 1 st

Row 1 (WS): Knit.

Row 2 (RS): Yoco, knit to end—1 st inc'd; 2 sts.

Row 3: Knit.

Rows 4–33: Rep [Rows 2 & 3] 15 times—15 sts inc'd; 17 sts.

Rows 34–35: Knit.

Row 36: K2tog, knit to end—1 st dec'd; 16 sts.

Row 37: Knit.

Rows 38–65: Rep [Rows 36 & 37] 14 times—14 sts dec'd; 2 sts.

Row 66: K2tog—1 st dec'd; 1 st.

Inner Triangles (BIa–BId)

Lay out BOTs as in Figure 4, being careful not to twist. Tie CO and BO tails tog to form a circle. **Note:** For Inner Triangles, stitches are generated for all Triangles first, working clockwise around the circle formed by the BOT shapes. Then the BI shapes are worked individually, in counterclockwise order around the circle. The first row of each BI is a WS row.

Pm at midpoint of the long edge of each BOT as shown in Figure 4. Attach yarn specified in Figure 2 at m at red triangle on long edge of BOTd. Working clockwise on the RS, *with dpn, pu&k 11 sts evenly from m to next corner, 1 st in corner, and 11 evenly from corner to next m (23 sts total bet m's). Rep from * 3 more times—92 sts.

Turn to WS. *Work [BI] over next 23 sts (bet m's)* (BIa). Rep bet * and * 3 more times (BIb–BId). Cut yarn.

B Inner Triangle (BI) - Method B—23 sts

Row 1 (WS): K12, w&t.
Row 2: K1, w&t—1 st bet wraps.
Row 3: Knit to wrap, w&t—2 sts bet wraps.
Rows 4–22: Rep [Row 3] 19 times—21 sts bet wraps.
Row 23: Knit to m, sm. Do not cut yarn.

Square (BS in Figure 4)

Turn to RS. Attach yarn specified in Figure 2. Work [BS].

B Square (BS) - Method B—92 sts dec'ing to 4 sts

Worked in the round on circular needles.

Note: Change to dpns when needed to accommodate sts. When working on dpns, do not pm's; on dec rounds, work to 2 sts bef end of dpn. The cdd's use the last 2 sts from the current dpn and the 1st st from the following dpn. The final cdd crosses the BOR.

Rnd 1: Purl.
Rnd 2: *Knit to last 2 sts on dpn, cdd; rep from * 3 times—8 sts dec'd; 84 sts.
Rnd 3: Purl.

Rnds 4–21: Rep [Rnds 2 & 3] 9 times; 72 sts dec'd; 12 sts rem.
Rnd 22: Rep [Rnd 2]—8 sts dec'd; 4 sts.
Cut yarn, leaving a 10"/24 cm tail. Thread tail onto tapestry needle and insert through all loops on needle. Pull tightly, cut yarn, and fasten off securely.

Continue at **Assembly**.

ASSEMBLY – METHODS A AND B

Arrange blocks as shown in Figure 5. For blocks made with Method A, orient all blocks so that A1a is at the top. For blocks made with Method B, blocks are symmetrical, so no special orientation is required.

With C and tapestry needle, sew blocks tog into vertical strips using mattress st, and then sew strips tog.

Figure 5: *Assembly Layout*

BORDERS

Top Border

On RS, attach A at top-right corner of blanket.
 Pu&k 24 sts on the edge of each Outer Triangle
 along the top edge of the blanket—240 sts.
Knit 11 rows. BO loosely.

Bottom Border

Rep as for Top Border, attaching A at bottom-
 left corner of blanket.

Right Border

On RS, attach A at bottom-right corner of
 Bottom Border. Pu&k 7 sts on Bottom Border,
 336 sts on the RS of the blanket (24 sts on the
 edge of each Outer Triangle), and 7 sts on the
 right edge of Top Border—350 sts.
Knit 11 rows. BO loosely.

Left Border

Rep as for Right Border attaching A at top-left
 corner of Top Border.

FINISHING

Weave in ends.

Granada

The beautiful tile patterns of the Alhambra in Granada, Spain, find expression in this blanket made of mitered squares.

Techniques

▲ ⌦ ♯

Size
51 x 51"/130 x 130 cm

Yarn
Red Heart Super Saver Multis, worsted (100% acrylic; 236 yd./215 m; 5 oz./141 g):

A: 11 skeins Macaw (variegated turquoise, navy and teal) #3944

Red Heart Super Saver Solids, worsted (100% acrylic; 364 yd./333 m; 7 oz./198 g):

B: 3 skeins Dusty Grey (medium gray) #340
C: 3 skeins Aran (off-white) #313
D: 3 skeins Soft Navy (navy) #387
E: 3 skeins Turqua (turquoise) #512

Needles
US Size 8/5 mm, 40"/100 cm circular needles and dpns

Notions
Stitch holders, stitch markers, tapestry needle

Gauge
17 sts and 34 rows = 4"/10 cm in garter st

Note
- The blanket is composed of mitered squares, mitered triangles, and an outside-in square. Units and Cross are composed of a set of shapes, with stitches picked up and knit from previously completed shapes. A block is formed from a set of Units. The Units are sewn to the Cross to form the blanket face (see Figure 6). The borders are picked up and knit on the edges of the blanket face.

Blanket Instructions

Mitered Squares (M1) — Make 48
With A, CO 37 sts and work [MS].

Mitered Square (MS)—37 sts dec'd to 1 st

See Figure 1 for illustration and orientation reference.

On RS, pm after 19th st.

Rows 1 (RS) & 2 (WS): Knit.

Row 3: Knit to 2 sts bef m, rm, cdd, pm, knit to end—2 sts dec'd; 35 sts.

Rows 4–37: Rep [Rows 2 & 3] 17 times—34 sts dec'd; 1 st.

Cut yarn and fasten off.

Units

Make 4 each of Units 1–5, in the colors shown in Figure 2, Refer to Figure 3 for Unit construction. Begin each Unit by arranging its MS1 shapes as shown, orienting according to arrows, and then work additional shapes of each Unit in the order below.

Note: *Leave a long tail at CO to sew seams in Units 1, 2, & 4 (see Figure 3).*

MS2 (used in Unit 1)

On RS, in space labeled "MS2," attach B. Pu&k 18 sts to corner, CO 1 at corner, and pu&k 18 sts to next corner—37 sts. Work [MS].

LT1 (used in Units 2–4)

On RS, in each space labeled "LT1," attach yarn at red triangle. Pu&k 18 sts to corner, CO 1 st in corner, pu&k 18 sts to next corner—37 sts. Work [LT].

Large Triangle (LT)—37 sts dec'ing to 1 st

On RS, pm after 19th st.
Row 1 (WS): Knit.
Rows 2–17: Rep [Rows 1 & 2 of Tr] 8 times—32 sts dec'd; 5 sts.
Row 18: K1, cdd, rm, k1—2 sts dec'd; 3 sts.
Row 19: Cdd—2 st dec'd; 1 st.
Cut yarn and fasten off.

Triangle (Tr)

Row 1 (RS): K2tog, knit to 2 sts bef m, rm, cdd, pm, knit to last 2 sts, ssk—4 sts dec'd.
Row 2: Knit.
Rep [Rows 1 & 2] for pattern.

LT2 (used in Units 1–4)

On RS, in each space labeled "LT2," attach yarn at red triangle. Pu&k 18 sts to corner, 1 st in corner, and 18 sts to next corner—37 sts. Work [LT].

Ed1 (used in Units 1–4)

On RS, in each space labeled "Ed1," with color specified in Figure 2, CO 19, pu&k 18 sts from red triangle to next corner—37 sts. Work [LT].

Ed2 (used in Units 1–4)

On RS, in each space labeled "Ed2," attach yarn at red triangle. Pu&k 18 sts to corner, CO 19—37 sts. Work [LT].

CT (used in Unit 5)

With D, CO37, leaving a long tail for sewing. Work [LT].

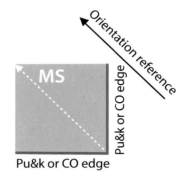

Figure 1: *Mitered Square (M) Orientation Reference*

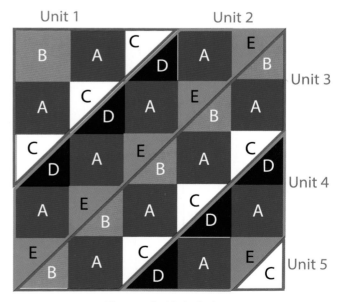

Figure 2: *Unit Colors*

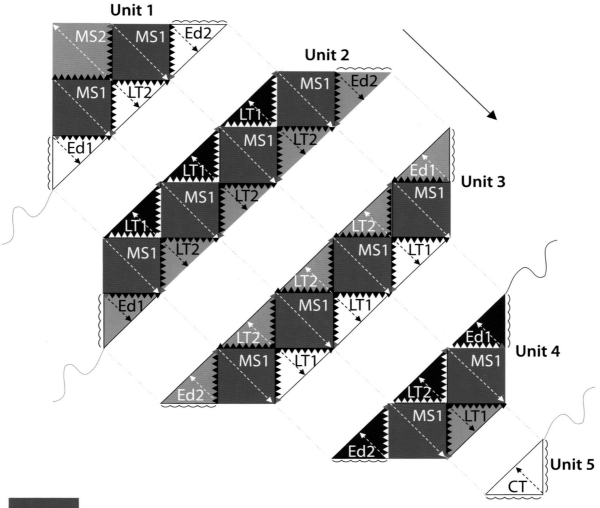

Figure 3: *Unit Construction and Assembly into Blocks*

Figure 4:
Arm Construction

Blocks — Make 4

Arrange one each of Units 1, 2, 3, and 4 as shown in Figure 3, orienting according to arrows. Using whip st, sew Units tog as shown using long tails of Ed1's and CT, and matching up corners as shown by dashed lines in Figure 3.

Arm — Make 4

See Figure 4 for Arm colors and construction.

PS1

With A, CO18, work [PS], and do not BO.
Cut A.

Plain Square (PS)—18 sts
Rows 1–36: Knit.

VS1

With C, *CO 19 sts, knit 18 sts on needle, CO 19 sts—56 sts. Work [VS]. Cut yarn and fasten off.

V-square (VS)—56 sts dec'ing to 1 st.

On RS, pm after 19th and 38th sts.
Row 1 (WS): Knit.
Row 2 (RS): K2tog, (knit to 2 sts bef m, rm, cdd, pm) twice, knit to last 2 sts, ssk—6 sts dec'd; 50 sts.
Row 3: Knit.
Rows 4–17: Rep [Rows 2 & 3] 7 times—42 sts dec'd; 8 sts.
Row 18: Rm's. K1, cdd twice, k1—4 sts dec'd; 4 sts.
Row 19: K2tog twice—2 sts dec'd; 2 sts.
Row 20: K2tog—1 st dec'd; 1 st.
Cut yarn and fasten off.

ST1

On RS, attach D at location at red triangle on top-right corner of VS1. Pu&k 13 sts to corner, 1 st in corner, and 13 sts to end of edge—27 sts. Work [ST]. Cut yarn and fasten off.

Small Triangle (ST)—27 sts dec'ing to 1 st

On RS, pm after 14th st.
Row 1 (WS): Knit.
Rows 2–11: Rep [Rows 1 & 2 of Tr] 5 times—20 sts dec'd; 7 sts.
Row 12: Rm. K2tog, cdd, ssk—4 sts dec'd; 3 sts.
Row 13: Cdd—2 sts dec'd; 1 st.
Cut yarn and fasten off.

PS2

On RS, attach A at orange triangle at top-right corner of ST1. Pu&k 18 sts across top edge of ST1. Work [PS]. Cut yarn. Do not BO.*

VS2, ST2, and PS3

Rep bet * and * once, working VS2 in color E, ST2 in color C, and PS3 in A. Place sts on holder.

Cross

See Figure 5 for construction.
Arrange the 4 completed Arms as shown in Figure 5. Transfer each set of 18 Arm sts to a dpn—72 sts. On RS, attach C and work [OS].

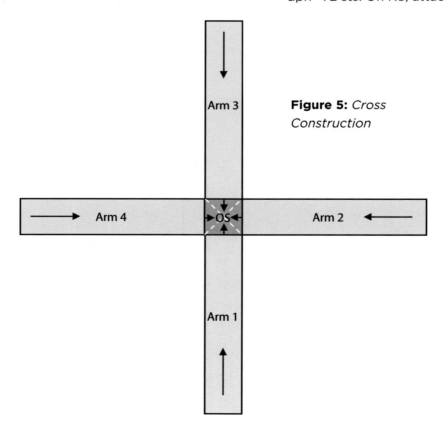

Figure 5: *Cross Construction*

Outside-In Square (OS)—72 sts dec'ing to 1 st

Worked in the round.

***

Note: The cdd's use the last 2 sts from the current dpn and the 1st st from the following dpn. The final cdd crosses the BOR.

***

Rnd 1: Knit.
Rnd 2: Purl.
Rnd 3: *Knit to last 2 sts on dpn, cdd, rep from * 3 more times—8 sts dec'd; 64 sts.
Rnd 4: Purl.
Rnds 5–18: Rep [Rnds 3 & 4] 7 times—56 sts dec'd; 8 sts.
Cut yarn, leaving a 10"/25 cm tail. Thread yarn through tapestry needle. Insert through all sts on needle. Pull to tighten and fasten securely.

ASSEMBLY

Lay out Blocks and Cross as shown in Figure 6, orienting pieces according to arrows. Using A and whip st, sew tog along dashed lines.

BORDERS

Top Border

On RS, attach C at top-right corner of blanket. Pu&k 18 sts per shape (square/triangle) edge—198 sts.
Row 1 (WS): Knit.
Row 2 (RS): Kf&b, knit to last st, kf&b—2 sts inc'd; 200 sts.

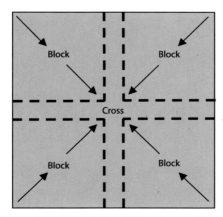

Figure 6: *Assembly of Blocks and Cross*

Rows 3–8: Rep [Rows 1 & 2] 3 times—6 sts inc'd; 206 sts.
Row 9: Knit.
Cut C, leaving a 10"/25 cm tail. Attach B.
Row 10 (RS): Rep [Row 2]—2 sts inc'd; 208 sts.
Rows 11–19: Rep [Rows 1–9]—8 sts inc'd; 216 sts.
BO all sts. Cut yarn, leaving a 10"/25 cm tail.

Bottom, Right, and Left Borders

Rep as for Top Border, attaching yarn at bottom-left corner, bottom-right corner, and top-left corners of blanket.

Border Seams

Using long tails left from binding off Borders, sew tog diagonal seams at corners of Borders using mattress st for garter st.

FINISHING

Weave in ends.

Hip to Be Square

Knit up this visually compelling blanket of squares in tints of your two favorite colors and white.

Techniques

Methods A & C:

Method B:

Method D:

Size

53 x 65.5"/135 x 166 cm

Yarn

Knit Picks Brava, worsted (100% premium
  acrylic; 218 yd./199 m; 3.53 oz./100 g):
A: 2 skeins Sky (pale blue) #28451
B: 6 skeins Solstice Heather (navy blue) #28452
C: 3 skeins Canary (yellow) #28416
D: 7 skeins White #28455
F: 1 skein Custard (pale yellow) #28426

Knit Picks Mighty Stitch Worsted (80% acrylic/
  20% superwash merino; 208 yd./190 m;
  3.53 oz./100 g):
E: 4 skeins Gulfstream (bright teal) #26827

Needles

US Size 7/4.5 mm, 40"/100 cm circular needles,
  US Size 7/4.5 mm dpns (for Methods B & D)

Notions

Stitch holders, stitch markers, tapestry needle

Gauge

19 sts and 38 rows = 4"/10 cm in garter st

Notes

- The blanket is worked in blocks that are sewn together. The border is picked up on the edge of the blanket.
- The blanket has two methods, A & B, for working the first 4 shapes (S1–S4) of a block, and two methods, C & D, for working the last 4 shapes (S6–S9) (see Figure 1).
- Method A is worked inside-out, starting with the small center square and picking up sts on the edges of completed shapes to create additional shapes.
- Method B works in the reverse order, outside-in, starting with the outer shape (S4) first, then working successive inner shapes, and finally working an outside-in center square in the round on dpns. The wrap & turn technique is used for some shapes.
- The 5th shape (S5) is worked the same for all methods. A square composed of Shapes 1–5, whether made with Method A or Method B, is referred to as "Square."
- Method B produces fewer yarn ends to weave in compared to Method A.
- Method C picks up sts on the outside of previously completed shapes and works back and forth, adding four stripes to each corner to create a block. These blocks are sewn together to complete the blanket face.
- Method D assembles groups of S1–S5 units and picks up sts on the edges to work 12 additional squares outside-in, changing colors to create the stripes. In triangular-shaped openings on the outside edges of the blanket, triangular shapes and corners are completed in the same manner.

- Method D produces fewer yarn ends to weave in compared to Method C.
- Borders are completed the same way for all methods.

Triangle (Tr) – All Methods

Row 1 (WS) and odd rows: Knit.
Row 2 (RS) and even rows: K2tog, knit to last 2 sts, ssk—2 sts dec'd.
Rep [Rows 1 & 2] for pattern.

Blanket Instructions

Square (Make 20 for either Method A or Method B)

METHOD A

Shapes 1–4 (A1 to A4)
Each octagon is composed of Shapes 1–4. See Figures 2 & 3 for construction.

Shape 1 (A1)
Using A, CO 8 sts.
Knit 16 rows.
Cut A but do not BO.

Shape 2 (A2)

A2a
Attach B.
Knit 12 rows.
BO loosely but do not cut B. Leave last st on needle.

A2b
On left edge of A2a at the red square in Figure 2, *skip the 1st garter st ridge, and then pu&k 5 sts on the left edge of A2a (one per garter st ridge) and 8 sts on the left edge of A1—14 sts. Knit 11 rows.
BO loosely but do not cut B. Leave last st on needle.

A2c
Rep from *, picking up sts on left edge of A2b and bottom edge of A1.

A2d
On the right edge of A2c, skip the 1st garter ridge, then pu&k 5 sts on the right edge of A2c, 8 sts on the right edge of A1, and 6 sts on the right edge of A2a—20 sts. Knit 11 rows.
BO loosely. Cut yarn and fasten off.

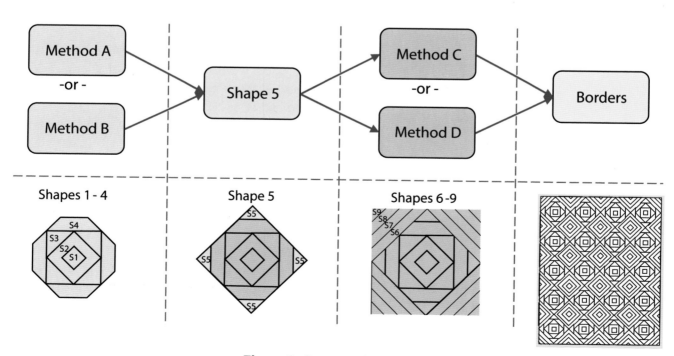

Figure 1: *Construction Options*

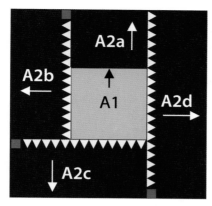

■ Last st from bindoff of previous A2 shape

Figure 2: *Method A: Construction of A1, and A2a to A2d*

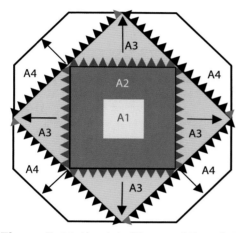

Figure 3: *Method A: Shapes A3 and A4*

Shape 3 (A3)

On the RS, on each edge of A2, attach yarn at
the green triangle in Figure 3 and pu&k 18 sts.
Work [Tr] until 4 sts rem, ending after a WS row
(knit as Row 1).
Next row (RS): K2tog, ssk—2 sts.
Next row: K2tog—1 st.
Cut C and fasten off.

Shape 4 (A4)

Working on the RS, on each long edge of A3
(red triangles in Figure 3), attach D and pu&k
13 sts evenly bef the point where A2 intersects
the edge, and 13 sts after the point—26 sts.
Work [Tr] until 14 sts rem, ending after a WS row.
BO loosely. Cut D and fasten off.
Continue at **Shape 5**.

METHOD B

Shapes 1–4 (B1–B4)

Each square is composed of Shapes 1–4. See
Figures 4, 5, and 6 for construction.

Shape 4 (B4)

Note: *CO for the first B4 (B4a) (starts at the red
dot in Figure 4).*

With D, CO 1 st.
Work [Trp] 4 times, without cutting yarn, to
make shapes B4a to B4d.

Trapezoid (Trp) – Method B—1 st inc'ing to 7,
dec'ing to 1

Note: *To keep track of rows, pm at end of
Row 12 (end of increases). Begin decreases
(at Row 41) when there are 14 garter st ridges
after the m.*

Row 1 (RS): Yoco, knit to end—1 st inc'd; 2 sts.
Row 2 (WS): Knit.
Rows 3–12: Rep [Rows 1 & 2] 5 times—5 sts
inc'd; 7 sts.
Rows 13–40: Knit.
Row 41 (RS): K2tog, knit to end—1 st
dec'd; 6 sts.
Row 42 (WS): Knit.
Rows 43–52: Rep [Rows 41 & 42] 5 times—5
sts dec'd; 1 st.
Do not cut yarn.

Shape 3 (B3)

Lay out B4's as in Figure 4, being careful not to
twist. Tie CO and BO tails tog to form a circle.
Pm at midpoint (bet the 13th and 14th ridges)
of the long edge of each B4.
On the RS, attach C to the left of the m on B4d
(at red dot in Figure 5). Working clockwise
on the long edges of the Trp's, *pu&k 10 sts
evenly to the corner, 1 st in corner, and 10 sts
from corner to next m—21 sts. Rep from * 3
times—84 sts.

Turn to WS. *Work [R] over next 21 sts (bet m's)* (B3a). Rep bet * and * 3 more times (B3b–B3d). Cut yarn.

Triangle (R) - Method B—21 sts

Row 1 (WS): Knit.
Row 2 (RS): Knit 11, w&t.
Row 3 (WS): K1, w&t next st—1 st bet wraps.
Row 4: Knit to wrap, w&t—2 sts bet wraps.
Rows 5–16: Rep [Row 4] 12 times—14 sts bet wraps.
Row 17: Knit to m.

Shape 2 (B2)

Attach B. Work [OS] until 44 sts rem ending after a Row 3. Cut B.

Shape 1 (B1)

Attach A. Work [OS] until 4 sts rem, ending after a Row 2.
Cut yarn, leaving a 10"/25 cm tail. Thread tail through tapestry needle and insert into all loops on needles. Pull tight, cut yarn, and fasten securely.
Continue at **Shape 5**.

Outside-In Square (OS) - Method B

Worked in the round.

Note: When working on dpns, do not pm's, and work to 2 sts bef end of dpn. The cdd uses the last 2 sts of 1 dpn and the 1st st of the next. The last cdd crosses the BOR.

Rnd 1: Purl.
Rnd 2: *Knit to last 2 sts bef m, rm, cdd, pm; rep from * 3 times—8 sts dec'd.
Rnd 3: Purl.
Rep [Rnds 2 & 3] for pattern.

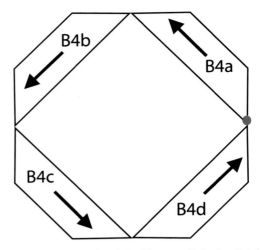

Figure 4: *Method B: Shapes B4a to B4d*

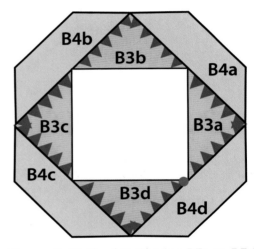

Figure 5: *Method B: Shapes B3a to B3d*

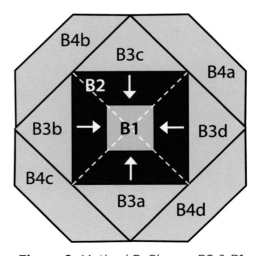

Figure 6: *Method B: Shapes B2 & B1*

Shape 5 (S5) – All Methods

On RS, at each of the 4 red triangles in Figure 7, attach E and pu&k 10 sts bef the point where Shape 3 intersects the edge and 10 sts after the point—20 sts.

Work [Tr] until 4 sts rem, ending after a WS row.

Next row: K2tog, ssk—2 sts.

Next row: K2tog—1 st.

Cut E and fasten off.

Continue at either **Method C** or **Method D** to complete and assemble blocks.

METHOD C

Shape 6

Use the color charts in Figure 8 for the number of blocks to complete using each of 5 different color schemes.

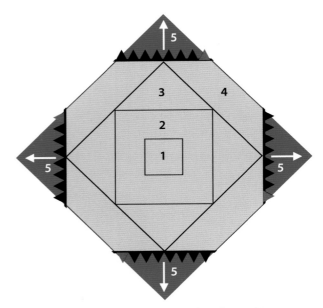

Figure 7: *All Methods: Shape 5*

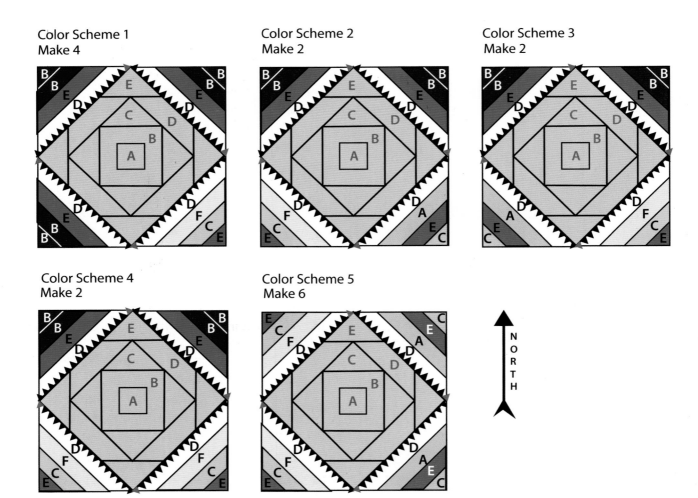

Color Scheme 1
Make 4

Color Scheme 2
Make 2

Color Scheme 3
Make 2

Color Scheme 4
Make 2

Color Scheme 5
Make 6

Figure 8: *Method C: Color Schemes and Construction for Completing Blocks*

Working on RS, on each edge of the Square formed by Shapes 1–5, attach D at the red triangle in Figure 8. Pu&k 14 sts on edge of Shape 5, 14 sts on edge of Shape 4, and 14 sts on Shape 5—42 sts.

*Work [Tr Rows 1 & 2] 10 times, and then work [Tr Row 1] once more; 10 sts dec'd.

Cut yarn, leaving a 10"/25 cm tail, and fasten off. Attach next yarn color specified in Figure 8.

Rep from * 3 times, but do not cut yarn on the final rep.

Next row (RS): K2tog, ssk—2 sts.

Next row: K2tog—1 st.

Cut yarn, leaving a 10"/25 cm tail, and fasten off.

Assembly of Blocks

Referring to the arrow North in Figure 8, arrange and orient the blocks as shown in Figure 9. Using the long tails of matching color and whip st, sew the blocks tog into four columns, aligning edges of similar shapes. Sew tog columns matching corners and aligning edges of similar shapes.

Continue at **Borders**.

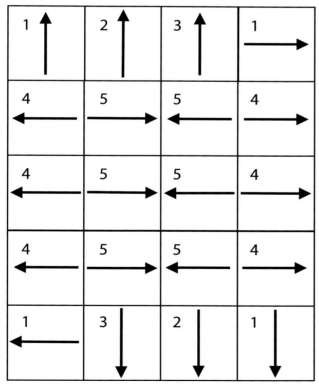

Figure 9: *Method C: Block Assembly Diagram*

METHOD D: SHAPES 6–8 (D6–D8)

Arrange the 20 completed Squares, formed by Shapes 1–5, into 5 rows of 4 Squares each as shown in Figure 10. If Squares were worked using Method A, orient them so that A2a is at the top. No special orientation is required for Squares worked with Method B.

Shape 6 (D6)

Note: *Begin on circ needle and then change to dpns and rm's when necessary to accommodate sts.*

Use color schemes D6a and D6b (see Figure 11).

Using circular needle, in each space labeled "D6a" and "D6b" in Figure 10, attach yarn specified in Figure 11 at a corner red triangle in Figure 10. *Pu&k 42 sts evenly along Square edge, pm, rep from * on other 3 edges—168 sts.

Join to work in the round.

*Work [OS Rows 2 & 3] 5 times—40 sts dec'd; 128 sts.

Cut yarn and fasten off. Attach next color specified in Figure 11.

Rep from * 3 times—120 sts dec'd; 8 sts.

Next rnd: Rm's; k2tog, 4 times—4 sts dec'd; 4 sts.

Next rnd: Purl.

Cut yarn, leaving a 10"/25 cm tail. Thread tail onto tapestry needle and insert through all loops. Pull to tighten and fasten off securely.

Shape 7

Use color scheme D7 (Figure 11).

On RS, in each space labeled "D7" in Figure 10, attach D at the red triangle. Pu&k 41 sts evenly to corner, 1 st in corner, pm, pu&k 41 sts to end of Square edge—83 sts.

*Work [HS Rows 2 & 3] 5 times; 20 sts dec'd—63 sts. Cut yarn and fasten off. Attach next yarn color.

Rep from * 3 times; 3 sts. Do not cut yarn on the final rep.

Note: *Yarn color does not change bet the last 2 reps.*

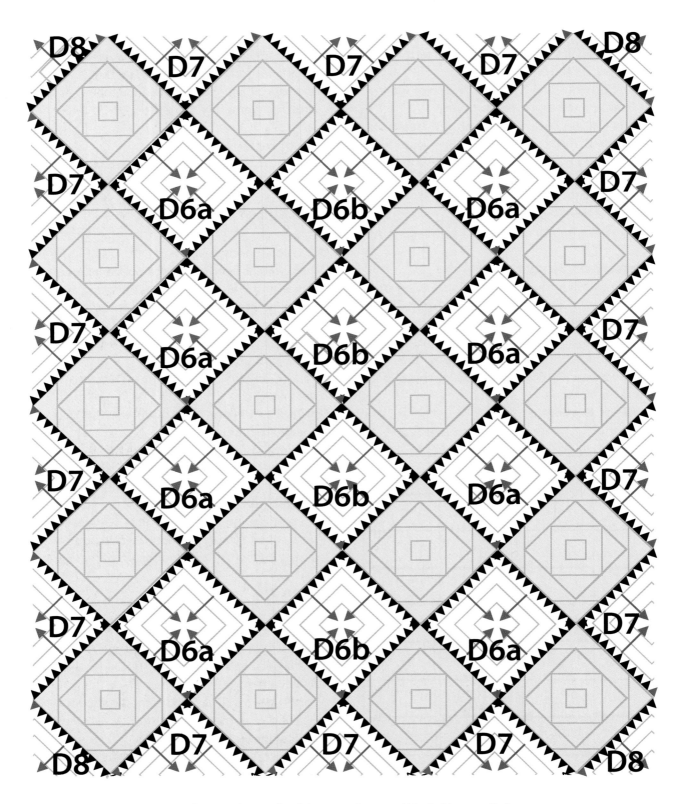

Figure 10: *Method D: Locations to Work Shapes 6–8*

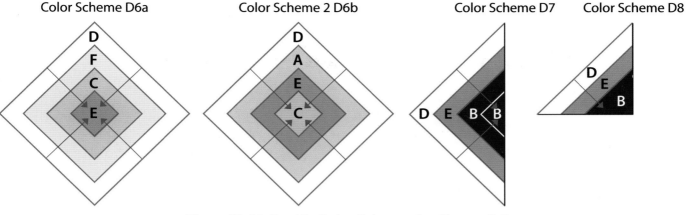

Color Scheme D6a Color Scheme 2 D6b Color Scheme D7 Color Scheme D8

Figure 11: *Method D: Color Schemes for Shapes 6–8*

Next row: Rm; cdd—2 sts dec'd; 1 st.
Cut yarn and fasten off.

Half Square (HS) – Method D
Row 1 (WS): Knit.
Row 2 (RS): K2tog, knit to 2 sts bef m, rm, cdd, pm, knit to 2 sts bef end, ssk—4 sts dec'd.
Row 3: Knit.
Rep [Rows 2 & 3] for pattern.

Shape 8

Use color scheme D8 (Figure 11).
On RS, in each space labeled "D8" in Figure 10, attach D at the red triangle. Pu&k 42 sts evenly along edge.
*Work [Tr Rows 1 & 2] 10 times, and then work [Tr Row 1] once more—10 sts dec'd; 32 sts. Cut yarn and fasten off. Attach next yarn color.
Rep from * 3 times—30 sts dec'd; 2 sts. On the last rep, do not work the final WS row (knit as Row 1) or cut yarn.

Note: *Yarn color does not change bet the last 2 reps.*

Next row (WS): K2tog—1 st.
Cut B and fasten off.
Continue at **Borders**.

BORDERS (ALL METHODS)

Tip: Pu&k 60 sts evenly along the edge of each large triangle and 30 sts on the edge of each small (corner) triangle.

Top Border

On RS, beginning at top-right corner, attach B and pu&k 240 sts evenly on top edge of assembled blanket.
Knit 11 rows. BO loosely. Cut and fasten off.

Bottom Border

Rep as for Top Border, beginning at bottom-left corner of blanket.

Left Border

On RS, beginning at top-left corner, attach B and pu&k 6 sts on Top Border, 300 sts along left edge of blanket, and 6 sts on Bottom Border—312 sts.
Knit 11 rows. BO loosely. Cut and fasten off.

Right Border

Rep as for Left Border, beginning at top-right corner of blanket.

FINISHING

Weave in ends.

Horizons

The color-shift and speckled yarns bring new textures to your home décor in this fresh take on the traditional striped blanket.

. . . .

Techniques

Size
57 x 71"/145 x 180 cm

Yarn
Yarns of Rhichard Devrieze, Fynn, worsted (100% merino wool; 175 yd./160 m; 3.0 oz./84 g):
A: 7 hanks Elfin Glen (speckled greens and teal)
B: 7 hanks Lake of Bays (speckled yellow, aqua, and orange)
C: 7 hanks Calabria (speckled dark orange, yellows, and blues)
D: 6 hanks Morning Mist (speckled yellow, cream, and light green)

Needles
US Size 8/5 mm, 40"/100 cm circular needles

Notions
Stitch holders, stitch markers, tapestry needle

Gauge
16 sts and 32 rows = 4"/10 cm in garter st

Note
• This no-sew blanket is worked from bottom to top as a sequence of diamond-shaped wedges, each of which is picked up from the edges of the previously completed diamonds. Garter stitch borders are added last, with stitches picked up from the blanket edges.

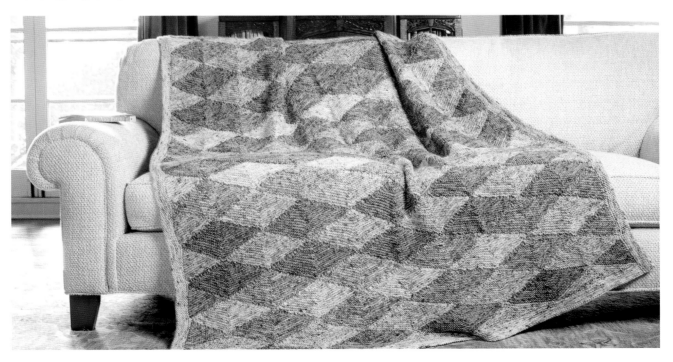

Blanket Instructions

A "Strip" refers to a horizontal band of diamonds and triangles worked in the same yarn color.

A color change occurs at the beginning of each strip. For yarn color to use for a strip, refer to Table 1 and Figure 1.

Make 35 Strips, beginning with the Foundation Strip (Strip 1) and then alternating bet even and odd Strips, using colors in Figure 1.

Foundation Strip (Strip 1)

With A, CO 25 sts. Work [RT]. Cut yarn and fasten off.

*With A, CO 49 sts. Work [DW]. Cut yarn and fasten off. Rep from * 3 times. With A, CO 25 sts. Work [LT]. Cut yarn and fasten off.

With RS facing, arrange completed pieces as shown in Figure 2.

Right Triangle (RT)—25 sts dec'ing to 1 st

Row 1 (RS): Knit.
Row 2 (WS): Ssk, knit to end—1 st dec'd; 24 sts.
Row 3: Knit to last 2 sts, ssk—1 st dec'd; 23 sts.
Row 4: Knit.
Row 5: K2tog, knit to last 2 sts, ssk—2 sts dec'd; 21 sts.
Row 6: Ssk, knit to end—1 st dec'd; 20 sts.
Row 7: Knit.
Rows 8–10: Rep [Rows 2-4]—2 sts dec'd; 18 sts.
Rows 11–28: Rep [Rows 5-10] 3 times—15 sts dec'd; 3 sts.
Row 29: K1, ssk—1 st dec'd; 2 sts.
Row 30: Ssk—1 st dec'd; 1 st.

Diamond Wedge (DW)—49 sts dec'ing to 1 st

Row 1 (RS): K24, pm, knit to end.
Row 2 (WS): Ssk, knit to last 2 sts, k2tog—2 sts dec'd; 47 sts.
Row 3: K2tog, knit to last 2 sts, ssk—2 sts dec'd; 45 sts.
Row 4: Knit.
Row 5: K2tog, knit to 1 st bef m, rm, cdd, pm, knit to last 2 sts, ssk—4 sts dec'd; 41 sts.
Row 6: Rep [Row 2]—2 sts dec'd; 39 sts.
Row 7: Knit.
Rows 8–10: Rep [Rows 2-4]—4 sts dec'd; 35 sts.
Rows 11–28: Rep [Rows 5-10] 3 more times—30 sts dec'd; 5 sts.
Row 29: K2tog, k1, ssk—2 sts dec'd; 3 sts.
Row 30: Cdd—2 sts dec'd; 1 st.
Cut yarn and fasten off.

Left Triangle (LT)—25 sts dec'ing to 1 st

Row 1 (RS): Knit.
Row 2 (WS): Knit to last 2 sts, k2tog—1 st dec'd; 24 sts.
Row 3: K2tog, knit to end—1 st dec'd; 23 sts.
Row 4: Knit.
Row 5: K2tog, knit to last 2 sts, ssk—2 sts dec'd; 21 sts.
Row 6: Knit to last 2 sts, k2tog—1 st dec'd; 20 sts.
Row 7: Knit.
Rows 8–10: Rep [Rows 2-4]—2 sts dec'd; 18 sts.
Rows 11–28: Rep [Rows 5-10] 3 times—15 sts dec'd; 3 sts.
Row 29: K2tog, k1—1 st dec'd; 2 sts.
Row 30: K2tog—1 st dec'd; 1 st.
Cut yarn and fasten off.

Figure 1 shows a diagram with diamonds labeled with strip numbers and colors:

A
35-B
34-A
33-C
32-D
31-C
30-B
29-A
28-B
27-A
26-C
25-D
24-C
23-B
22-A
21-B
20-A
19-C
18-D
17-C
16-B
15-A
14-B
13-A
12-C
11-D
10-C
9-B
8-A
7-B
6-A
5-C
4-D
3-C
2-B
1-A
B

Key: Strip #-Color

Figure 1: *Strip Color Assignments*

Even-Numbered Strips (2–34)

Note: *Pu&k 2 sts per garter st ridge for two ridges then 1 st per garter st ridge. On Strip 2, add the center st with a bli (see "Glossary") instead of picking up a st 2 strips below.*

*With color specified in Figure 1 and starting on the right edge of prev Strip, pu&k 24 sts on the top edge of RT, pm, 1 st at the peak of DW two Strips below, and 24 sts on the right edge of the adjacent DW—49 sts.

Work [DW Rows 2–30].

Rep from * 4 times to work 4 additional DWs in locations shown in Figure 3 to complete Strip.

Strip 1	A	Strip 8	A	Strip 15	A	Strip 22	A	Strip 29	A
Strip 2	B	Strip 9	B	Strip 16	B	Strip 23	B	Strip 30	B
Strip 3	C	Strip 10	C	Strip 17	C	Strip 24	C	Strip 31	C
Strip 4	D	Strip 11	D	Strip 18	D	Strip 25	D	Strip 32	D
Strip 5	C	Strip 12	C	Strip 19	C	Strip 26	C	Strip 33	C
Strip 6	A	Strip 13	A	Strip 20	A	Strip 27	A	Strip 34	A
Strip 7	B	Strip 14	B	Strip 21	B	Strip 28	B	Strip 35	B

Table 1: *Yarn Colors for Strips*

LT — DW — DW — DW — DW — RT

Figure 2: *Foundation Strip*

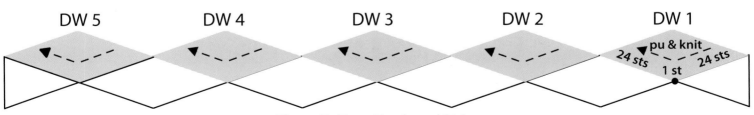

DW 5   DW 4   DW 3   DW 2   DW 1

pu & knit
24 sts   1 st   24 sts

Figure 3: *Even-Numbered Strips*

Odd-Numbered Strips (3–35)

With color specified in Figure 1 and starting on the right edge of the previous strip, pu&k 25 sts evenly on the top edge of the rightmost DW. Work [RT, Rows 2–30].

Rep from * for Even-Numbered Strips 4 times to work 4 DWs in locations shown in Figure 4.

Pu&k 25 sts on the top edge of the leftmost DW of the prev strip as shown in Figure 3. Work [LT, Rows 2–30].

Triangle Inserts

*On RS, with A, starting at top-right edge of blanket, pu&k 24 sts on top edge of RT, pm, 1 st in peak of DW two Strips below, and 24 sts on top-right edge of DW—49 sts. Work [TI].

Rep from * 4 times, working 4 more TIs in locations as specified in Figure 5.

With B, rep from * to work 5 TIs on bottom edge of blanket.

Triangle Insert (TI)—49 sts dec'ing to 45 sts

Row 1 (WS): Knit 24 sts, pm, knit to last 3 sts, w&t.

Row 2: Knit to last 3 sts, w&t—43 sts bet wraps.

Row 3: Knit to 3 sts bef wrap, w&t—40 sts bet wraps.

Row 4: Knit to st bef m, rm, cdd, pm, knit to 3 sts bef wrap, w&t—2 sts dec'd; 47 sts, 35 sts bet wraps.

Rows 5–9: Rep [Row 3]—20 sts bet wraps.

Row 10: Rep [Row 4]—2 sts dec'd; 45 sts, 15 sts bet wraps.

Rows 11–14: Rep [Row 3]—3 sts bet wraps.

Row 15: Knit to end.

Cut yarn and fasten off. Transfer sts to holder.

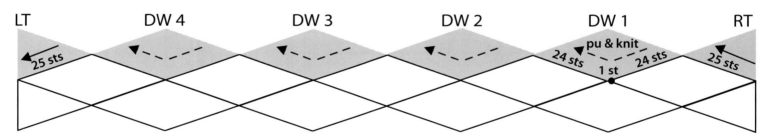

Figure 4: *Odd-Numbered Strips*

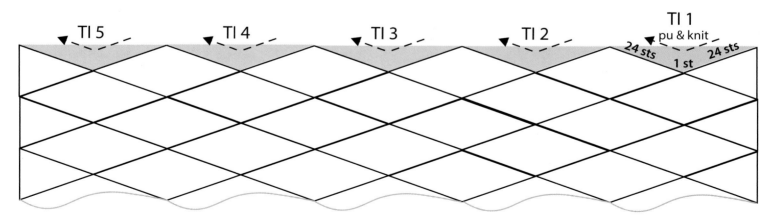

Figure 5: *Triangle Inserts Worked on Top and Bottom Edges of Blanket*

BORDERS

Top Border

On RS, attach D and starting at the top-right corner of the blanket, transfer TI sts from holders to needle and pm bet each set of sts—225 sts.

Row 1 (RS): *K14, k2tog, knit to 16 sts bef next m, k2tog; rep from * 4 times—10 sts dec'd; 215 sts. Rm's.

Knit 11 rows. BO loosely. Cut yarn and fasten off.

Bottom Border

Work as for Top Border, starting at the bottom-left corner of blanket.

Right Border

On RS, attach D and starting at the bottom-right corner of the blanket, pu&k 7 sts on Bottom Border, 15 sts evenly across each RT edge, and 7 sts on Top Border—284 sts.

Knit 11 rows. BO loosely. Cut yarn and fasten off.

Left Border

Work as for Right Border, starting at the left corner of the Top Border.

FINISHING

Weave in ends and block if desired.

Kaleidoscope

Interconnecting whirling disks in a rainbow of colors provide motion on this small rectangular blanket.

. . . .

Techniques

Method A: ▲ [symbol]

Method B: ▲ [symbol] ♯

Size

51.5 x 66.5"/131 x 169 cm

Yarn

Valley Yarns, Valley Superwash, worsted (100% extra fine merino; 97 yd./88 m; 1.76 oz./50 g):

A: 2 balls Crimson (red) #968
B: 1 ball Forest (green) #600
C: 2 balls Blue Mist (dark blue-green) #391
D: 2 balls Colonial Blue (medium blue) #502
E: 2 balls Golden Girl (yellow-orange) #300
F: 5 balls Soft Yellow (yellow) #023
G: 4 balls Spring Leaf (chartreuse) #694
H: 3 balls Ice Blue (light blue) #563
I: 3 balls Teal (light blue-green) #522
J: 1 ball Sriracha (orange-red) #302
K: 1 ball Manic Panic (hot pink) #304
L: 2 balls Classic Navy (navy blue) #571
M: 1 ball Mulberry (light burgundy) #321
N: 2 balls Plum (dark magenta) #320
O: 2 balls Misty Lilac (light dusty purple) #263
P: 2 balls Orchid (light purple-red) #024
Q: 7 balls Black (black) #220

Needles

US Size 8/5 mm, 40"/100 cm circular needles, US Size 8/5 mm dpns (for Method B)

Notions

Stitch markers, stitch holders, tapestry needle

Gauge

17 sts and 34 rows = 4"/10 cm in garter st

Notes

• This blanket is worked in blocks. Each block begins with the central square, and stitches for outer shapes are picked up from the edges of inner, completed shapes. The blocks are sewn together. The borders are added by picking up stitches from the edges of the assembled squares.

• Make color changes at the beginning of each shape by cutting current yarn and tying on new yarn color. For color assignments for shapes, refer to Figure 2.

• There are two construction methods for completing the corners of blocks. Method A works back and forth, decreasing to 1 stitch. Method B works the corners of four adjacent blocks in the round on dpns, as an outside-in square. Edge triangles and corners complete the blanket face.

Blanket Instructions

Block (Make 12)

Each Block is composed of Shapes 1–7.
See Figure 2 for colors and Figure 3 for
construction.

Shape 1 (S1)

With A, CO 16.
Knit 32 rows.
Cut A.

Shape 2 (S2)

Attach B.
Row 1 (RS): Knit.
*Work [Tr] until 2 sts rem.
Next row (WS): K2tog—1 st.
Cut yarn and fasten off.*
On left, bottom, and right edges of S1, with yarn
color specified in Figure 2, pu&k 16 sts. Rep
bet * and *.

Triangle (Tr) – Both Methods

Row 1 (WS): Knit.
Row 2 (RS): K2tog, knit to last 2 sts, ssk—2
sts dec'd.
Rep [Rows 1 & 2] for patt.

Shape 3 (S3)

*On one edge of S2 (blue edge in Figure 3), with
yarn color specified in Figure 2, pu&k 12 sts bef
the point where S1 intersects the edge, and 11
sts after the point—23 sts.
Work [Tr], until 7 sts rem, ending after a WS row.
Place 7 sts on holder. Cut yarn.
Rep from * on the three other edges of S2.

Shape 4 (S4)

Rep from * for Shape 3 on edges of S3 (green
edge in Figure 3).

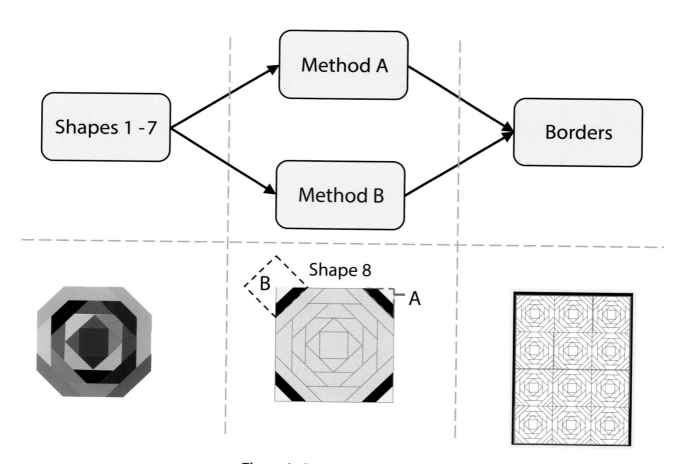

Figure 1: *Construction Options*

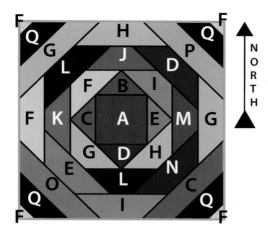

Figure 2: *Color Chart*

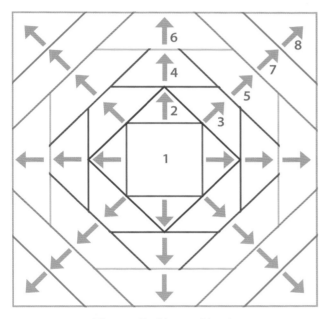

Figure 3: *Shape Chart*

Shape 5 (S5)

*On one long edge of S4 (purple edge in Figure 3), with yarn color specified in Figure 2, pu&k 12 sts, knit 7 sts from holder for S3, pu&k 11 sts—30 sts.

Work [Tr] until 14 sts rem, ending after a WS row. Place 14 sts on holder. Cut yarn.

Rep from * on the other three long edges of S4.

Shape 6 (S6)

Rep from * for Shape 5 on edges of S5 (yellow edge in Figure 3). Cut yarn, leaving a 10″/25 cm tail, and fasten off.

Shape 7 (S7)

*On one long side of S6 (magenta edge in Figure 3), with yarn color specified in Figure 2, pu&k 12 sts, knit 14 sts from holder for S5, pu&k 11 sts—37 sts.

Work [Tr], until 23 sts rem, ending after WS row. Cut yarn, leaving a 10″/25 cm tail, and fasten off.

Continue at either **Method A** or **Method B** to complete remaining shapes and assemble.

METHOD A

Shape 8 (S8)

On each S7 (teal edge in Figure 3), with Q, work [Tr] until 9 sts rem, ending after a WS row. Cut Q, leaving a 10″/25 cm tail, and fasten off. Attach F.

Work [Tr] until 3 sts rem, ending after a WS row.

Next row (RS): Cdd—1 st.

Cut yarn, leaving a 10″/25 cm tail, and fasten off.

Assembly

Referring to the arrow North in Figure 2, arrange and orient the blocks as shown in Figure 4. Using the long tails and whip st, sew the blocks tog into three columns and then sew columns tog, aligning edges of similar shapes.

Continue at **Borders.**

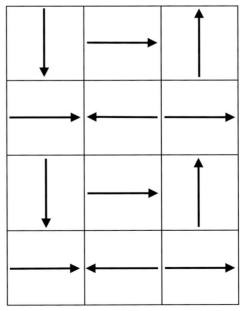

Figure 4: *Method A: Assembly Diagram*

METHOD B

Shape 8 Square, Triangle and Corner (8S, 8T, and 8C)

Orient Blocks as shown by arrows in Figure 5. On RS, using matching long tails and mattress st, sew blocks on dotted lines in Figure 5. If preferred, sewing may be piecemeal, sewing just the blocks adjacent to the Shape to be worked next.

Shape 8 Square (8S)

In each of the openings labeled "8S" in Figure 5, attach Q at red triangle. Working clockwise on the RS with a dpn, *pu&k 21 sts evenly to next corner; rep from * 3 times—84 sts, 21 sts on each dpn.

Work [OS]. Cut yarn, leaving a 10"/25 cm tail. Thread tail onto tapestry needle. Insert needle through rem sts, pull to tighten, and fasten securely.

Outside-In Square (OS) – Method B—84 sts dec'ing to 4 sts

Worked in the round.

Note: *The cdd uses the last 2 sts of 1 dpn and the 1st st of the next. The last cdd crosses the BOR.*

Rnd 1: Purl.

Rnd 2: *Knit to 2 sts bef end of dpn, cdd; rep from * 3 times—8 sts dec'd; 76 sts.

Rnds 3–12: Rep [Rnds 1 & 2] 5 times—40 sts dec'd; 36 sts.

Cut Q. Attach F.

Rnds 13–20: Rep [Rnds 1 & 2] 4 times—32 sts dec'd; 4 sts.

Figure 5: *Method B: Construction Diagram*

Shape 8 Triangle (8T)

In each of the openings labeled "8T" in Figure 5, attach Q at red triangle. On RS with circ needle, pu&k 21 sts on edge to corner, 1 st in corner, pm, and pu&k 21 on next edge—43 sts.

Work [HS]. Cut yarn, leaving a 10"/25 cm tail, and fasten off.

Half Square (HS) – Method B—43 sts dec'ing to 1 st

Row 1 (WS): Knit.
Row 2 (RS): K2tog, knit to 2 sts bef m, rm, cdd, pm, knit to 2 sts bef end, ssk—4 sts dec'd; 39 sts.
Rows 3–12: Rep [Rows 1 & 2] 5 times—20 sts dec'd; 19 sts.
Cut Q, leaving a 10"/25 cm tail, and fasten off. Attach F.
Rows 13–18: Rep [Rows 1 & 2] 3 times—12 sts dec'd; 7 sts.
Row 19: Knit. Rm.
Row 20: K2tog, cdd, ssk—4 sts dec'd; 3 sts.
Row 21: Cdd—2 sts dec'd; 1 st.

Shape 8 Corner (8C)

Worked back and forth.

In each of the openings labeled "8C" in Figure 5, attach Q at red dot. On RS, pu&k 21 sts evenly to next corner.

Work [Tr] until 9 sts rem, ending after a WS row. Cut Q, leaving a 10"/25 cm tail.

Attach F. Work [Tr] until 3 sts rem, ending after a WS row.

Next row (RS): Cdd—2 sts dec'd; 1 st.

Cut yarn, leaving a 10"/25 cm tail, and fasten off.

Continue at **Borders.**

BORDERS – BOTH METHODS

Top Border

On RS, with Q, pu&k 64 sts per Block on top edge of blanket—192 sts.

Tip: Divide Block edge into 4 equal lengths, mark and pu 16 sts bet m's.

Row 1 (WS): K1, kf&b, knit to last st, kf&b, k1—2 sts inc'd; 194 sts.
Row 2 (RS): Knit.
Rows 3–16: Rep [Rows 1 & 2] 7 times—14 sts inc'd; 208 sts.
Row 17: Rep [Row 1] once more—2 sts inc'd; 210 sts.
Cut Q, leaving a 10"/25 cm tail for sewing corner seam, and attach F.
Row 18: Rep [Row 2] once.
Rows 19–26: Rep [Rows 1 & 2] 4 times—8 sts inc'd; 218 sts.
Row 27: Rep [Row 1].
BO. Cut yarn, leaving a 10"/25 cm tail, and fasten off.

Bottom Border

Rep as for Top Border.

Left Border

With Q, pu&k 64 sts per Block along left edge of blanket—256 sts.
Rep as for Top Border, ending with 282 sts.

Right Border

Rep as for Left Border.
Using whip st and long tails, sew Border corners tog.

FINISHING

Weave in ends.

Metropolitan

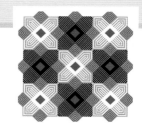

Let the striped geometrics of this blanket bring a touch of urban sophistication to your home.

. . . .

Techniques

Size
64 x 64"/163 x 163 cm

Yarn
Red Heart Sweet Home, super chunky (100% polyester; 193 yd./177 m; 10.5 oz./298 g):
A: 2 skeins Merlot (red) #E891–0915
B: 2 skeins Ink (black) #E891–0217
C: 3 skeins Steel (medium gray) #E891–0411
D: 3 skeins Snow (white) #E891–0110

Needles
US Size 11/8 mm, 3 straight needles and dpns

Notions
Stitch markers, tapestry needle

Gauge
7.5 sts and 15 rows = 4"/10 cm in garter st

Notes
- This blanket is worked in modules starting with the four Star-8s. The completed Star-8s are joined by working five Star-4s that are picked up on the sides of the Star-8s. Blanket edges are filled in with additional shapes (see Figure 1).
- On striped shapes, carry nonworking yarn up the edge until next use.
- When 3 markers are in use, there are special stitch counts at the end of each row as follows: (sts from beg to 1st m—# sts bet 1st m and 2nd m—# sts bet 2nd m and 3rd m—# sts from 3rd m to end of row).

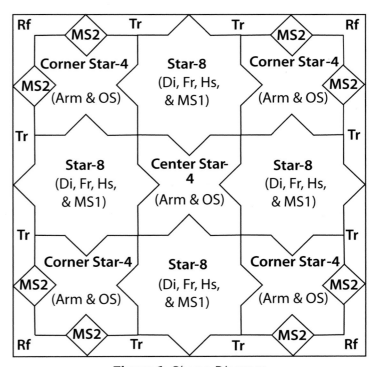

Figure 1: *Shape Diagram*

Blanket Instructions

Star-8s (Make 4)

A Star-8 consists of 4 shapes: Di, Fr, Hs, and MS1.

Diamond (Di)

With A, CO 1 st. Work [Di].

> **Diamond (Di)**—1 st inc'ing to 10 sts, dec'ing to 1 st
>
> **Rows 1–9:** Yoco, knit to end—9 sts inc'd; 10 sts.
> **Rows 10–11:** Knit.
> **Rows 12–20:** K2tog, knit to end—9 sts dec'd; 1 st.
> Pm on last st to mark northern tip of diamond. Cut yarn and fasten off.

Frame (Fr)

See Figure 2 for Frame construction. Frame is worked counterclockwise in the order Fr-a, Fr-b, Fr-c, and Fr-d.

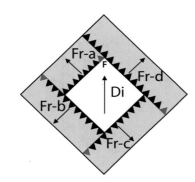

Figure 2: *Construction of Shapes Di, and Fr (Fr-a – Fr-d)*

Fr-a

With RS facing, attach B to the fasten-off point of Di (red triangle on shape Fr-a), and pu&k 8 sts to next corner.
Knit 5 rows.
BO, leaving last st on needle.

Fr-b

On next edge, starting at the red triangle on Fr-b, *pu&k 2 sts on the short edge of Fr-a and 8 sts evenly on edge of Di—11 sts.
Knit 5 rows.
BO, leaving last st on needle.

Fr-c

Starting at the red triangle on Fr-c, rep from * of Fr-b, picking up sts on the short edge of Fr-b.

Fr-d

On the next edge, starting at the red triangle on Fr-d, pu&k 2 sts on short edge of Fr-c, 8 sts evenly on next edge of Di, and 3 sts on short edge of Fr-a—14 sts.
Knit 5 rows and do not BO. Do not cut B.

House (Hs)

Attach C.
Knit 1 row. Work [Hs].
On each of the other 3 sides of Fr, attach C at next corner of Fr at red triangle in Figure 3, pu&k 14 sts on edge. Work [Hs].

> **House (Hs)**—14 sts dec'ing to 1 st
>
> **Row 1 (WS):** With C, knit.
> **Rows 2 & 3:** With B, knit.
> **Rows 4 & 5:** With C, knit.
> **Rows 6–17:** Rep [Rows 2–5] 3 times.
> **Rows 18 & 19:** Rep [Rows 2 & 3].
> **Row 20:** With C, k2tog, knit to last 2 sts, ssk—2 sts dec'd; 12 sts.
> **Row 21:** Knit.
> **Rows 22 & 23:** With B, rep [Rows 20 & 21]—2 sts dec'd; 10 sts.
> **Rows 24–31:** Rep [Rows 20–23] 2 times—8 sts dec'd; 2 sts.
> **Row 32:** With C, knit.
> **Row 33:** K2tog—1 st dec'd; 1 st.
> Cut yarns and fasten off.

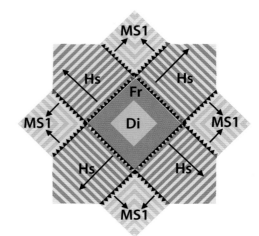

Figure 3: *Shapes Hs & MS1 Construction*

Mitered Square 1 (MS1)

In each of the 4 openings created by the sides of adjacent Hs's (MS1 in Figure 3), attach A at corner of Hs at red triangle. Pu&k 10 sts evenly to inner corner, 1 st in corner, pm, pu&k 10 sts—21 sts. Work [MS].

Mitered Square (MS)—21 sts dec'ing to 1 st

Row 1 (WS): Knit.

Row 2 (RS): With C, knit to 2 sts bef m, rm, cdd, pm, knit to end—2 sts dec'd; 19 sts.

Row 3: Knit.

Row 4: With A, Rep [Row 2]—2 sts dec'd; 17 sts.

Rows 5–16: Rep [Rows 1–4] 3 times—12 sts dec'd; 5 sts.

Rows 17–18: Rep [Rows 1 & 2]—2 sts dec'd; 3 sts.

Row 19: Cdd—2 sts dec'd; 1 st.

Cut yarn and fasten off.

Star-4s (Make 4)

A Star-4 consists of 2 shapes: Arm and OS.

Arm

Arrange the Star-8s as shown in Figure 4.

Note: *Referring to Figure 4, there are five Star-4s created from Shapes Arm and OS. In each, four Arms are worked and then sts are picked up on the edges of each Arm to work OS in the round*

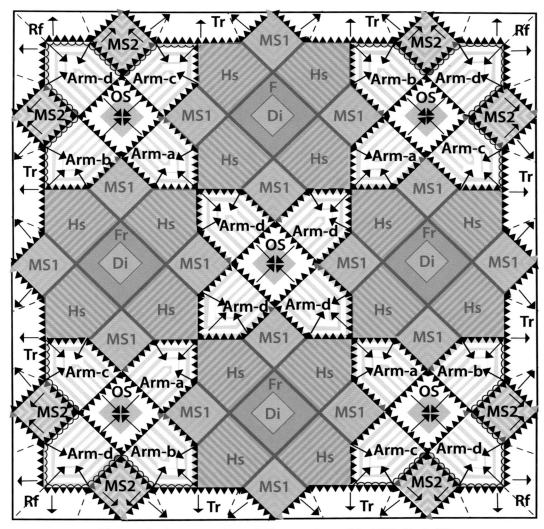

Figure 4: *Construction of Shapes Arm, OS, MS2, Tr, & Rf*

on dpns. There are four different types of Arms, **Arm-a** to **Arm-d**, shown on Figure 4, that differ only in the method used for generating stitches, depending on where the Arm resides on the blanket layout. Next to an existing shape, pu&k; where there is no existing shape, CO.

Arm-a

With C, *pu&k 10 st on edge, pm; rep from * 2 more times, pu&k 10 sts on last edge—40 sts. Work [Arm].

Arm-b

Attach C at the red triangle, *pu&k 10 sts on edge, pm; rep from * once more, CO 10 sts, pm, CO 10 sts—40 sts. Work [Arm].

Arm-c

Attach C at the red semicircle, *CO 10 sts, pm; rep from * once more, pu&k 10 sts next edge, pm, pu&k 10 sts on last edge—40 sts. Work [Arm].

Arm-d

Attach C at the red semicircle, *CO 10 sts, pm; rep from * 2 more times, CO 10 sts—40 sts. Work [Arm].

Arm—40 sts dec'ing to 0 sts

Row 1 (WS): Knit.
Change to D.
Row 2 (RS): Knit to 2 sts bef 2nd m, k2tog, ssk, knit to end—2 sts dec'd; 38 sts (10-9-9-10).
Row 3: Knit.
Change to C.
Row 4: *Knit to 2 sts bef m, k2tog, ssk; rep from * 2 more times, knit to end—6 sts dec'd; 32 sts (9-7-7-9).
Row 5: Knit.
Rows 6–9: Rep [Rows 2–5]—8 sts dec'd; 24 sts (8-4-4-8).
Rows 10 & 11: Rep [Rows 2 & 3]—2 sts dec'd; 22 sts (8-3-3-8).

Row 12: Rm 2nd and 3rd m's. Knit to 2 sts bef 1st m, k2tog, cdd twice, ssk, knit to end—6 sts dec'd; 16 sts.

Row 13: Knit.

Row 14: Knit 1 st bef 1st m, rm, k2tog, ssk, knit to end—2 sts dec'd; 14 sts.

Row 15: Knit 7, and then 3-needle BO of all sts. Cut yarn and fasten off.

Outside-In Square (OS)

In each of the 5 openings labeled "OS" in Figure 4, attach D at the purple triangle. *With dpn, pu&k 14 sts, pm; rep from * 3 times—56 sts. Work [OS].

Outside-In Square (OS)—56 sts dec'ing to 8 sts

Work in the round on dpns.

Rnd 1 and all odd (WS) rnds: Purl.

Rnd 2 (RS): *Ssk, knit to 2 sts bef end of dpn, k2tog; rep from * 3 more times—8 sts dec'd; 48 sts.

Rnds 4–7: Rep [Rnds 2 & 3] 2 times—16 sts dec'd; 32 sts.

Cut D and attach C.

Rnds 8–13: Rep [Rnds 2 & 3] 3 times—24 sts dec'd; 8 sts.

Cut C, leaving a 10"/25 cm tail. Thread tail onto needle and insert through all loops. Pull tightly and fasten off securely.

Edge Shapes

Mitered Square 2 (MS2)

In each of the 8 openings labeled "MS2" in Figure 4, attach A to rightmost corner at the green triangle. Pu&k 10 sts on edge, 1 st on the corner, pm, pu&k 10 sts on next edge—21 sts. Work [MS].

Trapezoid (Tr)

In each of the 8 spaces labeled "Tr" in Figure 4, attach D at the corner at the yellow triangle. Pu&k 10 sts on edge, pm, pu&k 20 sts on next edge, pm, and pu&k 10 sts on last edge—40 sts. Work [Tr].

Trapezoid (Tr)—40 sts dec'ing to 0 sts

Row 1 and all odd (WS) rows: Knit.

Row 2 (RS): K2tog, knit to last 2 sts, ssk—2 sts dec'd; 38 sts (9-20-9).

Row 4: *K2tog, knit to 2 sts bef m, ssk, rep from * twice more—6 sts dec'd; 32 sts (7-18-7).

Rows 5–8: Rep [Rows 1–4]—8 sts dec'd; 24 sts (4-16-4).

Rows 9–10: Rep [Rows 1 & 2]—2 sts dec'd; 22 sts (3-16-3).

Row 11: Knit.

Row 12: K3tog, k2tog, knit to 2 sts bef next m, ssk, sssk—6 sts dec'd; 16 sts (1-14-1).

Row 13: Rm's, k2tog, BO this st and all sts to last 2 sts on L needle, sl st on R needle to left, sk2p.

Cut yarn and fasten off.

Roof (R)

In each of the 4 spaces labeled "Rf" in Figure 4, attach D at the blue triangle. *Pu&k 10 sts on edge, pm; rep from * 2 more times, pu&k 10 sts on last edge—40 sts. Work [Rf].

Roof (Rf)—40 sts dec'ing to 0 sts

Row 1 and all odd (WS) rows: Knit.

Row 2 (RS): K2tog, knit to 1 st bef 2nd m, kf&b, kf&b, knit to last 2 sts, ssk (9-11-11-9).

Row 4: K2tog, knit to 2 sts bef 1st m, ssk, k2tog, knit to 1 st bef 2nd m, kf&b, kf&b, knit to 2 sts bef 3rd m, ssk, k2tog, knit to last 2 sts, ssk—4 sts dec'd; 36 sts (7-11-11-7).

Rows 5–8: Rep [Rows 1–4] 1 time—4 sts dec'd; 32 sts (4-12-12-4).

Rows 9–10: Rep [Rows 1 & 2]—(3-13-13-3).

Row 11: Knit.

Row 12: K3tog, k2tog, knit to 1 st bef next m, kf&b, kf&b, knit to 2 sts bef next m, ssk, sssk—4 sts dec'd; 28 sts (1-13-13-1). Rm's.

Row 13: K2tog, BO this st and all sts to last 2 sts on L needle, sl st on R needle to left, sk2p. Cut yarn and fasten off.

FINISHING

Weave in ends.

Perpetual Motion

A pinwheel of gorgeous colors appears to spin on this dramatic blanket.

. . . .

Techniques

Size
55.5 x 55.5"/141 x 141 cm

Yarn
Valley Yarns Haydenville, worsted (60%
  superwash merino wool/40% acrylic; 220
  yd./201 m; 3.5 oz./100 g):
A: 2 skeins Soft Grape (plum) #14
B: 3 skeins Lavender (light, dusty purple) #24
C: 6 skeins Teal (teal) #11
D: 1 skein Burgundy (burgundy) #10
E: 6 skeins Lake (light teal) #15
F: 1 skein Gold (gold) #27
G: 3 skeins Natural (off-white) #02

Needles
US Size 7/4.5 mm, 60"/150 cm and 40"/100 cm
  circular needles

Notions
Stitch markers, tapestry needle

Gauge
19 sts and 38 rows = 4"/10 cm in garter st

Note
• This blanket is worked from the center out
  starting with the individual blades of the
  pinwheel, each of which is picked up from
  the edges of the previously completed
  blade. Diamonds and corners fill out the
  center square. The Striped Border is worked
  separately and sewn on.

Blanket Instructions

Center
See Figure 1 for construction and colors. C1–4
  refer to the Blade colors beginning from the
  outermost.

Blade 1 (B1)
With C1 for Blade 1 in Figure 1, *CO 72 sts, pm,
  rep from * once more, CO 42 sts, leaving a
  32"/81 cm tail—186 sts.
Work [Blade].

Blades 2–8 (B2–B8)
With C1 for the Blade as specified in Figure 2, CO
  40 sts, pm, CO 40 sts, pu&k 30 sts along edge
  ab (see Figure 1) of prev Blade, pm, and 70 sts
  along edge **bc** of prev Blade—180 sts. Work
  [Blade] starting at Row 2 (WS).

Blade (B)—186 sts dec'ing to 0 sts

Row 1 (RS): With C1, k2tog, *knit to 2 sts bef m, ssk, k2tog; rep from * once more, knit to 2 sts bef end, ssk—6 sts dec'd; 180 sts.

Row 2 (WS): Knit.

Rows 3–18: Rep [Rows 1 & 2] 8 times—48 sts dec'd; 132 sts.

Cut C1. Attach C2.

Rows 19–36: Rep [Rows 1 & 2] 9 times—54 sts dec'd; 78 sts.

Cut C2. Attach C3.

Rows 37–40: Rep [Rows 1 & 2] 2 times—12 sts dec'd; 66 sts.

Row 41: Rm, sl2, k2tog, p2sso, knit to 2 sts bef m, ssk, k2tog, knit to 2 sts bef end, ssk—6 sts dec'd; 60 sts.

Row 42: Knit.

Row 43: K2tog, knit to 2 sts bef m, ssk, k2tog, knit to 2 sts bef end, ssk—4 sts dec'd; 56 sts.

Row 44: Knit.

Rows 45–54: Rep [Rows 43 & 44] 5 times—20 sts dec'd; 36 sts.

Cut C3. Attach C4.

Rows 55–70: Rep [Rows 43 & 44] 8 times—32 sts dec'd; 4 sts.

Row 71: Knit.

Cut yarn, leaving a 10"/25 cm tail. Thread yarn end through tapestry needle and then insert needle through all sts on needle and fasten off securely.

Using whip stitch and the long CO tail of B1, sew B1 and B8 tog along dashed line shown in Figure 2.

Diamonds (DI)

In each of the 8 spaces labeled "DI" in Figure 3, attach G at red triangle at tip of Blade, and pu&k 41 sts evenly along edge to next corner, 1 st in corner, pm, and 41 sts to next corner—83 sts. Work [DI].

Diamond (DI)—83 sts dec'ing to 0 sts

Row 1 and all WS (odd) rows to 53: Knit.

Row 2 (RS): K2tog, knit to last 2 sts, ssk—2 sts dec'd; 81 sts.

Row 4: K2tog, knit to 2 sts bef m, rm, cdd, pm, knit to last 2 sts, ssk—4 sts dec'd; 77 sts.

Rows 5–52: Rep [Rows 1–4] 12 times—72 sts dec'd; 5 sts.

Row 54: K1, cdd, k1—2 sts dec'd; 3 sts.

Row 55 (WS): Cdd—2 sts dec'd; 1 st.

Cut yarn and fasten off.

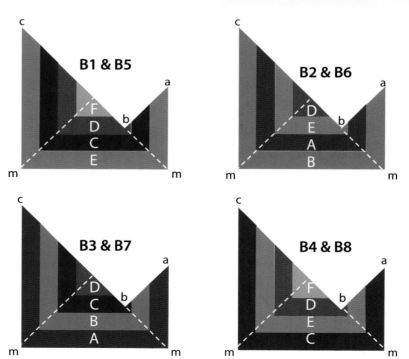

Figure 1: *Blade Color Schemes, Marker Positions, and Attachment Locations*

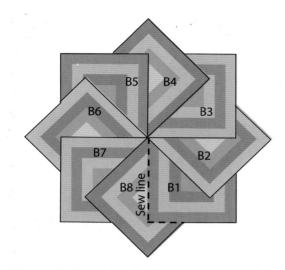

Figure 2: *Sew Line for Attaching B1 and B8*

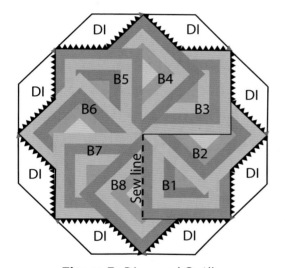

Figure 3: *Diamond Outline*

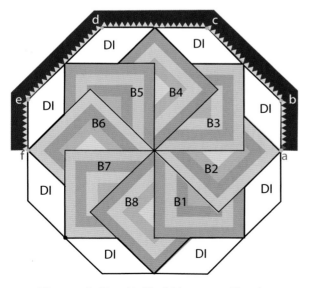

Figure 4: *Top Half of Hexagon Border*

HEXAGON BORDER

Top Half

Attach C at point **a** in Figure 4. Using the longer circular needles, pu&k 42 sts bet point **a** and **b**, pm, 84 sts along each of edges **bc**, **cd**, and **de**, placing m at each point, and 42 sts bet point **e** and **f**—336 sts.

Row 1 (WS): Knit.

Row 2 (RS): *Knit to 1 st bef m, bli, k1, k1, bli; rep from * 3 more times, knit to end—8 sts inc'd; 344 sts.

Rows 3 & 4: Knit.

Rows 5–16: Rep [Rows 1–4] 3 times—24 sts inc'd; 368 sts.

Rows 17–18: Knit.

Row 19 (WS): BO 46 sts from **f** to **e**, rm, knit and place 92 sts bet **e** and **d** on holder, rm, BO 92 sts bet **d** and **c**, rm, knit and place 92 sts bet **c** and **b** on holder, rm, BO rem 46 sts bet **b** and **a**. Cut yarn, leaving a 10"/25 cm tail, and fasten off.

Bottom Half

Rep Top Half beg at point **a** in Figure 5.

Using whip st and long tails, sew open edges of the Top Half and Bottom Half of Hexagon.

Corners (CR)

For each set of sts on holder from Hexagon Border (bet each pair of points **a** and **b** in Figure 6), transfer 92 sts from holders to needle. Attach E on RS. Work [CR].

Corner (CR)—92 sts dec'ing to 0 sts

Row 1: Knit.

Row 2: K2tog, knit to last 2 sts, ssk—2 sts dec'd; 90 sts.

Rows 3–46: Rep [Rows 1 & 2] 44 times—88 sts dec'd; 2 sts.

Cut yarn, leaving a 10"/25 cm tail. Thread yarn through tapestry needle. Insert needle through all sts on needle and fasten off securely.

STRIPED BORDER

See Figure 7 for construction. See inset for details. Bright blue lines are the beg and end of Strips.

Strip 1

With E, CO on 31 sts. Knit 1 row.

Work [BT1].

*On RS, attach B on right edge of completed BT1 at red triangle in Figure 7; pu&k 31 sts evenly. Work [BT2].

Attach E on left edge of BT2 at orange triangle, pu&k 31 sts evenly. Work [BT1].*

Rep bet * and * 4 times.

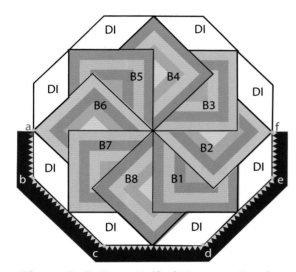

Figure 5: *Bottom Half of Hexagon Border*

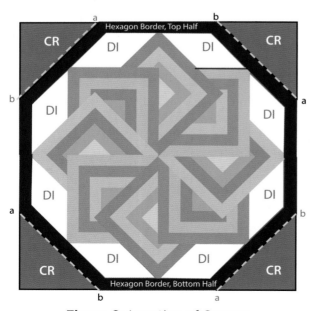

Figure 6: *Location of Corners*

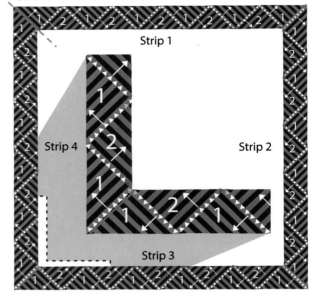

Figure 7: *Striped Border Construction*

Border Triangle 1 (BT1)—31 sts dec'ing to 1 st

Carry nonworking yarn along the edge.

Row 1 (WS): Knit.

Change to C.

Row 2 (RS): Knit to last 2 sts, ssk—1 st dec'd; 30 sts.

Row 3: Knit.

Change to E.

Rows 4–5: Rep [Rows 2 & 3]—1 st dec'd; 29 sts.

Change to C.

Rows 6–61: Rep [Rows 2–5] 14 times—28 sts dec'd; 1 st.

Cut yarn and fasten off.

Border Triangle 2 (BT2)—31 sts dec'ing to 1 st

Carry nonworking yarn along the edge.

Row 1 (WS): Knit.

Change to C.

Row 2 (RS): K2tog, knit to end—1 st dec'd; 30 sts.

Row 3: Knit.

Change to B.

Rows 4–5: Rep [Rows 2 & 3]—1 st dec'd; 29 sts.

Change to C.

Rows 6–61: Rep [Rows 2–5] 14 times—28 sts dec'd; 1 st.

Cut yarn and fasten off.

Strip 2

On RS, on right edge of last BT1 of Strip 1 (bright blue line in Figure 7), attach E and pu&k 31 sts. Rep as for Strip 1, starting at Row 1.

Strips 3 & 4

Work as for Strip 2. Leave a 20"/50 cm tail when tying off the last BT1 of Strip 4.

Using whip st and the long tail, sew the last BT1 of Strip 4 to the first BT1 of Strip 1.

FINISHING

Match corners of Striped Border to Center Corners as shown in Figure 8. Pin and, using E and whip st, sew border and blanket face tog, starting at blue dot in Figure 8 and working counterclockwise. Weave in ends and block if desired.

Figure 8: *Final Assembly—attach border to blanket face*

Petals

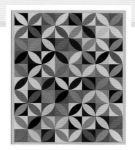

Gently curved petals form a garden of multicolored flowers.

Techniques

Size
60 x 73"/152 x 185 cm

Yarn
Patons Alpaca Blend, chunky (60% acrylic/22% wool/10% nylon/8% alpaca; 155 yd./142 m; 3.5 oz./100 g):
A: 3 skeins Baltic (navy blue)
B: 3 skeins Lagoon (dark teal)
C: 3 skeins Oats (taupe)
D: 3 skeins Iceberg (light teal)
E: 5 skeins Sable (chocolate brown)
F: 3 skeins Butternut (yellow-orange)
G: 5 skeins Birch (light taupe)
H: 3 skeins Maize (light yellow)
I: 3 skeins Yam (rusty orange)
J: 3 skeins Tiger Eye (medium brown)

Needles
US Size 8/5 mm, 40"/100 cm circular needles

Notions
US J-10/6 mm crochet hook, scrap yarn or holder for provisional CO, tapestry needle

Gauge
13 sts and 26 rows = 4"/10 cm in garter st

Notes
- The blanket face is worked in blocks with crochet edges, which are sewn together. The petal shapes are worked using wrap & turn technique. The borders are picked up and knit after the blocks are sewn together.
- This blanket uses the same shapes and general design as the Carnival blanket on page 1 but is worked in a different gauge and colors.

Blanket Instructions

Block
Make 80 Blocks using the color combinations in Figure 2 and Table 1. A Block consists of a Petal (P) and two Triangles (T1, T2), and is finished with a single-crochet edging. See Figure 1 for construction and colors.

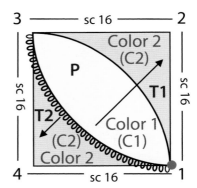

Figure 1: *Color and Construction Chart for Block*

Petal Color (C1)	T1 & T2 Color (C2)									
	A	B	C	D	E	F	G	H	I	J
A		1		2			1		1	1
B	1		1	1		1			1	1
C				4	1				2	3
D	1	3	2						1	
E		2		2		1			1	
F	1		2		1		3	1		1
G	2	1			4	3			1	1
H	1	3			1	2			2	
I				1				4		2
J	4			1	2			1		

Table 1: *Color Combinations in Blocks*

Petal (P)

With C1, provisionally CO 30 sts.

Work [P]. Cut C1.

Petal (P)—30 sts

Row 1 (RS): K19, w&t.

Row 2 (WS): K8, w&t.

Rows 3 & 4: Knit to 3 sts after wrap, w&t.

Rows 5–8: Knit to 1 st after wrap, w&t.

Rows 9–12: Knit to wrap, w&t.

Rows 13–16: Knit to 1 st bef wrap, w&t.

Rows 17–19: Knit to 2 sts bef wrap, w&t.

Rows 20 & 21: Knit to 4 sts bef wrap, w&t.

Row 22: K4.

Note: Row 22 ends in the middle of the row.

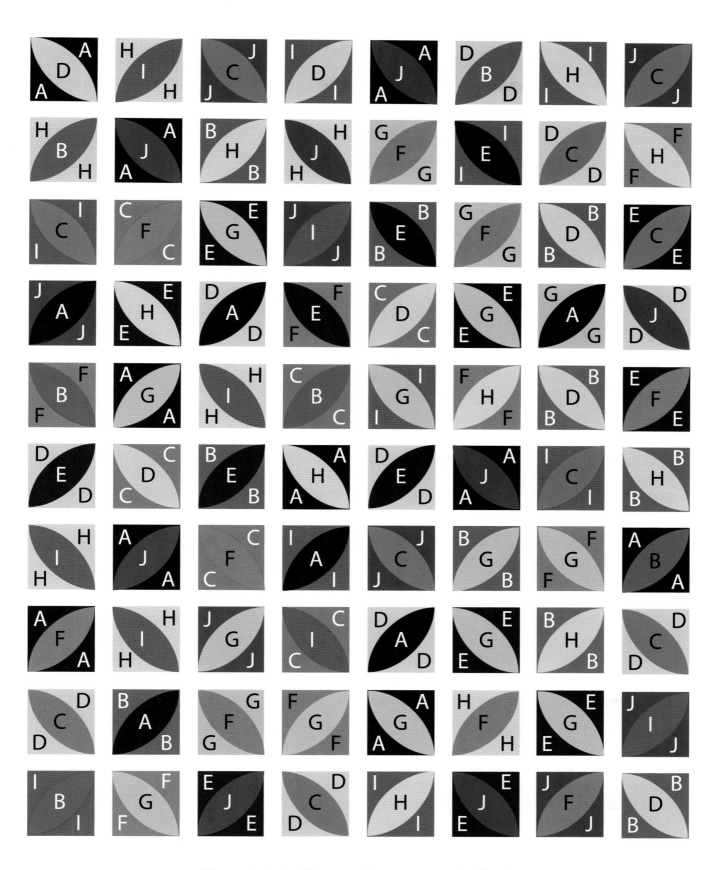

Figure 2: *Color Chart and Arrangement for Blocks*

Triangle 1 (T1)

Turn work to RS, slip sts one by one from R to L needle. Attach C2 at beg of row, leaving a 100"/254 cm tail.

Work [T].

Tip: *Wind long tails into a ball or hank and secure with a stitch marker so that they stay wound while the block is worked.*

Triangle 2 (T2)

Transfer 30 provisional sts to needle. On RS, attach C2, leaving a 100"/254 cm tail.

Work [T].

> **Triangle (T)—30 sts inc'ing to 34 sts dec'ing to 1 st**
>
> **Setup row (RS):** K7, *kf&b, k4; rep from * 3 more times, knit to end—4 sts inc'd; 34 sts.
> **Row 1 (WS):** BO3, knit to end—3 sts dec'd; 31 sts.
> **Rows 2–4:** Rep [Row 1]—9 sts dec'd; 22 sts.
> **Rows 5–10:** BO2, knit to end—12 sts dec'd; 10 sts.
> **Row 11:** Knit.
> **Row 12:** Knit to last 2 sts, ssk—1 st dec'd; 9 sts.
> **Rows 13–19:** Rep [Row 12] 7 times—7 sts dec'd; 2 sts.
> **Row 20:** Ssk—1 st dec'd; 1 st.
> Cut yarn, leaving a 25"/64 cm tail, and fasten off.

Crochet Edge

At corners 1 and 3 in Figure 1, with the long C2 CO tails, use a tapestry needle to take a st in the corner of the Block's adjacent T and fasten securely.

On RS, with crochet hook and C2 tail from T2, starting at 1 (red dot) in Figure 1, sc16 to next corner (1 st for each BO or dec st), sc2 in corner, sc16 to next corner, sl st in corner. Drop tail from T2 and pick up tail from T1. Rep bet **. Sl st in first st to finish. Cut yarn and fasten off.

ASSEMBLY

Lay out Blocks as shown in Figure 2. Using T1/T2 CO tails, sew tog blocks into vertical strips, and then sew strips tog. Catch only the back leg of the sl st edge when sewing seams.

BORDERS

Top Border

On RS, attach G at top-right corner of blanket. Pu&k 22 sts per block edge—176 sts.
Row 1 (WS): Knit.
Row 2 (RS): Kf&b, knit to last st, kf&b—2 sts inc'd; 178 sts.
Rows 3–8: Rep [Rows 1 & 2] 3 times—6 sts inc'd; 184 sts.
Row 9: Knit.
Cut, leaving a 10"/25 cm tail. Attach E.
Row 10: Rep [Row 2]—2 sts inc'd; 186 sts.
Rows 11–19: Rep [Rows 1–9]—8 sts inc'd; 194 sts.
BO all sts. Cut yarn, leaving a 10"/25 cm tail.

Bottom Border

On RS, attach G at bottom-left corner of blanket. Work as for Top Border.

Right Border

On RS, attach G at bottom-right corner of blanket. Pu&k 22 sts per block edge—220 sts.
Work [Rows 1–19] as for Top Border, ending with 238 sts.

Left Border

On RS, attach G at top-left corner of blanket. Work as for Right Border.

FINISHING

Using long tails left from Border BOs, sew tog diagonal seams at corners of Borders, using mattress st for garter st. Weave in ends.

Picnic

In the heart of winter, the stars and checks of this blanket remind us of warm, sunny days and picnics to come.

. . . .

Techniques

Method A: ▲

Method B: ▲ ♯

Method C: ⟝₀

Method D: ⟝₀ ♯

Size
50.5 x 67"/128 x 170 cm

Yarn
Paintbox Yarns Simply Aran (100% acrylic; 201 yd./184 m; 3.5 oz./100 g):

A: 4 skeins Slate Grey (medium gray) #205
B: 2 skeins Pistachio Green (light, dusty green) #224
C: 1 skein Racing Green (dark green) #227
D: 1 skein Duck Egg Blue (light blue) #235
E: 1 skein Neon Pink (neon pink) #256
F: 1 skein Banana Cream (light yellow) #220
G: 1 skein Red Wine (burgundy) #215
H: 1 skein Kingfisher Blue (medium blue) #234
I: 1 skein Blush Pink (medium coral/pink) #253
J: 2 skeins Dusty Lilac (lavender) #246
K: 1 skein Royal Blue (bright navy) #240
L: 1 skein Mustard Yellow (bright gold) #223
M: 1 skein Pansy Purple (bright purple) #247
N: 4 skeins Paper White (bright white) #200
O: 1 skein Rose Red (bright red) #213

Needles
US Size 8/5 mm, 40"/100 cm circular needles and dpns (for Method B)

Notions
Stitch markers, tapestry needle

Gauge
18 sts and 36 rows = 4"/10 cm in garter st

Notes
- Figure 1 illustrates the construction(s) of the blanket. There are two methods for working Crosses and Quarter Crosses: Method A uses more pu&k and is worked back and forth. Method B uses more edge decreases, a square worked outside-in, and a short seam.
- There is a single method for turning Crosses into octagons and Quarter Crosses into trapezoids by adding wedges.
- There are also two methods for assembling the blanket: Method C, which requires more sewing, uses plain garter stitch squares that are then arranged between the octagons and trapezoids and sewn into strips. In Method D, the diagonal edges of the octagons and trapezoids are sewn together to make the blanket face; then outside-in squares are worked to fill in spaces.
- Following either assembly method, corner pieces are picked up and knit as triangles.
- The border is worked by picking up sts on the edges of the completed blanket face.

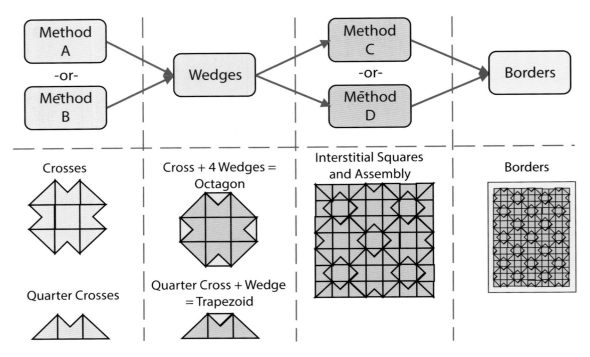

Figure 1: *Construction Options*

Method A -or- Method B → Wedges → Method C -or- Method D → Borders

Crosses

Quarter Crosses

Cross + 4 Wedges = Octagon

Quarter Cross + Wedge = Trapezoid

Interstitial Squares and Assembly

Borders

Blanket Instructions

CROSSES

Make 18—1 in each of the 18 Color Schemes (CS) listed in Table 1. Use Method A or Method B. Column headings correspond to named shapes in Figures 2 & 3. An Octagon is composed of a Cross (worked with either Method A or Method B) and four Wedges.

METHOD A

See Figure 2.

Square A (SA)

Using yarn color specified in Table 1 for S, work [Sq] but do not bind off. Cut yarn and fasten off.

Square (Sq) – Methods A & C—19 sts

CO 19 sts. Knit 38 rows.
BO loosely. Cut yarn and fasten off.

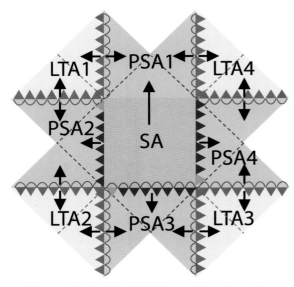

Figure 2: *Method A: Cross Construction*

Pointed Squares (PSA1–PSA4)

PSA1

With yarn color specified in Table 1 for PS, CO 18 sts. On RS work across SA sts: k1, pm, k9, bli, k9, pm; then CO 18—56 sts. Work [PSA].

PSA2

With yarn color specified in Table 1 for PS, CO 18 sts. Starting at the orange triangle in space labeled "PSA2" in Figure 2, pu&k 1 st along edge of SA, pm, pu&k 19 sts to next corner, pm, CO 18—56 sts. Work [PSA].

PSA3 & PSA4

Rep as for PSA2 in spaces labeled "PSA3" and "PSA4."

Pointed Square A (PSA) – Method A—56 sts dec'ing to 4 sts

Row 1 (WS): Knit.

Row 2 (RS): K2tog, *knit to 2 sts bef m, rm, cdd, pm; rep from * 1 more time, knit to last 2 sts, ssk—6 sts dec'd; 50 sts.

Row 3: Knit.

Rows 4–17: Rep [Rows 2 & 3] 7 times—42 sts dec'd; 8 sts.

Row 18: K2tog twice, ssk twice—4 sts dec'd; 4 sts.

Cut yarn, leaving a 10"/25 cm tail. Thread yarn through tapestry needle and insert needle through 4 rem sts. Pull tight and fasten off securely.

CS	Color for:			CS	Color for:			CS	Color for:		
	S (A/B)	PS (A/B)	LT (A/B) & CW		S (A/B)	PS (A/B)	LT (A/B) & CW		S (A/B)	PS (A/B)	LT (A/B) & CW
GFA	G	F	A	CIA	C	I	A	NIO	N	I	O
EDA	E	D	A	HDA	H	D	A	NJC	N	J	C
CBA	C	B	A	GLA	G	L	A	NBM	N	B	M
KJA	K	J	A	KFA	K	F	A	NFG	N	F	G
GIA	G	I	A	GJA	G	J	A	NLE	N	L	E
EHA	E	H	A	KHA	K	H	A	NBK	N	B	K

Table 1: *Color Schemes for Octagons*

Large Triangles (LTA1–LTA4)

LTA1–LTA4

Attach yarn color specified in Table 1 for LT at point of PSA indicated by the red triangles in Figure 2, leaving a 15"/38 cm tail. Pu&k 18 sts to corner, 1 st in the corner of SA, pm, and 18 sts along right edge of next PSA to next corner—37 sts. Work [T].

> **Triangle (T)** – Methods A & B—odd number of sts
>
> **Row 1 (WS):** Knit.
> **Row 2 (RS):** K2tog, knit to 2 sts bef m, rm, cdd, pm, knit to last 2 sts, ssk—4 sts dec'd.
> **Row 3:** Knit.
> Rep [Rows 2 & 3] until 3 sts rem.
> **Next row (RS):** Cdd—2 sts dec'd; 1 st.
> Cut yarn, leaving a 10"/25 cm tail. Thread yarn onto tapestry needle and insert through rem sts on needle. Pull to tighten and fasten off securely.

Continue at **Quarter Crosses**.

METHOD B
See Figure 3.

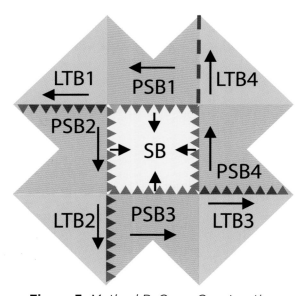

Figure 3: *Method B: Cross Construction*

Pointed Squares (PSB1–PSB4) and Large Triangles (LTB1–LTB4)

PSB1

CO 19 sts in color specified in Table 1 for PS. Work [PSB].

> **Pointed Square B (PSB)** – Method B—19 sts dec'ing to 10 sts, inc'ing to 19 sts
>
> **Row 1 (RS):** Knit.
> **Row 2 (WS):** Knit to last 2 sts, ssk—1 st dec'd; 18 sts.
> **Rows 3–18:** Rep [Rows 1 & 2] 8 times—8 sts dec'd; 10 sts.
> **Row 19:** Yoco, knit to end—1 st inc'd; 11 sts.
> **Row 20:** Knit.
> **Rows 21–36:** Rep [Rows 19 & 20] 8 times—8 sts inc'd; 19 sts.
> Do not BO. Cut yarn and fasten off.

LTB1

Attach yarn color specified in Table 1 for LT. Work [LTB]. Cut yarn and fasten off.

> **Large Triangle B (LTB)** – Method B—19 sts dec'ing to 1 st
>
> **Row 1 (RS) & 2 (WS):** Knit.
> **Row 3:** K2tog, knit to end—1 st dec'd; 18 sts.
> **Row 4:** Knit.
> **Rows 5–38:** Rep [Rows 3 & 4] 17 times—17 sts dec'd; 1 st.
> Cut yarn, leaving a 20"/50 cm tail, and fasten off.

PSB2 and LTB2

Attach yarn color specified in Table 1 for PS at red triangle at the corner of LTB1. Pu&k 19 sts to corner. Work [PSB], beg with Row 2.
Attach yarn for LT and work [LTB].

PSB3 and LTB3, and PSB4 and LTB4

Work as for PSB2 and LTB2, attaching yarn at red triangle of prev completed LTB.
After LTB4, cut yarn, leaving a 20"/50 cm tail.
Use BO tail of LTB4 to sew tog the CO edge of PSB1 and left edge of LTB4 along the dashed line in Figure 3, matching corners.

Square B (SB)

On RS, attach yarn color specified in Table 1 for S at the orange triangle on left corner of PSB1 in Figure 3. Working clockwise, *pu&k 17 sts to the next corner, 1 st in corner, pm; rep from * 3 more times—72 sts. Work [OSB].

Outside-In Square (OSB) – Method B—72 sts dec'ing to 8 sts

Worked in the round on circular needles.

Note: *Change to dpns when needed to accommodate sts. When working on dpns, do not pm's. On dec rounds, work to 2 sts bef end of dpn. The cdd uses the last 2 sts of 1 dpn and the 1st st of the next. The last cdd crosses the BOR.*

Rnd 1: Purl.
Rnd 2: *Knit to 2 sts bef m, rm, cdd, pm; rep from * 3 times—8 sts dec'd; 64 sts.
Rnd 3: Purl.
Rnds 4–17: Rep [Rnds 2 & 3] 7 times—56 sts dec'd; 8 sts. Rm's.
Cut yarn, leaving a 10"/25 cm tail. Thread yarn through tapestry needle and insert needle through rem sts. Pull tight and fasten off securely.

Continue at **Quarter Crosses**.

Quarter Crosses

Make 10—1 in each of the Color Schemes (CS) listed in Table 2. Column headings in Table 2 correspond to named shapes in Figures 4 & 5. Use Method A or Method B.

	Color for:	
CS	**PS(A/B)**	**LT(A/B) & QW**
BG	B	G
LO	L	O
DC	D	C
JK	J	K
DJ	D	J

	Color for:	
CS	**PS(A/B)**	**LT(A/B) & QW**
IE	I	E
BC	B	C
HE	H	E
BL	B	L
JK	J	K

Table 2: *Color Schemes for Trapezoids*

METHOD A

See Figure 4.

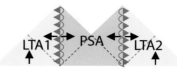

Figure 4: *Method A: Quarter Cross*

PSA

With yarn color specified in Table 2 for PS, CO 56 sts. Pm's after 19th st from beg of row and 18 sts from end of row on RS. Work [PSA].

LTA1

Attach yarn color specified in Table 2 for LT at the red triangle at the top-left corner of PSA in Figure 4. Pu&k 18 sts to corner. CO 1 st, pm, CO 18 sts—37 sts. Work [T].

LTA2

With yarn color specified in Table 2 for LT, CO 19 sts, pm. Starting at the red triangle at bottom-right corner of PSA, pu&k 18 sts on edge to next corner—37 sts. Work [T].

Continue at **Wedges**.

METHOD B

See Figure 5.

Figure 5: *Method B: Quarter Cross*

LTB1

With yarn color specified in Table 2 for LT, CO 19 sts. Work [LTB].

PSB & LTB2

Attach yarn color specified in Table 2 for PS at the red triangle at the top corner of LTB1 in Figure 5. Work as for PSB2 and LBT2 for Method B Crosses.

Continue at **Wedges**.

Wedges

Cross Wedge (CW)

Used to transform Crosses into Octagons. Make 4 per Cross.

On RS, in each shape labeled "CW" in Figure 6, attach yarn color specified in Table 1 for CW at red triangle, leaving a 15"/38 cm tail. *Pu&k 10 sts to corner, 1 st in corner, pm, and 10 sts to next corner—21 sts. Work [T].*

Quarter Cross Wedge (QW)

Make 1 on each Quarter Cross to create a Trapezoid.

Attach yarn color specified in Table 2 for QW at red triangle in shape labeled "QW" in Figure 7, leaving a 15"/38 cm tail. Rep bet * and * of Cross Wedge.

Assembly

Use Method C or Method D.

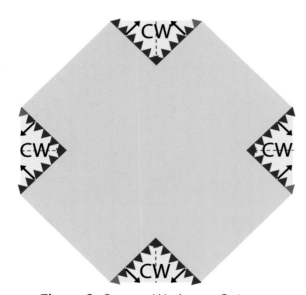

Figure 6: *Cross + Wedges = Octagon*

Figure 7: *Quarter Cross + Wedge = Trapezoid*

METHOD C

With N, work [Sq] 17 times to make 17 squares, leaving 15"/38 cm tails at CO and BO.

Strips 1–7

Arrange 18 Octagons, 6 Trapezoids (along long sides), and 17 Squares as shown in Figure 8. Orient BO edges of the S's to be at the top. If Center Squares were worked using Method A, orient Center Squares with CO edges at the bottom. Using long tails of S's and whip st, sew Octagons and Squares tog on green dotted lines, matching corners.

Assembling Strips

Arrange strips 1–7 and the 4 remaining Trapezoids as shown in Figure 8. Using long tails from Ts and whip st, sew tog strips and shapes along red dotted lines, matching corners.

Continue at **Corners and Borders**.

METHOD D

Arrange 18 Octagons and 10 Trapezoids as shown in Figure 9. Using whip st, sew tog along dotted lines using long tails of LTBs and matching corners.

Interstitial Squares (IS)

On RS, attach N at red triangle in each of the 17 spaces labeled "IS" in Figure 9. *Pu&k 17 sts to next corner, 1 st in corner, pm; rep from * 3 more times—72 sts. Work [OS].

Continue at **Corners and Borders**.

CORNERS AND BORDERS

Corners

Attach yarn color specified in Figure 10 at red triangles and pu&k 25 sts to next corner. Work [CR].

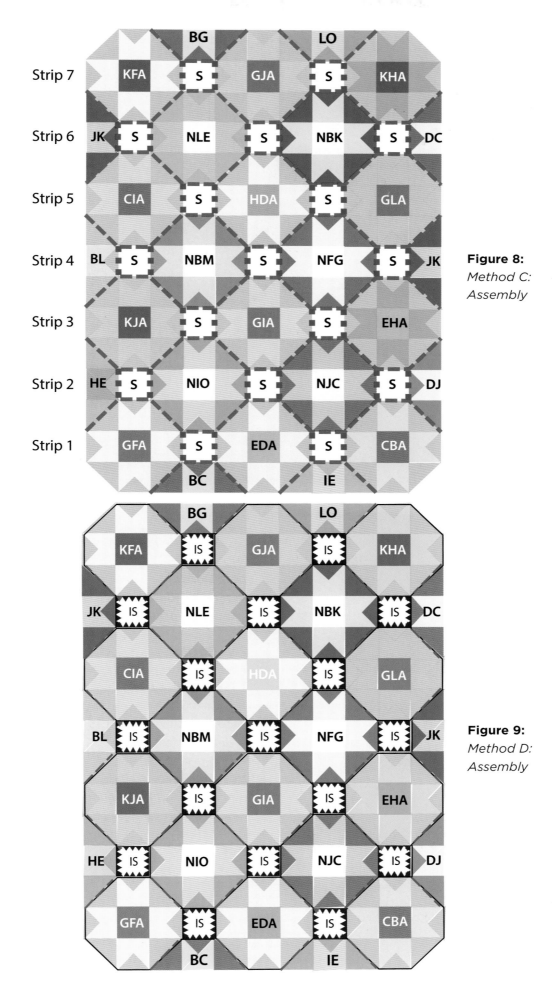

Figure 8:
Method C: Assembly

Figure 9:
Method D: Assembly

Corner (CR)—25 sts dec'ing to 1 st

Row 1 (WS): Knit.

Row 2 (RS): K2tog, knit to last 2 sts, ssk—2 sts dec'd; 23 sts.

Row 3: Knit.

Rows 4–25: Rep [Rows 2 & 3] 11 times—22 sts dec'd; 1 st.

Cut yarn, leaving a 10"/25 cm tail. Thread yarn onto tapestry needle and insert through rem sts on needle. Pull to tighten and fasten off securely.

Borders

Right Border

Attach N at bottom-right corner of completed blanket and pu&k 19 sts on the edge of each shape—285 sts. Knit 15 rows. BO loosely. Cut yarn and fasten off.

Left Border

Rep as for Right Border, attaching yarn at the top-left corner of completed blanket.

Top Border

Attach N at top-right corner of Right Border. Pu&k 9 sts on edge of Border, 19 on the edge of each shape, and 9 on edge of Left Border—227 sts. Knit 15 rows. BO loosely. Cut yarn and fasten off.

Bottom Border

Rep as for Top Border, attaching yarn at the bottom-left corner of the Left Border.

FINISHING

Weave in ends.

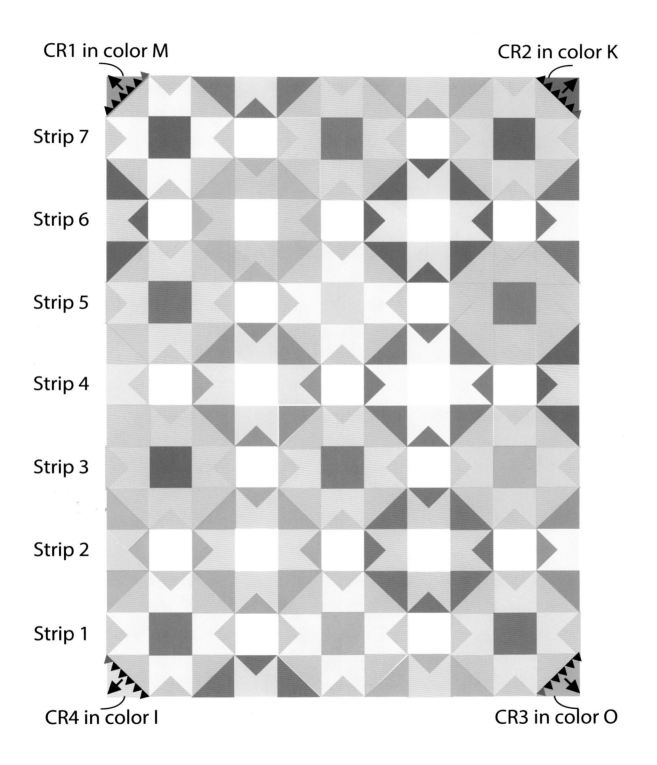

Figure 10: *Corners*

Prisma

Explore the magic of light and color with this joyously colored lap robe.

Techniques

Method A: ⊼ ▲

Method B: ▲ ✧ ♯

Size

40.5 x 60"/103 x 152 cm

Yarn

Malabrigo Worsted (100% merino wool; 210 yd./192 m; 3.5 oz./100 g):

A: 2 hanks Marine (dark blue) #062
B: 2 hanks Water Green (light green) #083
C: 2 hanks Jewel Blue (medium blue) #032
D: 2 hanks Vermillion (red) #024
E: 2 hanks Shocking Pink (bright pink) #184
F: 1 hank Sauterne (gold) #022
G: 2 hanks Pollen (light yellow) #019
H: 1 hank Red Mahogany (burgundy) #610

Needles

US Size 8/5 mm, 40"/100 cm circular needles, US Size 8/5 mm dpns (for Method B)

Notions

Stitch holders, stitch markers, tapestry needle

Gauge

18 sts and 36 rows = 4"/10 cm in garter st

Note

- There are two methods for constructing this blanket, shown in Figure 1. In Method A, the blanket is worked in blocks that are then sewn together. In Method B, a set of crosses is worked, each starting with an inside-out square. The blanket face is filled in with outside-in squares between the crosses. There is no sewing in Method B. For both methods, border sts are picked up on the edges of the completed blanket.

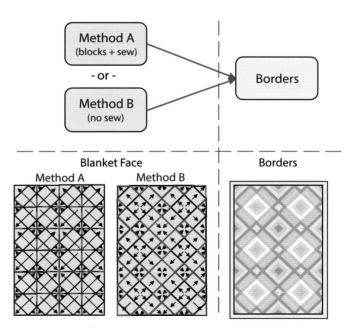

Figure 1: *Construction Options*

Blanket Instructions

METHOD A

Block — Make 24 total

See Figure 2 for colors and construction.

Increasing Triangle (IT)

With D, CO 2 sts. Work [IT], leaving a 10"/25 cm tail with each color.

Increasing Triangle (IT) – Method A—2 sts inc'ing to 40 sts

Row 1 (RS): Kf&b twice—2 sts inc'd; 4 sts.
Row 2 (WS): K1, kf&b twice, k1—2 sts inc'd; 6 sts.
Row 3: Kf&b, knit to end—1 st inc'd; 7 sts.
Rows 4–12: Rep [Row 3] 9 times—9 sts inc'd; 16 sts.
Cut D and attach E.
Rows 13–24: Rep [Row 3] 12 times—12 sts inc'd; 28 sts.
Cut E and attach G.
Rows 25–36: Rep [Row 3] 12 times—12 sts inc'd; 40 sts.
Cut G, leaving a 10"/25 cm tail.

Rectangle (Rt)

Attach D and work [Rt].

Rectangle (Rt) – Methods A & B—40 sts

Rows 1 (RS)–12 (WS): Knit.
Cut D and attach E.
Rows 13–24: Knit.
Cut E and attach C.
Rows 25–36: Knit.
Cut C and attach A.
Rows 37–48: Knit.
Cut A.

Decreasing Triangle (DT)

Attach B. Work [DT], leaving a 10"/25 cm tail with each.

Decreasing Triangle (DT) – Methods A & B—40 sts dec'ing to 2 sts

Row 1 (RS): K2tog, knit to last 2 sts, ssk—2 sts dec'd; 38 sts.
Row 2 (WS): Knit.
Rows 3–12: Rep [Rows 1 & 2] 5 times—10 sts dec'd; 28 sts.
Cut B and attach C.
Rows 13–24: Rep [Rows 1 & 2] 6 times—12 sts dec'd; 16 sts.
Cut C and attach A.
Rows 25–36: Rep [Rows 1 & 2] 6 times—12 sts dec'd; 4 sts.
Row 37: Rep [Row 1]—2 sts dec'd; 2 sts.
Cut C, leaving a 10"/25 cm tail. Thread yarn onto tapestry needle and insert through 2 rem sts. Pull tightly and tie off securely.

Edge Triangles (ET)

ET1

On RS of each isohedral hexagon, attach H at red triangle in Figure 2. Pu&k 24 sts (1 st per garter st ridge) across edge of Rt. Knit 1 row (WS). Work [SP].

Small Point (SP) – Method A—24 sts dec'ing to 2 sts

Row 1 (RS): K2tog, knit to last 2 sts, ssk—2 sts dec'd; 22 sts.
Row 2 (WS): Knit.
Rows 3–10: Rep [Rows 1 & 2] 4 times—8 sts dec'd; 14 sts.
Cut H and attach F.
Rows 11–22: Rep [Rows 1 & 2] 6 times—12 sts dec'd; 2 sts.
Cut F, leaving a 10"/25 cm tail. Thread yarn onto tapestry needle and insert through rem sts. Pull tightly and tie off securely.

ET2

Rep as for ET1, attaching yarn at green triangle in Figure 2.

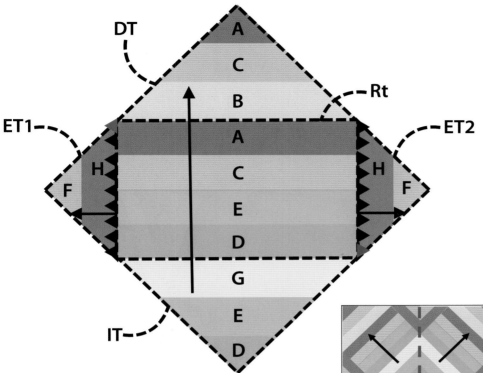

Figure 2: *Method A: Construction and Colors for Block*

Assembly

Arrange 24 Blocks as shown in Figure 3. Using long tails of matching color yarn and whip st, sew blocks along the red dotted lines to make horizontal strips. Using long tails, sew strips tog along blue dotted lines. When sewing, match similar colored stripes.

Continue at **Borders**.

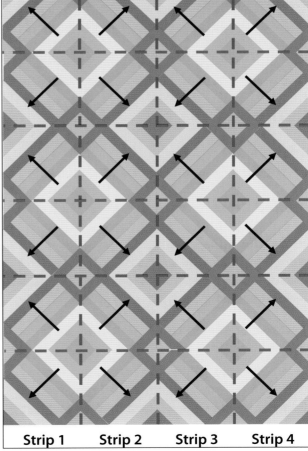

Figure 3: *Method A: Assembly*

METHOD B

Crosses

See Figure 4 for colors and construction.

Pointed Cross — *Make 4*

Inside-Out Square (IS)

Work [IS]. Place last 120 sts onto 3 separate
holders (40 sts each) and continue with 1st 40
sts on needle.

> **Inside-Out Square (IS)** – Method B—8 sts
> inc'ing to 160 sts
>
> Worked in the round. Start on dpns and then
> switch to circular needle when required to
> accommodate sts, placing m after each set
> of dpn sts.
> With D, CO 8 using pinhole cast-on (see
> "Glossary"), divided evenly over 4 dpns.

Rnd 1: *Kf&b, knit to 1 st bef m or end of
dpn, kf&b, rep from * 3 more times—8 sts
inc'd; 16 sts.

Rnd 2: *Pf&b, purl to 1 st bef m or end of
dpn, pf&b, rep from * 3 more times—8 sts
inc'd; 24 sts.

Rnd 3: Rep [Rnd 1]—8 sts inc'd; 32 sts.

Rnd 4: Purl.

Rnds 5–12: Rep [Rnds 3 & 4] 4 times—32 sts
inc'd; 64 sts.

Cut D and attach E.

Rnds 13–24: Rep [Rnds 3 & 4] 6 times—48 sts
inc'd; 112 sts.

Cut E and attach G.

Rnds 25–36: Rep [Rnds 3 & 4] 6 times—48 sts
inc'd; 160 sts.

Cut G.

Arms

Pointed Arm (A1)

Attach D and work [Rt]; attach B and work [DT], using colors specified in Figure 4.

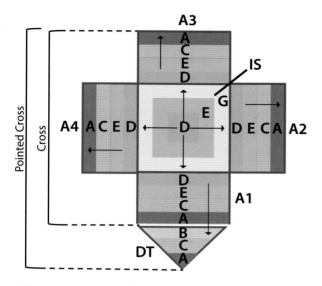

Figure 4: *Method B: Construction of Crosses*

Arms (A2–A4)

For each set of 40 sts on holders, transfer sts to needle. Attach D, work [Rt], and return 40 sts to holder.

Plain Cross — *Make 2*

Inside-Out Square (IS)

Work as for Pointed Cross, Inside-Out Square (IS).

Arms (A1–A4)

Work all four as for Pointed Cross, A1, A2–A4.

Interstitial Diamonds and Triangles

Large Interstitial Diamonds (LID)

See Figure 5 for construction.

Arrange the 4 Pointed and 2 Plain Crosses as shown in Figure 5. In each of the 2 center spaces labeled "LID," beginning at bottom corner on RS (orange dot), transfer 40 sts from each Arm to circ needle and pm after each set—160 sts.

On RS, attach B and work [ID] until 112 sts rem. Cut B.

Attach C and work [ID] until 64 sts rem. Cut C.

Attach A and work [ID] until 8 sts rem.

Cut yarn, leaving a 10"/25 cm tail. Thread yarn onto tapestry needle and insert through rem sts. Pull tightly and fasten off securely.

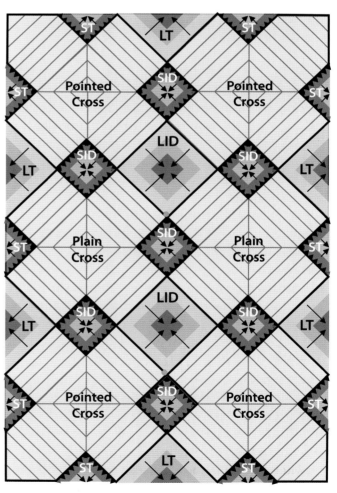

Figure 5: *Method B: Locations of LIDs, SIDs, LTs, and STs*

Small Interstitial Diamond (SID)

On RS, in each of the 7 spaces labeled "SID," at the red triangles in Figure 5, attach H. *Pu&k 24 sts to next corner, and 1 st in corner, pm; rep from * 3 more times—100 sts.

Purl 1 rnd. Work [ID] until 60 sts rem. Cut H.

Attach F and work [ID] until 12 sts rem.

Next rnd: *K2tog, rep from * to end—6 sts dec'd; 6 sts.

Cut yarn, leaving a 10"/25 cm tail. Thread yarn onto tapestry needle and insert through rem sts. Pull tightly and fasten off securely.

Interstitial Diamond (ID) – Method B

Worked in the round. When working on dpns, do not pm; work to 2 sts before end of dpn.

Rnd 1: *K2tog, knit to 2 sts bef m, ssk, sm; rep from* 3 more times—8 sts dec'd.

Rnd 2: Purl.

Rep [Rnds 1 & 2] as specified.

Large Triangles (LT)

Working on RS, in each of the 6 spaces labeled "LT" in Figure 5, working left to right, transfer 40 sts on holder from left Arm to needle, pm, pu 1 st in the corner of SID, and then transfer 40 sts on holder from holder from right Arm to needle—81 sts.

Work [Tr] until 57 sts rem. Cut B.

Attach C and work [Tr] until 33 sts rem. Cut C.

Attach A and work [Tr] until 5 sts rem.

Next row: K1, cdd, k1—2 sts dec'd; 3 sts.

Cut yarn, leaving a 10"/25 cm tail. Thread yarn onto tapestry needle and insert through rem sts. Pull tightly and fasten off securely.

Triangle (Tr) – Method B

Row 1 (RS): K2tog, knit to 2 sts bef m, rm, cdd, pm, knit to last 2 sts, ssk—4 sts dec'd.

Row 2 (WS): Knit.

Rep [Rows 1 & 2] as specified.

Small Triangles (ST)

In each of the 10 spaces labeled "ST" in Figure 5, attach H at red triangle. Pu&k 24 sts (one per garter st ridge) to corner, 1 st in the corner, pm, and 24 sts (one per garter st ridge) on the next edge—49 sts.

Knit 1 row (WS). Work [Tr] until 29 sts rem. Cut H.

Attach F and work [Tr] until 5 sts rem.

Next row: K1, cdd, k1—2 sts dec'd; 3 sts.

Cut yarn, leaving a 10"/25 cm tail. Thread yarn onto tapestry needle and insert through rem sts. Pull tightly and fasten off securely.

Continue at **Borders.**

BORDERS

Top Border

On RS, attach G at top-right corner of blanket. *Pu&k 9 sts on next color strip and 8 sts on following color strip; rep from * 9 more times—170 sts. Knit 11 rows. BO loosely.

Note: *A triangle counts as 2 strips.*

Bottom Border

Work as for Top Border, attaching yarn at bottom-left corner of blanket.

Right Border

On right side of blanket, attach G at the bottom-right corner of the Bottom Border. Pu&k 7 sts on border edge, 255 sts on blanket (alternating 8 and 9 sts per color strip as for Top), and 7 sts on border edge—269 sts. Knit 11 rows. BO loosely.

Left Border

Rep as for Right Border, attaching yarn at the top-left corner of the Top Border.

FINISHING

Weave in ends.

Pueblo

Bring some "South of the Border" to any room with this colorful design.

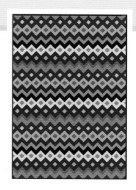

- -

Technique

Sizes
Small (Large): 42 x 60"/107 x 152 cm (55 x 88"/140 x 224 cm)

Yarn
Malabrigo Worsted Merino (100% kettle-dyed pure merino wool; 210 yd./192 m; 3.5 oz./100 g):
A: 2 (3) hanks Azul Profundo (dark blue) #150
B: 2 (2) hanks Jewel Blue (medium blue) #032
C: 2 (2) hanks Rhodesian Ridgeback (burnt orange) #123
D: 2 (3) hanks Burgundy (dark red) #041
E: 1 (1) hank Sunset (yellow-orange) #096
F: 2 (3) hanks Butter (light yellow) #061
G: 3 (4) hanks VAA (dark teal) #051
H: 2 (2) hanks Lettuce (yellow-green) #037
I: 2 (2) hanks Forest (dark green) #145
J: 2 (3) hanks Moss (moss green) #505
K: 1 (1) hank Frank Ochre (yellow) #035

Note: This yarn line is kettle-dyed, so check with the store that yarns are from the same dye lot.

Needles
US Size 7/4.5 mm, 40"/100 cm circular needles

Notions
Stitch holders or waste yarn, stitch markers, tapestry needle

Gauge
18 sts and 36 rows = 4"/10 cm in garter st

Notes
- Blanket is worked in one piece from bottom to top using a traditional chevron pattern and mitered squares. See Figures 3 & 4 for complete construction. Borders are picked up from completed blanket face and worked separately.
- There are 2 size options, differing in the number of horizontal and vertical pattern repeats. Directions are for the Small size, with changes for the Large size in parentheses.

Blanket Instructions

See Figure 1 for construction (left) and colors (right). Dashed area is repeated 8 (11) times horizontally and 2 (3) times vertically between the Base and End strips.

Note: When working the mitered square (MS) Strips, thread long tails of adjacent shapes on tapestry needle, insert into last st of prev shape and then back into the last st of current shape. Pull to tighten, and tie off.

Base Strip

Corners [CR] and Increasing Wedges [IW]

See Figure 2 for construction.

With A, CO 1 st. Work [CR], and leave sts on needle; pm. Cut yarn and fasten off—15 sts.

*With A, CO 1 st. Work [IW], and leave sts on needle; pm. Cut yarn and fasten off—28 sts inc'd.

Rep from * 7 (10) more times—196 (280) sts inc'd; 239 (323) sts.

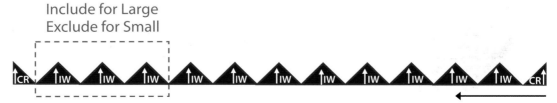

Figure 1: *Construction (left) and Yarn Colors (right)*

With A, CO 1 st. Work [CR], and on Row 14, work one k2tog in center of row. Leave sts on needle. Cut yarn and fasten off—14 sts inc'd; 253 (337) sts.

Note: At this point, there should be 8 (11) completed IWs on the needle with a CR on either end.

Corner (CR)—1 st inc'ing to 15 sts

Row 1 (WS): Knit.
Row 2 (RS): Kyok—2 sts inc'd; 3 sts.
Row 3: Knit.
Row 4: Kf&b, knit to last st, kf&b—2 sts inc'd; 5 sts.
Rows 5–14: Rep [Rows 3 & 4] 5 times—10 sts inc'd; 15 sts.
Row 15: Knit.

Increasing Wedge (IW)—1 st inc'ing to 28 sts

Row 1 (WS): Kf&b—1 st inc'd; 2 sts.
Row 2 (RS): Kf&b, pm, kf&b—2 sts inc'd; 4 sts.
Row 3: Knit.
Row 4: Kf&b, knit to 1 st bef m, kf&b, kf&b, knit to last st, kf&b—4 sts inc'd; 8 sts.
Rows 5–14: Rep [Rows 3 & 4] 5 times—20 sts inc'd; 28 sts.
Row 15: Knit.

Main Strips

Turn work to RS.

St1

On RS, attach B. Work [St]. Cut B.

Include for Large
Exclude for Small

Figure 2: *Base Strip Construction*

St2

On RS, attach C. Work [St]. Cut C.

Strip (St)—253 (337) sts

Row 1 (RS): Kf&b (knit to 2 sts bef m, rm, cdd, pm, knit to 1 bef next m, kyok, pm after yo) 8 (11) times; knit to 2 sts bef next m, rm, cdd, pm, knit to last st, kf&b.

Row 2 (WS): Knit.

Rows 3–14: Rep [Rows 1 & 2] 6 times.

MS1

On RS, attach D, leaving a 10"/25 cm tail, and work [MS] over 1st 29 sts (bet beg and 2nd m), omitting the kf&b in Row 1 and changing to E after 12 rows.

*On RS, attach D, and work [MS] over the next 28 sts, changing to E after 12 rows. Cut E.
Rep from * 7 (10) more times. Rm first 2 m's.

Mitered Square (MS)—28 sts dec'ing to 1 st

Row 1 (RS): Kf&b, knit to 2 sts bef m, rm, cdd, pm, knit to end—1 st dec'd; 27 sts.

Row 2 (WS): Knit.

Row 3: Knit to 2 sts bef m, rm, cdd, pm, knit to end—2 sts dec'd; 25 sts.

Row 4: Knit.

Rows 5–12: Rep [Rows 3 & 4] 4 times—8 sts dec'd; 17 sts.

Cut yarn. Attach next yarn color.

Rows 13–26: Rep [Rows 3 & 4] 7 times—14 sts dec'd; 3 sts.

Row 27: Rm. Cdd—2 sts dec'd; 1 st.

Cut yarn and fasten off.

US1

On RS, attach D at green triangle. Pu&k 15 sts to next corner, pm, *pu&k 14 sts to next corner, pm, rep from * 16 (22) more times—253 (337) sts. Work [US].

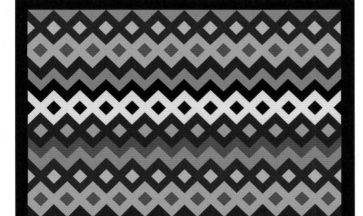

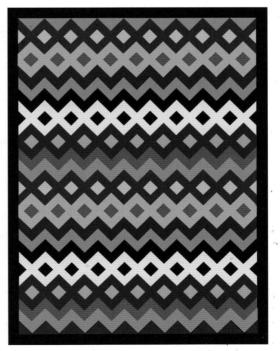

Figure 3: *Large Blanket*

Figure 4: *Small Blanket*

Upside-Down Strip (US)—253 (337) sts

Row 1 (WS): Knit.

Row 2 (RS): K2tog *knit to 1 st bef m, kyok, pm after yo, knit to 2 sts bef next m, rm, cdd, pm; rep from * 7 (10) more times; knit to 1 st bef next m, kyok, pm after yo, knit to last 2 sts, ssk.

Row 3: Knit.

Rows 4–11: Rep [Rows 2 & 3] 4 times.

RT1, MS2, and LT1

On RS, attach F and work [RT] over 1st 15 sts (bef 1st m), changing to G after 12 rows. Rm 1st m.

Right Triangle (RT)—15 sts dec'ing to 1 st

Row 1 (RS): K2tog, knit to end—1 st dec'd; 14 sts.

Row 2 (WS): Knit.

Rows 3–12: Rep [Rows 1 & 2] 5 times—5 sts dec'd; 9 sts.

Cut yarn. Attach next yarn color.

Rows 13–28: Rep [Rows 1 & 2] 8 times—8 sts dec'd; 1 st.

Cut yarn and fasten off.

*On RS, attach F and work [MS] over next 28 sts, changing to G after 12 rows. Rep from * 7 (10) more times.

On RS, attach F and work [LT] over last 14 sts (bet last m and end), changing to G after 12 rows. Rm next 2 m's.

Left Triangle (LT)—14 sts dec'ing to 1 st

Row 1 (RS): Kf&b, knit to last 2 sts, ssk—14 sts.

Row 2 (WS): Knit.

Row 3: Knit to last 2 sts, ssk—1 st dec'd; 13 sts.

Row 4: Knit.

Rows 5–12: Rep [Rows 3 & 4] 4 times—4 sts dec'd; 9 sts.

Cut yarn. Attach next yarn color.

Rows 13–28: Rep [Rows 3 & 4] 8 times—8 sts dec'd; 1 st.

Cut yarn and fasten off.

St3

Attach F at red triangle at the top corner of RT1. Pu&k 15 sts to next corner, pm, *pu&k 14 sts to next corner, pm; rep from * 16 (22) more times—253 (337) sts. Work [St Rows 2–12]. Cut F.

St4

Attach G. Work [St]. Cut G.

St5

Attach H. Work [St]. Cut H.

St6

Attach I. Work [St]. Cut I.

MS3

Rep as for MS1 attaching J and changing to D after 12 rows. Cut D.

US2

Rep as for US1 attaching J at red triangle.

RT2, MS4, and LT2

Rep as for RT1, MS2, and LT1, attaching A and changing to K after 12 rows for each shape. Cut K.

St7

Rep as for St3 attaching A at red triangle.

Rep from [St1] to [St7] 1 (2) more time(s).

End Strip

First DW

On RS, attach B and work [DW] over 1st 29 sts (bet beg and 2nd m), and omit the kf&b in the 1st st of Row 1.

Remaining DWs

*On RS, attach B and work [DW] over next 28 sts. Rep from * 7 (10) more times.

Decreasing Wedge (DW)—28 sts
dec'ing to 3 sts

Row 1 (RS): Kf&b, knit to 2 sts bef m, rm, cdd, pm, knit to end—1 st dec'd; 27 sts.

Row 2 (WS): Knit.

Row 3: K2tog, knit to 2 sts bef m, rm m, cdd, pm, knit to 2 sts from end, ssk—4 sts dec'd; 23 sts.

Row 4: Knit.

Rows 5–14: Rep [Rows 3 & 4] 5 times—20 sts dec'd; 3 sts.

Cut yarn, leaving a 10"/25 cm tail. Thread yarn onto tapestry needle, insert through rem sts, and fasten off.

BORDERS

Top Border

On RS, attach G at top-right corner of completed blanket. Pu&k sts along edges of 9 (12) DWs, alternating bet 19 and 20 sts per DW—175 (234) sts.
Knit 13 rows. BO loosely.

Bottom Border

On RS, attach G at bottom-left corner of completed blanket. Pu&k 10 sts on the edge of CR, 156 (214) sts along edges of 8 (11) IWs, alternating bet 19 and 20 per IW, and 9 (10) sts along final CR—175 (234) sts.
Knit 13 rows. BO loosely.

Right Border

On RS, attach G at bottom-right corner of Bottom Border. Pu&k 8 sts on edge of border, 256 (380) sts along edges of the 27 (40) Strips alternating bet 9 and 10 sts per Strip, and 8 sts on edge of Top Border—272 (396) sts.
Knit 13 rows. BO loosely.

Left Border

Repeat as for Right Border, attaching yarn at top-left corner of Top Border.

FINISHING

Weave in ends.

Pulsar

Nested chevrons and color-shifting striping make a vibrant statement piece for bedroom, lounge, or study.

∙∙

Techniques

⌐3 ♯

Size

58 x 58"/147 x 147 cm

Yarn

Cascade Yarns 128, superwash bulky (100% superwash wool; 128 yd./117 m; 3.5 oz./100 g):

A: 4 hanks Navy (navy blue) #854
B: 4 hanks Aporto (royal blue) #856
C: 7 hanks Pacific (aqua) #1960
D: 4 hanks Moss (moss green) #841
E: 3 hanks Ecru (off-white) #817

Needles

US Size 10/6 mm, 60"/150 cm, 40"/100 cm circular needles and dpns

Notions

US J-10/6 mm crochet hook, stitch markers, tapestry needle

Gauge

15 sts and 30 rows = 4"/10 cm in garter st

Notes

- This no-sew blanket is worked outside-in starting with individual triangles that are assembled on the larger circular needle. A crochet edge is added last.
- Start work using longest circular needle, changing to shorter length and then to dpns as needed to comfortably accommodate the stitches.
- In 2-color Color Bands, carry nonworking yarn at the back of the work between uses.
- Some brands of interchangeable circular needles have a "join" that you can buy to screw together two shorter cables to make a long cable.

Blanket Instructions

Note: *Although shown as solid color in figures, bands with 2-color names are actually striped.*

See Figure 1 for construction and color band colors.

Points

With A and circular needle, [(work [SP], leave on needle, turn to RS) 6 times, pm, work [CP] and leave on needle, pm] 4 times—1048 sts.

Side Point (SP)—1 st inc'ing to 40 sts

CO 1.
Row 1 (RS): Kf&b—1 st inc'd; 2 sts.
Row 2 (WS): Knit.
Row 3: CO 1, k2—1 st inc'd; 3 sts.
Row 4: CO 1, k1tbl, pm, k2—1 st inc'd; 4 sts.
Row 5: CO 1, knit to 1 st bef m, bli, k2 , bli, knit to end—3 sts inc'd; 7 sts.

Row 6: CO 1, k1tbl, knit to end—1 st inc'd; 8 sts.
Rows 7–22: Rep [Rows 5 & 6] 8 more times— 32 sts inc'd; 40 sts. Rm.
Cut yarn and fasten off.

Corner Point (CP)—1 st inc'ing to 22 sts

CO 1.
Row 1 (RS): Kf&b—1 st inc'd; 2 sts.
Row 2 (WS): Knit.
Row 3: CO1, k1tbl, knit to end—1 st inc'd; 3 sts.
Rows 4–22: Rep [Row 3] 19 times—19 sts inc'd; 22 sts.
Cut yarn and fasten off.

Turn work. Sl last 11 sts of the CP to R needle. Pm for BOR.

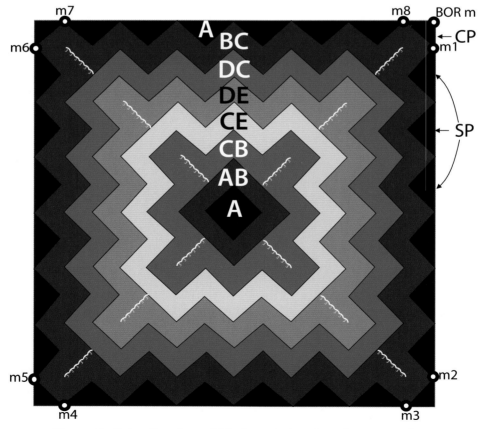

Figure 1: *Color Bands and Markers (m1–m8 and BOR marker)*

Color Band BC

Note: Rnd 1 joins the piece in the round; be sure sts are not twisted.

Attach B and work [Band], using B for C1 and C for C2—72 sts dec'd; 976 sts.

Band—72 sts dec'd

Note: This pattern uses a jogless join method at the end of rounds. See the chart of this method below.

Attach C1.

Rnd 1: With C1, (knit to 2 sts bef m, k2tog, *ssk, k17, bli, k2, bli, k17, k2tog, rep from * to next m, ssk) 4 times, knit to end of rnd; 8 sts dec'd.

Rnd 2: Purl to BOR m; sl last st back to L needle and drop C1. Attach C2 and knit st.

Rnd 3: (Knit to 2 sts bef m, k2tog, *ssk, k17, bli, k2, bli, k17, k2tog, rep from * to next m, ssk) 4 times, knit to last st, pick up knit st from rnd below, place on L needle and k2tog; 8 sts dec'd.

Rnd 4: Rep Rnd 2, dropping C2 and switching to C1 at end of rnd.

Rnds 5–18: Rep [Rnds 3 & 4] 7 times, changing colors every other rnd—56 sts dec'd.

Rnd 19: With C, rep Rnd 3, ending 21 sts bef end of rnd (after last bli), p17, p2tog twice—8 sts dec'd; 968 sts.
Work [CBO]—156 sts dec'd; 812 sts.
Cut B and fasten off.

Corner BO (CBO)—156 sts dec'd

Worked on the 5th ridge of color C2—a purl rnd.
*Sm, p1, move 1st m back 40 sts. Move 2nd m forward 40 sts, hold RS's together and 3-Needle BO 20 times, purl to next m; rep from * 3 more times—156 sts dec'd.

Color Band DC

Attach D.

Rnd 1 (Special Dec): With D, (knit to last 2 sts bef m, k2tog, [ssk, k17, bli, k2, bli, k17, k2tog] 4 times, ssk, k18, k2tog) 4 times—12 sts dec'd; 800 sts.

Rnds 2–18: Work [Band Rnds 2–18], using D for C1 and C for C2—64 sts dec'd; 736 sts.

Rnds 19–20: Rep [Band Rnds 3 & 4] once more—8 sts dec'd; 728 sts.
Cut C and fasten off.

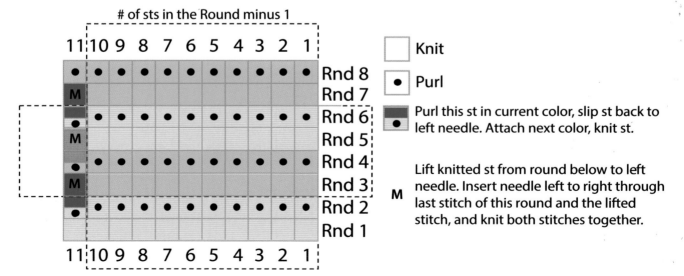

Figure 2: *Jogless Join*

Color Band DE

Rnds 1-18: Work [Band Rnds 3 & 4], attaching E in the 1st Rnd 4—72 sts dec'd; 656 sts.

Rnd 19: With E, rep Rnd 3, ending 21 sts bef end of rnd (after last bli), p17, p2tog twice—8 sts dec'd; 648 sts.

Work [CBO]—156 sts dec'd; 492 sts.

Cut D and fasten off.

Color Band CE

Attach C.

Rnd 1 (Special Dec): With C, (knit to last 2 sts bef m, k2tog, [ssk, k17, bli, k2, bli, k17, k2tog] 2 times, ssk, k18, k2tog) 4 times—12 sts dec'd; 480 sts.

Rnds 2-18: Work [Band Rnds 2-18], using C for C1 and E for C2—64 sts dec'd; 416 sts.

Rnds 19-20: Rep [Band Rnds 3 & 4] once more—8 sts dec'd; 408 sts.

Cut E and fasten off.

Color Band CB

Rnds 1-18: Work [Band Rnds 3 & 4], attaching B in the 1st Rnd 4—72 sts dec'd; 336 sts.

Rnd 19: With B, rep Rnd 3, ending 21 sts bef end of rnd (after last bli), p17, p2tog twice—8 sts dec'd; 328 sts.

Work [CBO]—156 sts dec'd; 172 sts.

Remove duplicate m's. Cut C and fasten off.

Color Band AB

Attach A.

Rnd 1 (Special Dec): With A, (knit to last 2 sts bef m, k2tog, knit to m, ssk, k18, k2tog) 4 times—12 sts dec'd; 160 sts.

Rnds 2-18: Work [Band Rnds 2-18], using A for C1 and B for C2—64 sts dec'd; 96 sts.

Rnds 19-20: Rep [Band Rnds 3 & 4] once—8 sts dec'd; 88 sts.

Cut B and fasten off.

Color Band A

Rnd 1: Work [Band Rnd 1]—8 sts dec'd; 80 sts.

Rnd 2: Purl.

Rnds 3-20: Rep [Rnds 1 & 2] 9 more times—72 sts dec'd; 8 sts.

Cut A, leaving an 8"/20 cm tail. Thread yarn through tapestry needle and then draw through rem 8 sts, pull, tighten, and tie securely.

FINISHING

On RS, attach A to blanket edge at the side corner of top-right CP (point **m8** in Figure 1). With crochet hook, *sc 16 evenly spaced along edge of each SP, 7 on side of CP, 2 in corner st of CP, and 7 on second side of CP; rep from * 3 more times. Sl st in first sc, cut yarn, and fasten off.

Weave in ends.

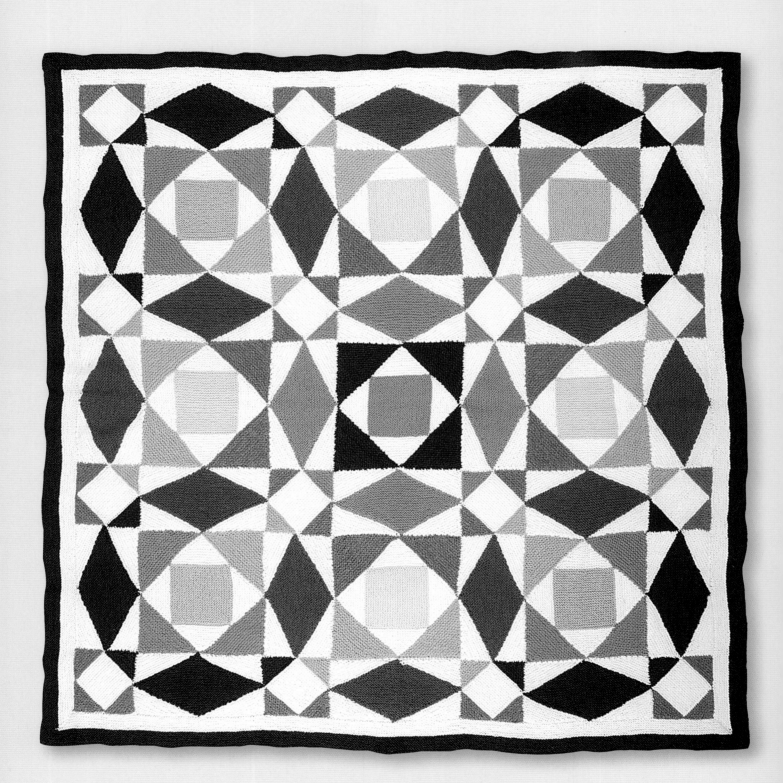

Ribbons

Simple triangles and squares are artfully arranged to create the illusion of intertwined ribbons.

. . . .

Techniques

Method A: ▲ 🖌

Method B: ▲ 🖌 ⊞

Size
57 x 57"/145 x 145 cm

Yarn
Ella Rae Superwash Classic, worsted (100% superwash wool; 220 yd./201 m; 3.5 oz./100 g):
A: 2 balls Light Blue (light blue) #6
B: 7 balls Vanilla (cream) #1
C: 2 balls Yellow Green (yellow-green) #79
D: 3 balls Elm Blue (medium blue) #82
E: 2 balls Yellow (light yellow) #4
F: 3 balls Driftwood Heather (dark gold) #108
G: 5 balls Deep Blue Sea Heather (dark blue) #139
H: 3 balls Dell Green Heather (dark green) #110

Needles
US Size 7/4.5 mm, 40"/100 cm circular needles, US Size 7/4.5 mm dpns (for Method B)

Notions
Stitch markers, tapestry needle

Gauge
20 sts and 40 rows = 4"/10 cm in garter st

Notes
- The blanket face is worked in square and rectangular blocks that are sewn together. The borders are picked up and knit after the blocks are sewn together. Corner seams are sewn after the borders are worked.
- There are three different block types in the blanket, numbered Blocks 1–3 (see Figure 1). Each of these block types can be made in one of two methods, A or B.
- Method A is worked inside-out, starting with the center shape back and forth. Stitches for outer shapes are picked up on the edges of previously completed shapes and knit outward.
- Method B is worked outside-in, starting with the outer shapes. Stitches for the center shape are picked up on the inner edges of the outer shapes and worked in the round outside-in. Method B generates fewer yarn ends to weave in.
- Both methods are assembled and work the borders in the same way.

Blanket Instructions

BLOCK 1
Make 9 in color schemes and counts specified in Figure 2. A Block 1 consists of a Square and 4 Inner Triangles (the Center), and 4 Outer Triangles.

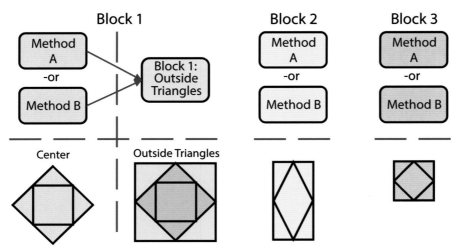

Figure 1: *Construction Options*

Center

Method A
See Figure 3 for construction.

Large Square A (LSA)
Work [LSA].

Large Square (LSA) – Method A—26 sts
CO 26 sts. Knit 52 rows. Cut yarn and fasten off.

Inner Triangles

ITA1
Attach yarn color specified in Figure 2.
Setup row (RS): K12, k2tog, knit to end—1 st dec'd; 25 sts.
Work [Tr].

Triangle (Tr) – Methods A & B (also used in Block 3)—odd number of sts dec'ing to 1 st
Row 1 (WS): Knit. **Row 2 (RS):** K2tog, knit to 2 sts bef end, ssk—2 sts dec'd. **Row 3:** Knit. Rep [Rows 2 & 3] until 3 sts rem. **Next row (RS):** Cdd—2 sts dec'd; 1 st. Cut yarn and fasten off, leaving a 15"/38 cm tail.

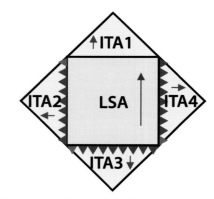

Figure 2: *Block 1 Color Schemes and Counts*

Figure 3: *Method A: Block 1 - Center Construction*

ITA2–ITA4
On the other 3 edges of LSA, attach yarn at red triangle in Figure 3. Pu&k 25 sts evenly to next corner (1 st for each garter st ridge along left and right edges and 1 for each CO st along bottom edge, skipping 1 ridge/CO st in the center of the edge). Work [Tr].
Continue at **Outside Triangles.**

Method B

See Figure 4 for construction.

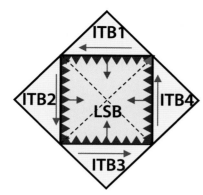

Figure 4: *Method B: Block 1 – Center Construction*

Inner Triangles (ITB1–ITB4)

With yarn color specified in Figure 2, work [TB] 4 times, with X = 12 sts. Do not cut yarn between ITBs. After ITB4, cut yarn and tie the CO tail of ITB1 to the BO tail of ITB4.

Triangle B (TB) – Method B (also used in Block 3)—1 st inc'ing to X sts dec'ing to 1 st

CO 1 st.
Row 1 (RS): Yoco, knit to end—1 st inc'd; 2 sts.
Row 2 (WS): Knit.
Rep [Rows 1 & 2] until there are X sts on needle.
Row 3: K2tog, knit to end—1 st dec'd.
Row 4: Knit.
Rep [Rows 3 & 4] until 1 st rem.

Large Square B (LSB)

On RS, attach yarn at corner at red triangle in Figure 4. Working clockwise with circular needle, *pu&k 24 sts evenly on edge of TB to next corner, pm; rep from * 3 more times—96 sts. Work [OSB].

Outside-In Square (OSB) – Method B (also used in Block 3)—dec'ing to 8 sts

Worked in the round.
Rnd 1: Purl.
Rnd 2: *Ssk, knit to 2 sts bef next m, k2tog; rep from * 3 more times—8 sts dec'd.
Rnd 3: Purl.

Rep [Rnds 2 & 3] until 8 sts rem.
Cut yarn, leaving a 10"/25 cm tail. Thread tail through tapestry needle and insert needle through all sts on needle. Pull tightly and fasten off securely.

Continue at **Outside Triangles.**

Outside Triangles – Both Methods

See Figure 5 for construction.

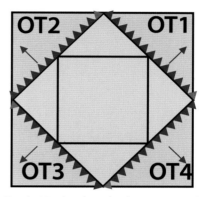

Figure 5: *Both Methods: Block 1 – Outside Triangles*

OT1–OT4

On RS, attach yarn in color specified in Figure 2 at the red triangles in Figure 5. Pu&k 37 sts to next corner. Work [Tr].

BLOCK 2

Make 24, in color schemes (CS) and quantities specified in Figure 6. Each Block 2 consists of a Diamond and 4 Wedges.

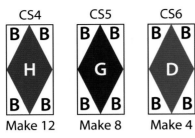

Figure 6: *Color Schemes (CS) for Block 2*

Method A

See Figure 7 for construction.

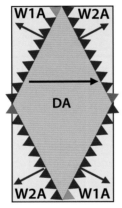

Figure 7: *Method A: Block 2 Construction*

Diamond

Work [DA].

Diamond (DA) – Method A—2 sts inc'ing to 52 sts, dec'ing to 2 sts

CO 2 sts.
Row 1 (WS): Knit.
Row 2 (RS): CO 2, knit to end—2 sts inc'd; 4 sts.
Rows 3–27: Rep [Row 2] 24 times—48 sts inc'd; 52 sts.
Row 28: BO 2, knit to end—2 sts dec'd; 50 sts.
Rows 29–53: Rep [Row 28] 24 times—48 sts dec'd; 2 sts.
Row 54: Knit.
BO loosely. Cut yarn and fasten off.

Wedges

W1A – Make 2

On RS, at each of the bottom and top corners of DA, attach B at orange triangle, and pu&k 29 sts to next corner. Work [W1A].

Wedge 1 (W1A) - Method A—29 sts dec'ing to 1 st

Row 1 (WS): K2tog, knit to end—1 st dec'd; 28 sts.
Row 2 (RS): Knit to last 2 sts, ssk—1 st dec'd; 27 sts.
Row 3: Rep [Row 1]—1 st dec'd; 26 sts.
Row 4: K2tog, knit to last 2 sts, ssk—2 sts dec'd; 24 sts.
Rows 5–20: Rep [Rows 1-4] 4 times—20 sts dec'd; 4 sts.
Row 21: K2tog, ssk—2 st dec'd; 2 sts.
Row 22: Ssk—1 st dec'd; 1 st.
Cut yarn and fasten off, leaving a 15"/38 cm tail.

W2A – Make 2

On RS, at each of the left and right corners of DA, attach B at red triangle and pu&k 29 sts to next corner. Work [W2A].

Wedge 2 (W2A) – Method A—29 sts dec'ing to 1 st

Row 1 (WS): Knit to last 2 sts, ssk—1 st dec'd; 28 sts.
Row 2 (RS): K2tog, knit to end—1 st dec'd; 27 sts.
Row 3: Rep [Row 1]—1 st dec'd; 26 sts.
Row 4: K2tog, knit to last 2 sts, ssk—2 sts dec'd; 24 sts.
Rows 5–20: Rep [Rows 1-4] 4 times—20 sts dec'd; 4 sts.
Row 21: K2tog, ssk—2 st dec'd; 2 sts.
Row 22: K2tog—1 st dec'd; 1 st.
Cut yarn and fasten off, leaving a 15"/38 cm tail.

Continue at **Block 3.**

Method B

See Figure 8 for construction.

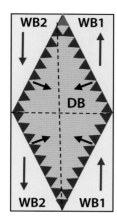

Figure 8: *Method B: Block 2 Construction*

Wedges

WB1 & WB2

CO 13 sts. Work [WB]. BO loosely, leaving last
st on needle. CO 12 sts and work [WB] again,
beginning at Row 2 (RS).

BO all sts loosely. Cut yarn and fasten off.

> **Wedges (WB)** – Method B—13 sts dec'ing to 1
> st, increasing to 13 sts

Rows 1 (WS)–3: Knit.

Row 4 (RS): Knit to last 2 sts, ssk—1 st
dec'd; 12 sts.

Rows 5–48: Rep [Rows 1–4] 11 times—11 sts
dec'd; 1 st.

Rows 49–53: K1.

Row 54: Kf&b—1 st inc'd; 2 sts.

Rows 55–57: Knit.

Row 58: Knit to last st, kf&b—1 st inc'd; 3 sts.

Rows 59–102: Rep [Rows 55–58] 11 times—11
sts inc'd; 13 sts.

Row 103: Knit.

Diamond

Arrange WB1 and WB2 as shown in Figure 8,
with RS facing, and tie tog BO and CO yarn
tails. Attach yarn for Diamond at the red
triangle in Figure 8, and, working clockwise,
*pu&k 29 sts to next corner, pm; rep from * 3
more times—116 sts. Work [DB].

> **Diamond (DB)** – Method B—116 sts
> dec'ing to 8 sts

Worked in the round; switch to dpns when
necessary.

Rnd 1: P2tog, purl to 2 sts bef 2nd m, ssp,
p2tog, purl to 2 sts bef end of rnd, ssp—4
sts dec'd; 112 sts.

Rnd 2: Ssk, knit to 2 sts bef 2nd m, k2tog, ssk,
knit to 2 sts bef end of rnd, k2tog—4 sts
dec'd; 108 sts.

Rnd 3: Rep [Rnd 1]—4 sts dec'd; 104 sts.

Rnd 4: *Ssk, knit to 2 sts bef next m, k2tog,
sm; rep from * 3 more times—8 sts
dec'd; 96 sts.

Rnds 5–20: Rep [Rnds 1–4] 4 times—80 sts
dec'd; 16 sts.

Rnds 21–22: Rep [Rnds 1 & 2] 1 time—8 sts
dec'd; 8 sts.

Cut yarn, leaving a 10"/25 cm tail. Thread
tail onto tapestry needle and insert needle
through all sts on needle. Pull tightly and
fasten off securely.

Continue at **Block 3.**

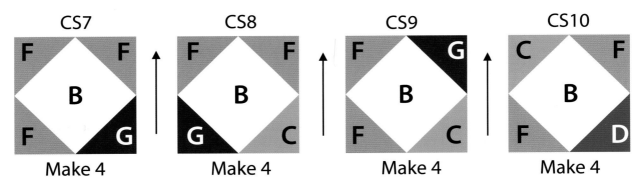

Figure 9: *Block 3 Color Schemes and Counts*

BLOCK 3

Make 16 in color schemes and counts specified in Figure 9. Each Block consists of a Square and 4 Triangles.

Method A

See Figure 10 for construction.

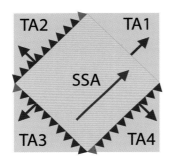

Figure 10: *Method A: Block 3 Construction*

Square

With B, work [SSA].

> **Small Square (SSA)** – Method A—19 sts
>
> CO 19 sts.
> Knit 38 rows.
> Cut yarn and fasten off.

Triangles (TA)

TA1

Attach yarn.
Setup row (RS): Knit.
Work [Tr].

TA2–TA4

At each red triangle in Figure 10, attach yarn and pu&k 19 sts to next corner. Work [Tr].
Continue at **Assembly.**

Method B

See Figure 11 for construction.

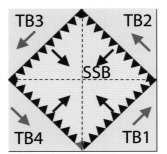

Figure 11: *Method B: Block 3 Construction*

Triangles (TB)

TB1–TB4

With colors specified in Figure 9, work [TB] (pattern stitch is on page 119) with X = 10 sts, 4 times. Cut yarn between TBs only when the following triangle is a different color.
Tie CO and BO tails of TBs tog to form a square as shown in Figure 11.

Square (SSB)

On RS, attach B at red triangle in Figure 11. Working clockwise with circular needle, *pu&k 18 sts to next corner, pm; rep from * 3 more times—72 sts. Work [OSB].
Continue at **Assembly.**

ASSEMBLY

Assemble Strips

Arrange 3 Block 2s and 4 Block 3s into each of the 4 Strip 2–3's as shown in Figure 12, and sew tog using whip st and long tails of matching yarn color, aligning corners of shapes.

Arrange 3 Block 1s and 4 Block 2s into each of the 3 Strip 1–2's as shown in Figure 12, and sew tog using whip st and long tails of matching yarn color.

Join Strips

Lay out strips as shown in Figure 12. Using whip st and matching yarn tails, sew tog, matching block corners.

BORDERS

On RS, at any corner of blanket, attach B and pu&k 52 sts along the edge of each Block 2 and 26 sts along the edge of each Block 3 across one side—260 sts.

Row 1 (WS): Knit.

Row 2 (RS): Kf&b, knit to last st, kf&b—2 sts inc'd; 262 sts.

Row 3: Knit.

Rows 4–13: Rep [Rows 2 & 3] 5 times—10 sts inc'd; 272 sts.

Cut B, leaving a 10"/25 cm tail. Attach D.

Rows 14–27: Rep [Rows 2 & 3] 7 times—14 sts inc'd; 286 sts.

BO loosely.

Cut D, leaving a 10"/25 cm tail.

Repeat for other 3 sides.

FINISHING

Use long tails of Borders to sew corner seams tog. Block to measurements. Weave in ends.

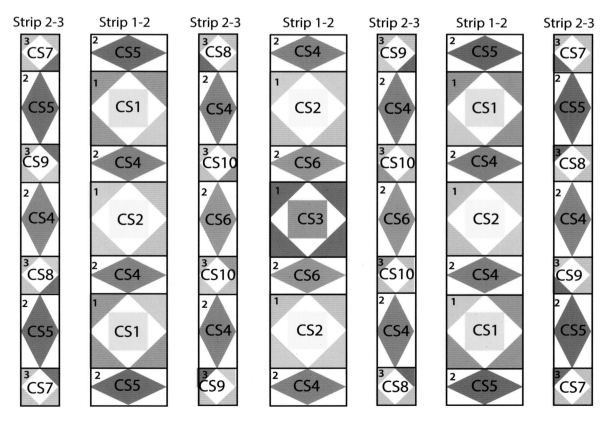

Figure 12: *Assembly*

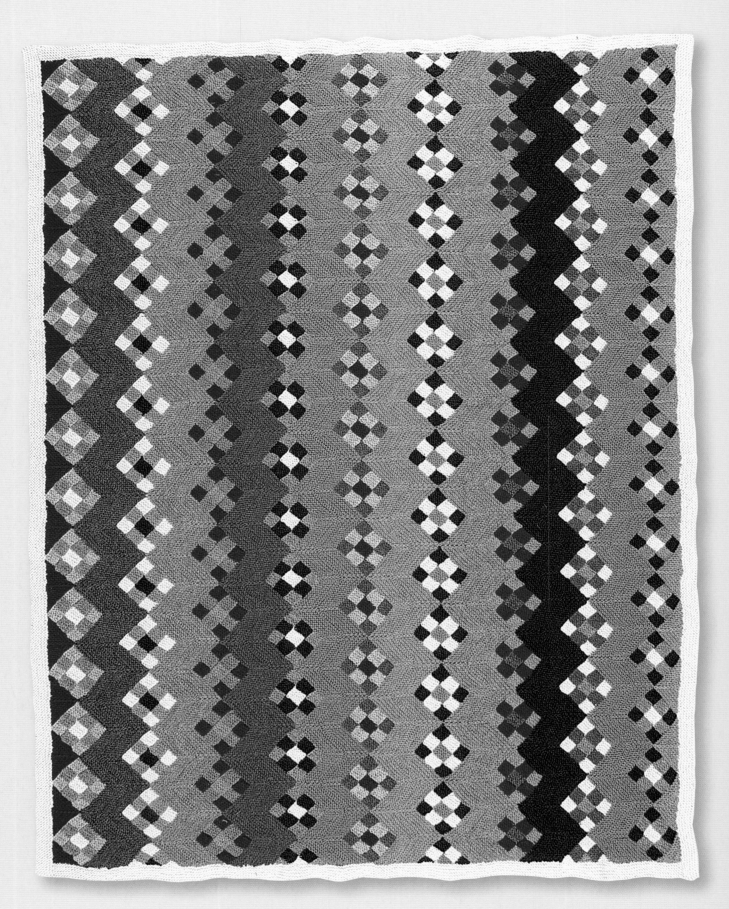

Ric Rac

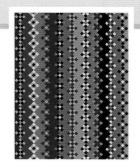

Cozy up under this checked and striped blanket in an array of complementary tones.

Techniques

Size
51 x 64.5"/130 x 164 cm

Yarn
Knit Picks Wool of the Andes Superwash, worsted (100% superwash wool; 110 yd./100 m; 1.75 oz./50 g):

A: 2 skeins Fjord Heather (light turquoise) #26316
B: 7 skeins Bamboo Heather (avocado green) #26315
C: 5 skeins Oyster Heather (light beige) #26317
D: 4 skeins Brass Heather (gold) #26319
E: 5 skeins Solstice Heather (dark blue-purple) #26300
F: 3 skeins Hollyberry (garnet) #26325
G: 5 skeins Cadet (turquoise) #26339
H: 4 skeins Amethyst Heather (plum) #26313
I: 3 skeins Mineral Heather (purple-gray) #26312

Needles
2 US Size 7/4.5 mm, 40"/100 cm circular needles

Notions
Stitch markers, bobbins, tapestry needle

Gauge
19 sts and 38 rows = 4"/10 cm in garter st

Notes
- Construction starts with knitting individual blocks and half blocks and assembling them into strips of two types: Strip 1 consists of only blocks, and Strip 2 has a half block at the top and bottom and blocks in between (see Figures 3–5).
- Adjacent strips are attached with 8 zigzag columns. There are two zigzag types: Zigzag 1 is worked on the edge of a Strip 1, and Zigzag 2 on the edge of a strip 2. Both are worked by picking up sts on the edges of strips. The zigzags are joined together into columns with a 3-needle BO.
- After all strips are assembled with columns, triangles are worked on sides and corners of the blanket.
- The borders are picked up on the edges of the completed blanket.
- As there are many yarn ends in this blanket, it might be desirable to weave them in as blocks/half blocks are completed rather than at the end of assembly.
- Charts for block and half block are at the end of the pattern.

Tip: Working Intarsia (used on Blocks and Half Blocks)

Follow pattern instructions for introducing colors and transitioning between colors. For convenience, wind 2–3 yards/meters of each yarn color onto a bobbin. When transitioning between colors, move both yarns to the WS of work. Working in garter st, this method requires moving the yarns forward on WS rows and leaving yarns in the back on RS rows. Twist the yarns around each other so they interlock, and then continue with the new color. Twisting yarns closes the hole that would otherwise form when transitioning between colors.

Blanket Instructions

BLOCKS AND HALF BLOCKS

Work [Block] and [Half Block] for Strips 1 to 9 in the color combinations and quantities specified in Figures 1 & 2.

Block—15 sts

See Block in Figure 1 for color arrangement.

CO 5 with 1 bobbin of C1; CO 5 with 1 bobbin of C2; CO 5 with 2nd bobbin of C1—15 sts.

Row 1 (WS): K5 with C1, twist C1 & C2 on WS, k5 with C2, twist C2 & 2nd strand of C1 on WS, k5.

Rows 2–9: Rep [Row 1] 8 times.

Cut C1 & C2.

Attach C2 at beg and C3 after 5 sts.

Row 10: Rep [Row 1], using C2 for C1, and C3 for C2.

Rows 11–19: Rep [Row 10] 9 times.

Cut C2 & C3.

Attach C1 at beg and C2 after 5 sts.

Rows 20–29: Rep [Row 1] 10 times.

BO sts in like color.

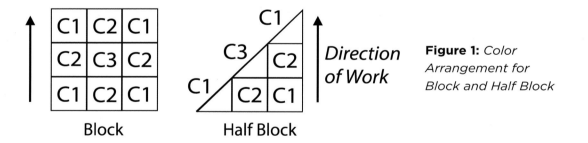

Figure 1: *Color Arrangement for Block and Half Block*

Figure 2: *Block and Half Block Color Assignments and Quantities for Strips*

Half Block—15 sts dec'ing to 1 st

See Half Block in Figure 1 for color chart.

CO 5 with 1 bobbin of C1; CO 5 with 1 bobbin of C2; CO 5 with 2nd bobbin of C1—15 sts.

Row 1 (WS): With C1, knit to color change, twist C1 & C2 on WS, k5 with C2, twist C2 & 2nd strand of C1 on WS, knit to end.

Row 2: K5 with C1, twist C1 & C2 on WS, k5 with C2, twist C2 & 2nd strand of C1 on WS, knit to last 2 sts, ssk—1 st dec'd; 14 sts.

Rows 3-8: Rep [Rows 1 & 2] 3 times—3 sts dec'd; 11 sts.

Row 9: Rep [Row 1].

Cut C1 & C2. Attach C2 at beg and C3 after 5 sts. Continue to twist colors at the color change.

Row 10: With C2, k5, with C3 knit to last 2 sts, ssk—1 st dec'd; 10 sts.

Row 11: With C3, knit to color change, twist C2 & C3 on WS, k5 with C2.

Rows 12-19: Rep [Rows 10 & 11] 4 times—4 sts dec'd; 6 sts.

Cut C2 & C3. Attach C1.

Row 20: Knit to last 2 sts, ssk—1 st dec'd; 5 sts.

Row 21: Knit.

Rows 22-27: Rep [Rows 20 & 21] 3 times—3 sts dec'd; 2 sts.

Row 28: Ssk—1 st dec'd; 1 st.

Cut yarn and fasten off.

STRIP ASSEMBLY

Arrange blocks for Strip 1 as shown in Figure 3, orienting blocks according to arrows. Tie tog the CO and BO tails of adjacent blocks to form strips.

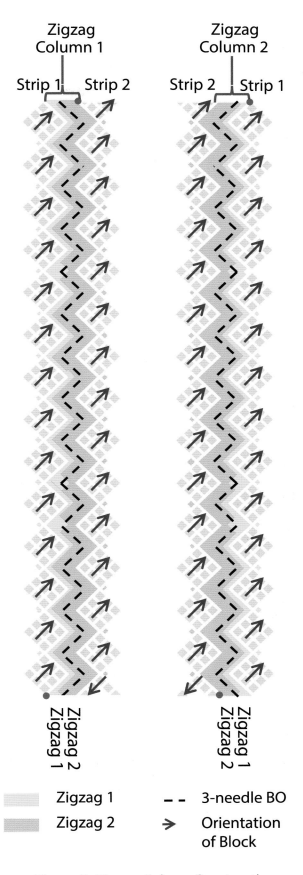

Figure 3: *Zigzag Column Construction*

Zigzag Column 1

See Figure 4 for yarn colors for Zigzags.

Zigzag 1

On RS, on the right edge of Strip 1, attach yarn at red dot in Figure 3. With 1st circular needle, *pu&k 15 sts to next corner, pm; rep from * 27 more times—420 sts. Work [Z1]; cut yarn.

Zigzag 1 (Z1)—420 sts

Row 1 (WS): Knit.

Row 2 (RS): *K2tog, knit to 1 st bef m, kf&b, kf&b, knit to 2 sts bef m, ssk; rep from * to end.

Rows 3–10: Rep [Rows 1 & 2] 4 times.

Row 11: Knit. Leave sts on needle.

Zigzag 2

On RS, the left edge of Strip 2, attach yarn at red dot in Figure 3. With 2nd circular needle, *pu&k 15 sts to next corner, pm; rep from * 27 more times—420 sts. Work [Z2]; do not cut yarn.

Zigzag 2 (Z2)—420 sts

Row 1 (WS): Knit.

Row 2 (RS): *Kf&b, knit to 2 sts bef next m, ssk, k2tog, knit to 1 st bef next m, kf&b; rep from * to end.

Rows 3–10: Rep [Rows 1 & 2] 4 times.

Row 11: Knit. Leave sts on needle.

Join Zigzags

Turn the two circular needles with Zigzag sts so that RSs are together. Working from the end with the yarn attached, 3-needle BO all sts loosely.

Tip: Use the markers, which are still in place, to help align the sts. Rm's as encountered.

Zigzag Columns 2–8

Work remaining Columns as for Column 1, working [Z1] on edges of Strip 1s and [Z2] on edges of Strip 2s (see Figures 3 & 4).

Side Triangles

In each of the 13 triangular-shaped openings labeled "Tr" on the right blanket edge in Figure 5, attach yarn in color specified in Figure 5 at the red triangle. Pu&k 14 sts to next corner, 1 st in corner, pm, pu&k 14 sts to next corner. Work [T]. Rep on left blanket edge, attaching yarn specified in Figure 5 at green triangle.

Zigzag Col 1	Zigzag Col 2	Zigzag Col 3	Zigzag Col 4	Zigzag Col 5	Zigzag Col 6	Zigzag Col 7	Zigzag Col 8
Strip 1	Strip 2	Strip 1	Strip 2	Strip 1	Strip 2	Strip 1	Strip 2	Strip 1

I   B H   G D   B E   G

Figure 4: *Zigzag Colors*

Figure 5: *Locations and Colors for Triangles (Tr) & Small Triangles (ST)*

Triangle (T)—29 sts dec'ing to 1 st

Row 1 (WS): Knit.

Row 2 (RS): K2tog, knit to 2 sts bef m, rm, cdd, pm, knit to 2 sts bef end, ssk—4 sts dec'd; 25 sts.

Rows 3–12: Rep [Rows 1 & 2] 5 times—20 sts dec'd; 5 sts. Rm.

Row 13: Knit.

Row 14: K1, cdd, k1—2 sts dec'd; 3 sts.

Row 15: Cdd—2 sts dec'd; 1 st.

Cut yarn and fasten off.

Corner Triangles

On each diagonal corner of the blanket labeled "ST" in Figure 5, attach yarn in color specified in Figure 5 at the red or green triangle. Pu&k 15 sts and work [ST].

Small Triangle (ST)—15 sts dec'ing to 1 st

Row 1 (WS): Knit.

Row 2 (RS): K2tog, knit to 2 sts from end, ssk—2 sts dec'd; 13 sts.

Rows 3–12: Rep [Rows 1 & 2] 5 times—10 sts dec'd; 3 sts.

Row 13: Knit.

Row 14: Cdd—2 sts dec'd; 1 st.

Cut yarn and fasten off.

BORDERS

Top Border

On RS, attach C at top-right corner of blanket. Pu&k 11 sts on edge of 1st ST, 16 sts on the edge of each pair of Z's, 20 sts on the edge of each Half Block, and 11 sts on the edge of last ST—230 sts.

Knit 11 rows. BO loosely.

Bottom Border

Attach C at bottom-left corner of blanket. Rep as for Top Border.

Right Border

Attach C at bottom-right corner of Bottom Border. Pu&k 6 sts on edge of Bottom Border (1 per garter st ridge), 11 sts on 1st ST, 21 sts on each Tr, 11 sts on last ST, and 6 sts on edge of Top Border (1 per garter st ridge)—307 sts.

Knit 11 rows. BO loosely.

Left Border

Attach C at top-right corner of Top Border. Rep as for Right Border.

FINISHING

Weave in ends.

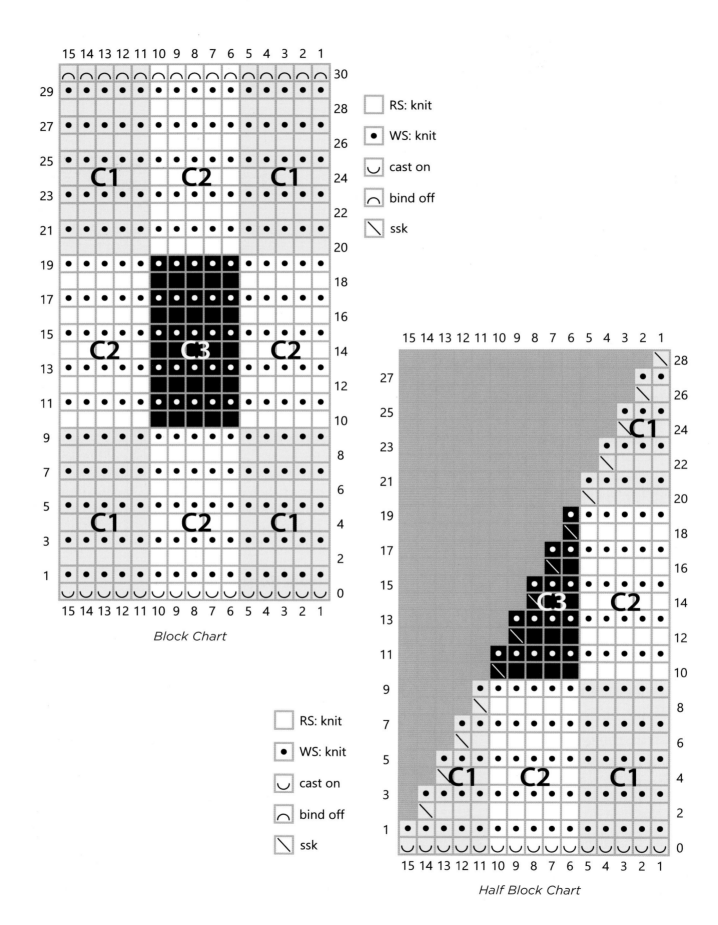

Block Chart

RS: knit
• WS: knit
⌣ cast on
⌢ bind off
╲ ssk

Half Block Chart

Rivers

With a flowing design in classic colors, this blanket will warm up your evenings relaxing on the front porch or stargazing from the dock.

Techniques

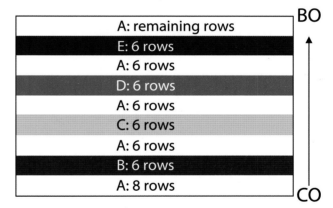

Size
51.5 x 70"/131 x 178 cm

Yarn
Berroco Vintage Chunky (52% acrylic/40% wool/8% nylon; 136 yd./124 m; 3.5 oz./100 g):
A: 14 skeins Mochi (white) #6101
B: 3 skeins Indigo (blue) #61182
C: 3 skeins Sunny (yellow) #6121
D: 3 skeins Sour Cherry (red) #6134
E: 3 skeins Mistletoe (green) #6152

Needles
2 US Size 10/6 mm, 40"/100 cm short-tip circular needles

Notions
9 removable markers (6 in one color or shape (m1's) and 3 in a different color or shape (m2's)), stitch holders, tapestry needle

Gauge
13 sts and 26 rows = 4"/10 cm in garter st

Notes
- This blanket is worked in 7 separate pieces—6 striped edge pieces and a center single-colored rectangle—and seamed.
- Follow the sequence shown in Figure 1 when working shapes S1, S2, and Eddy. Cut colors B, C, D, and E at each color change. Yarn A may be cut or carried up by twisting together with the working yarn at beg of each RS row.

	BO
A: remaining rows	
E: 6 rows	
A: 6 rows	
D: 6 rows	
A: 6 rows	
C: 6 rows	
A: 6 rows	
B: 6 rows	
A: 8 rows	CO

Figure 1: *Stripe Sequence*

Blanket Instructions

See Figure 2 for colors and construction. Markers of type 1 (m1's), placed during CO, represent locations of decreases and are indicated by green dots. Markers of type 2 (m2's), placed in Row 2 of Pattern sts, represent locations of increases and are indicated by orange dots.

S-Shape 1 — Make 2

With A, and leaving a 20"/50 cm tail, CO 29, place marker 1 (pm1), (CO 57, pm1) twice, CO 31—174 sts total. Do not join. Work [S1].

S-Shape 1 (S1)—174 sts

Row 1 and all odd rows (WS): Knit.

Row 2 (RS): *Knit to 2 sts bef m1, rm1, cdd, pm1; rep from * 2 more times, knit to last 3 sts, (kyok, pm2 after yo) 3 times.

Row 4: *Knit to 2 sts bef m1, rm1, cdd, pm1; rep from * 2 more times; **knit to 1 st bef next m2, rm2, kyok, pm2 after yo; rep from ** 2 times.

Rows 5–56: Rep [Rows 3 & 4] 26 times following Stripe Sequence.

Row 57: Rm's. Knit and place first 3 sts on holder; BO rem sts loosely. Cut yarn, leaving a 20"/50 cm tail.

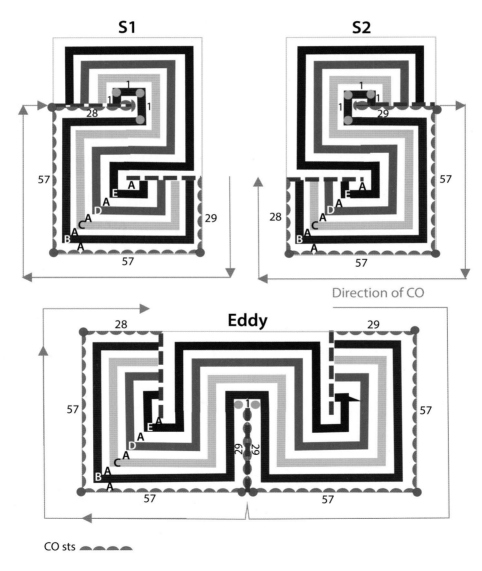

Figure 2: *CO Edges, Colors, and Seams for S1, S2, and Eddy*

S-Shape 2 — Make 2
With A, leaving a 20"/50 cm tail, CO 32, pm1, (CO 57, pm1) twice, CO 28—174 sts total. Do not join. Work [S2].

S-Shape 2 (S2)—174 sts
Row 1 and all odd rows (WS): Knit.
Row 2 (RS): (Kyok, pm2 after yo) 3 times, *knit to 2 sts bef m1, rm1, cdd, pm1; rep from * 2 more times, knit to end.
Row 4: *Knit to 1 st bef next m2, rm2, kyok, pm2 after yo; rep from * 2 more times, **knit to 2 sts bef next m1, rm1, cdd, pm1; rep from ** 2 times, knit to end.
Rows 5–56: Rep [Rows 3 & 4] 26 times following Stripe Sequence.
Row 57: Rm's; BO loosely to last 3 sts; knit and place last 3 sts on holder. Cut yarn, leaving a 20"/50 cm tail.

Eddy — Make 2
With A, leaving a 20"/50 cm tail, CO 29, pm1, (CO 57, pm1) twice, CO 29, pm2, CO 1, pm2, CO 29, pm1, (CO 57, pm1) twice, CO 28—344 sts total. Work [Eddy].

Eddy—344 sts dec'ing to 120 sts
Row 1 and all odd rows (WS): Knit.
Row 2 (RS): *Knit to 2 sts bef next m1, rm1, cdd, pm1; * rep bet * and * 2 times, (work to 1 st bef next m2, rm2, kyok, pm2 after yo) 2 times, rep bet * and * 3 more times, knit to end—8 sts dec'd; 336 sts.
Rows 3–56: Rep [Rows 1 & 2] 27 times following Stripe Sequence—216 sts dec'd; 120 sts.
Row 57: Rm's. Knit and place first 3 sts on holder, BO loosely to last 3 sts, knit and place last 3 sts on holder. Cut yarn, leaving a 20"/50 cm tail.

Outside-In Rectangle (OR) — Make 1

With A, *CO 113, pm1, CO 57, pm1; rep from * once—340 sts. Work [OR].

Note: If preferred, the rectangle (OR) can be worked by picking up sts along the insides of the other shapes after they have been sewn together. Assemble S1s, S2s, and Eddys as below, and then pu&k the number of CO sts below, beginning at the lower right corner of the center space.

Outside-In Rectangle (OR)—340 sts dec'ing to 116 sts

Worked in the round.

Rnd 1 and all odd rows: Purl.

Rnd 2: *Knit to m, rm1, cdd, pm1; rep from * 3 more times—8 sts dec'd; 332 sts.

Note: The last dec crosses BOR.

Rnds 3–56: Rep [Rnds 1 & 2] 27 times—216 sts dec'd; 116 sts.

Rnd 57: P58. Turn RSs together, and using 2nd needle, 3-needle BO all sts. Cut yarn and fasten off.

ASSEMBLY

Using long tails from COs and BOs and whip st, sew inner seams on S1, S2, and Eddy pieces along purple lines shown in Figure 2. Tie off, and then insert needle through 3 sts on holders. Pull tight and then fasten off securely. Arrange pieces as shown in Figure 3. Using whip st and A, sew tog edges along purple dashed lines and then along green dashed lines.

FINISHING

Weave in ends.

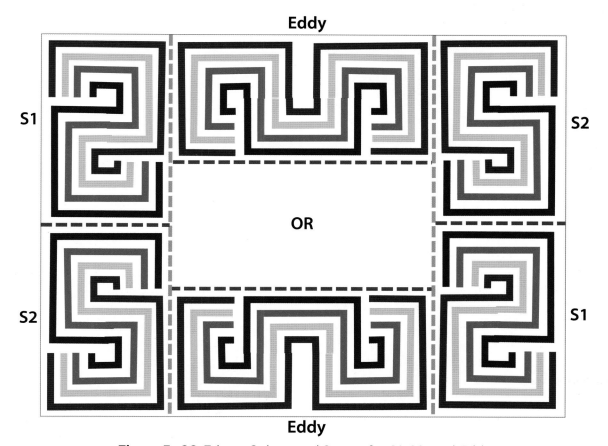

Figure 3: *CO Edges, Colors, and Seams for S1, S2, and Eddy*

Shadow Play

Diagonal elements make an eye-catching statement in dark and light gem tones.

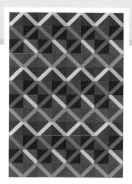

· ·

Techniques

Size

57.5 x 83.5"/146 x 212 cm

Yarn

Plymouth Worsted Merino Superwash (100% superwash fine merino; 218 yd./199 m; 3.5 oz./100 g):

A: 1 hank Teal (teal) #0062
B: 1 hank Pink (coral pink) #0021
C: 1 hank Green (forest green) #0004
D: 1 hank Cornflower (medium blue) #0019
E: 1 hank Pesto (avocado green) #0078
F: 1 hank Slate (gray-teal) #0070
G: 1 hank Plum (plum) #0015
H: 1 hank Light Orchid (light pink) #0085
I: 1 hank Violet (violet) #0064
J: 1 hank Celantro (light avocado green) #0017
K: 1 hank Burgundy (burgundy) #0016
L: 1 hank Natural (off-white) #0001
M: 1 hank Purple (true purple) #0024
N: 1 hank Dusty Violet (light gray-purple) #0034
O: 1 hank Denim (medium gray-blue) #0022
P: 2 hanks Lavender (light gray-purple) #0018

Needles

US Size 7/4.5 mm, 40"/100 cm circular needles, 10"/25 cm straights or shorter circular needles

Notions

Tapestry needle

Gauge

18 sts and 36 rows = 4"/10 cm in garter st

Note

- This blanket is worked in diagonally knit blocks. Each block has a dark background with a lighter colored stripe. The blocks are sewn together; then borders are added by picking up sts from the edges of the assembled blocks.

Blanket Instructions

Work [Block] 12 times in each of the 8 combinations of MC and CC in Table 1.

Combination #	MC	CC
1	A	B
2	C	D
3	E	F
4	G	H

Combination #	MC	CC
5	I	J
6	K	L
7	M	N
8	O	P

Table 1: *Color Combinations for Block*

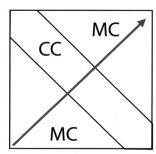

Figure 1: *Block Colors and Construction*

Block—1 st inc'ing to 43 sts, dec'ing to 1 st

Note: *See Figure 1. When cutting current yarn color, leave a 10"/25 cm tail for sewing blocks. You can also carry yarn along edge until next use, twisting tog with working yarn at beg of each RS row.*

With MC, make slipknot and place on needle.
Row 1 (RS): Yoco, knit to end—1 st inc'd; 2 sts
Rows 2–34: Rep [Row 1] 33 times—33 sts inc'd; 35 sts.
Cut MC and attach CC.
Rows 35–42: Rep [Row 1] 8 times—8 sts inc'd; 43 sts.
Row 43: K2tog, knit to end—1 st dec'd; 42 sts.
Rows 44–50: Rep [Row 43] 7 times—7 sts dec'd; 35 sts.
Cut CC and attach MC.
Rows 51–84: Rep [Row 43] 34 times—34 sts dec'd; 1 st.
Cut MC and fasten off, leaving a 20"/50 cm tail.

ASSEMBLY

Note: *Use mattress stitch for all sewing.*

*On RS, lay out 1 block in each of the 8 color combinations as shown in Step 1 of Figure 2.

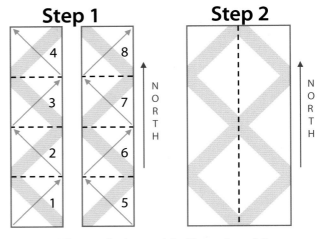

Figure 2: *Assembly Steps 1 and 2*

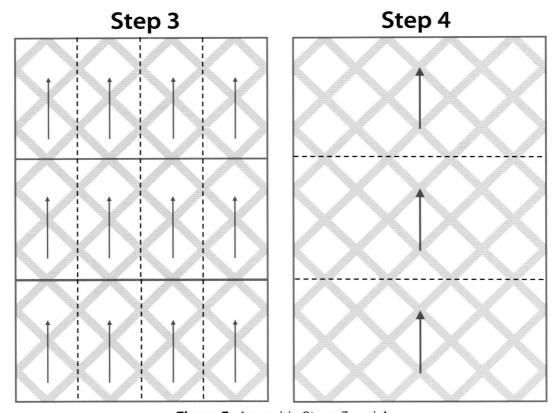

Figure 3: *Assembly Steps 3 and 4*

Using tails of matching color, sew on dashed lines shown in Steps 1 & 2. Rep from * 11 times, to create 12 groups of 8 blocks.

*On RS, lay out 4 groups of 8 blocks as shown in Assembly Step 3 in Figure 3. Using tails of matching color, sew along dashed lines shown in Step 3. Rep from * 2 more times, to create 3 groups of 32 blocks.

Lay out groups of 32 blocks as shown in Assembly Step 4 in Figure 3. Sew on dashed lines in Step 4 to complete assembly.

BORDERS

Right Border

On RS, attach P to the bottom-right corner of the blanket.

Pu&k 30 sts on the edge of each block—360 sts. Knit 15 rows. BO loosely.

Left Border

Rep as for Right Border, attaching yarn at the top-left corner of the blanket.

Top Border

On RS, attach P to top-right corner of Right Border. Pu&k 9 sts on border, 30 sts on each block, and 9 sts on the last border—258 sts. Knit 15 rows. BO loosely.

Bottom Border

Rep as for Top Border, attaching yarn at the bottom-left edge of the Left Border.

FINISHING

Weave in ends and block if desired.

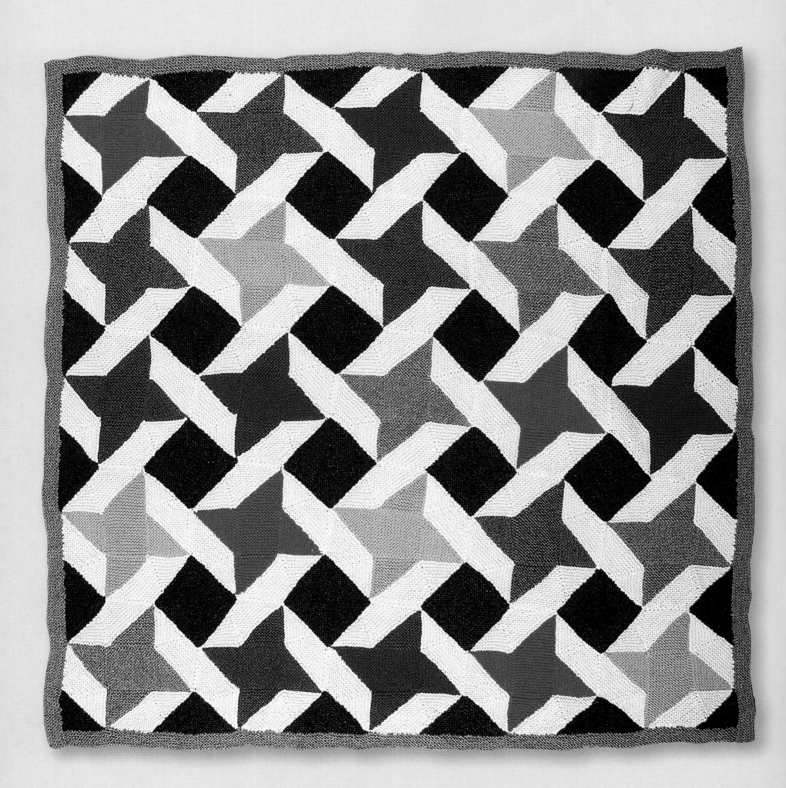

Starry Skies

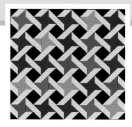

A star-studded sky on a dark night is the inspiration for this gem of a blanket.

. . . .

Techniques

Method A: ▲

Method B: ⊃

Method C: ▲ ⟋

Method D: ▲ ⟋ ⊞

Size

63 x 63"/160 x 160 cm

Yarn

Lion Brand Heartland, worsted (100% acrylic; 251 yd./230 m; 5 oz./142 g):

A: 1 skein Yellowstone (yellow) #158
B: 2 skeins Glacier Bay (aqua) #105
C: 1 skein Isle Royale (violet) #189
D: 1 skein Hotsprings (purple) #147
E: 1 skein Olympic (blue) #109
F: 1 skein Redwood (red) #113
G: 6 skeins Acadia (ecru) #098
H: 3 skeins Black Canyon (black) #153

Needles

US Size 8/5 mm, 40"/100 cm circular needles, 10"/25 cm straights and 5 dpns (Method D)

Notions

Stitch markers, tapestry needle

Gauge

15 sts and 30 rows = 4"/10 cm in garter st

Notes

- See Figure 1 for construction methods. There are two methods, A and B, for working the 4-Point Stars.
- In Method A, a center square is worked, and then triangles are worked from sts picked up on the edges of the square.
- In Method B, the 4-Point Star is worked as a single unit using wrap & turn short rows, completed with a short, sewn seam.
- For both methods, once the 4-Point Stars are complete, trapezoids are worked to transform the star into an octagon shape. Trapezoids are picked up from the edges of the 4-Point Star. Once the octagons are complete, either Method C or Method D is used to complete the blanket face.
- In Method C, sts are picked up on the diagonal edges of the octagons and triangles are worked to transform the octagon into a square (blocks). The blocks are then sewn together to complete the blanket face.
- In Method D, the octagons are sewn together after trapezoids are complete. Square shapes between octagons are filled by picking up sts on the edges of openings and working a square outside-to-center. Triangles and corners are picked up to fill spaces on the edges of the blanket face.
- For both methods, the borders are worked by picking up sts on the edges of the completed blanket face.
- Methods B and D generate fewer ends to weave in.

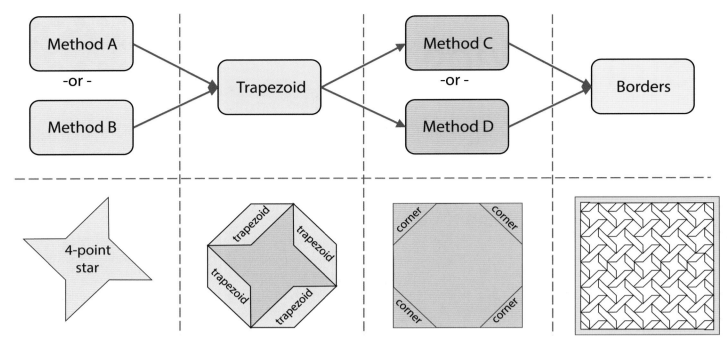

Figure 1: *Construction Options*

Blanket Instructions

4-Point Stars

Make 25 4-Point Stars in the colors and
quantities in Figure 2.

METHOD A

Make 4-Point Star using decreases and pu&k.

Square

Work [Sq]. Do not cut yarn or BO.

> **Square (Sq)** – Method A—15 sts
>
> CO 15 sts.
> Knit 30 rows.

Triangles (Tr)

See Figure 3 for construction.

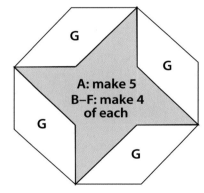

Figure 2: *Octagon Colors and Quantities*

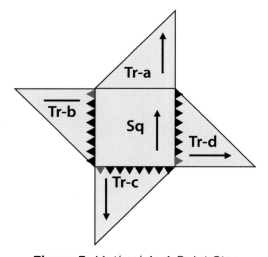

Figure 3: *Method A: 4-Point Star*

Tr-a

Knit 1 row. Work [Tr].

> **Triangle (Tr)** – Method A—15 sts dec'ing to 1 st
>
> **Row 1 (WS):** Knit.
> **Row 2 (RS):** Knit to last 2 sts, ssk—1 st
> dec'd; 14 sts.
> **Row 3:** Knit.
> **Rows 4–29:** Rep [Rows 2 & 3] 13 times—13 sts
> dec'd; 1 st.
> Cut yarn and fasten off.

Tr-b, Tr-c, and Tr-d

On RS, at each of the locations indicated by the
red triangle in Figure 3, attach yarn and pu&k
15 sts on edge of Sq (1 per garter st ridge or 1
per CO st)—15 sts. Work [Tr].

Continue at **Trapezoids**.

METHOD B

4-Point Star is worked as a single unit using w&t
technique. See Figure 4.

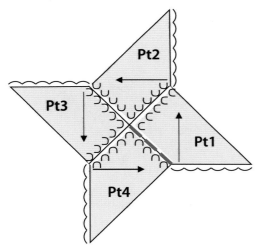

Figure 4: *Method B: 4-Point Star*

Point 1 (Pt1)

With yarn color specified in Figure 2, work [FP].
Do not cut yarn.

> **Foundation Point (FP)** – Method B—14
> sts inc'ing to 15 sts, dec'ing to 9 sts,
> inc'ing to 23 sts

Using simple CO (see "Glossary"), CO 14 sts.
Row 1 (WS): Yoco, knit to end—1 st
inc'd; 15 sts.
Row 2 (RS): Knit.
Row 3: Yoco, knit to last 2 sts, ssk.
Rows 4–15: Rep [Rows 2 & 3] 6 times.
Row 16: Knit to last st, w&t.
Row 17: Knit to last 2 sts, ssk—1 st
dec'd; 14 sts.
Row 18: Knit to 1 st bef wrap, w&t.
Row 19: Rep [Row 17]—1 st dec'd; 13 sts.
Rows 20–27: Rep [Rows 18 & 19] 4 times—4
sts dec'd; 9 sts.
Row 28: Rep [Row 18].
Row 29: Ssk, CO 14 using a Simple CO—23 sts.

Points 2–4 (Pt2–Pt4)

Work [Pt] 3 times continuously, ending the final
rep after Row 28.
BO very loosely. Cut yarn, leaving a
15"/38 cm tail.
Using tail, and mattress st, sew tog BO edge
of last Point (Pt4) and bottom-left edge of
first Point (Pt1), shown as the red-dashed line
in Figure 4.

Continue at **Trapezoids**.

> **Point (Pt)** – Method B—23 sts, dec'ing to 9
> sts, inc'ing to 23 sts

See chart at end of the pattern.
Setup row (RS): Knit 15, w&t next st.
Row 1 (WS): Knit to last 2 sts, ssk—1 st
dec'd; 22 sts.
Row 2 (RS): Knit to 1 st past wrap, w&t.
Rows 3–14: Rep [Rows 1 & 2] 6 times—6 sts
dec'd; 16 sts.
Row 15: Rep [Row 1]—1 st dec'd; 15 sts.
Row 16: Knit to 1 st bef wrap, w&t.
Rows 17–28: Rep [Rows 15 & 16] 6 times—6 sts
dec'd; 9 sts.
Row 29: K1, CO 14 using Simple CO—23 sts.

Trapezoids (Trp)

Note: *Leave a long tail (12"/30 cm) when attaching for the first 2 consecutive Trps of each Octagon.*

On RS, at each of the outer points of one of the 4-Point Star shapes, attach G at red triangle in Figure 5. Pu&k 21 sts evenly to next corner, pm, and 15 sts (1 per garter st ridge) to next corner—36 sts. Work [Trp].

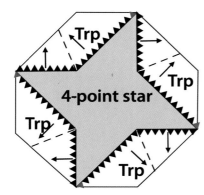

Figure 5: *Trapezoids (Trp) for All Methods*

Trapezoid (Trp)—36 sts dec'ing to 6 sts

Row 1 (WS): Knit.
Row 2 (RS): K2tog, knit to m, knit to last 2 sts, ssk—2 sts dec'd; 34 sts.
Row 3: Knit.
Row 4: K2tog, knit to 2 sts bef m, ssk, k2tog, knit to last 2 sts, ssk—4 sts dec'd; 30 sts.
Row 5: Knit.
Rows 6–21: Rep [Rows 2–5] 4 times—24 sts dec'd; 6 sts.
BO loosely.
Cut yarn and fasten off.

Continue at **Corners** with Method C or D.

Corners

METHOD C

On RS, on the long edge of each Trapezoid in spaces labled "CR" in Figure 6, attach H at the red triangle, leaving a 10"/25 cm tail. Pu&k 21 sts to next corner. Work [CR].

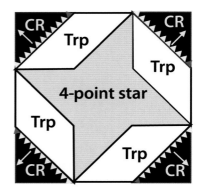

Figure 6: *Method C for Corners*

Corner (CR) – Method C & D—21 sts dec'ing to 1 st

Row 1 (WS): Knit.
Row 2 (RS): K2tog, knit to last 2 sts, ssk—2 sts dec'd; 19 sts.
Row 3: Knit.
Rows 4–19: Rep [Rows 2 & 3] 8 times—16 sts dec'd; 3 sts.
Row 20 (RS): Ccd—2 sts dec'd; 1 st.
Cut yarn and fast off.

Assembly

Lay out completed Square blocks according to the color arrangement in Figure 7. If the Octagons were worked with Method A, orient the CO edge of Sq to the bottom. Using mattress st and long tails of matching colors, sew the blocks tog into horizontal strips and then sew strips together, matching corners of shapes as shown.
Continue at **Borders**.

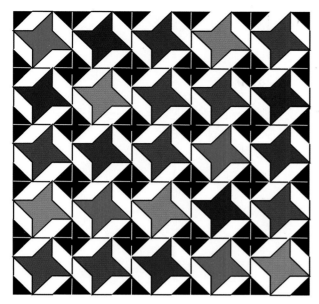

Figure 7: *Method C Assembly*

METHOD D

Assembly

Assemble the 25 completed Octagons as shown in Figure 8. If the Octagons were worked with Method A, orient the CO edge of Sq to the bottom. Using mattress st and long tails from Trps, sew along dashed lines.

Interstitial Squares

On RS, at each of the 16 square spaces labeled "IS" in Figure 8, attach H at the red triangle. *With dpn, pu&k 21 sts to next corner, rep from * 3 more times—84 sts. Work [IS].

Interstitial Square (IS) – Method D—84 sts dec'ing to 4 sts

Worked in the round.
Rnd 1: Purl.
Rnd 2: *K2tog, knit to last 2 sts on dpn, ssk; rep from * 3 times—8 sts dec'd; 76 sts.
Rnd 3: Purl.
Rnds 4–19: Rep [Rnds 2 & 3] 8 times—64 sts dec'd; 12 sts.
Rnd 20: Purl.
Rnd 21: Rm's. Cdd 4 times—8 sts dec'd; 4 sts.
Cut yarn, leaving a 10"/25 cm tail. Thread yarn through tapestry needle and insert needle through all loops. Pull tightly and fasten off securely.

Edge Triangles

On RS, at each of the 16 triangular spaces labeled "ET" in Figure 8, attach H at the red triangle. Pu&k 21 sts to next corner, pm, pu&k 21 sts to next corner—42 sts. Work [ET].

Edge Triangle (ET) – Method D—42 sts dec'ing to 4 sts

Row 1 (WS): Knit.
Row 2 (RS): K2tog, knit to 2 sts bef m, ssk, k2tog, knit to 2 sts bef end, ssk—4 sts dec'd; 38 sts.
Row 3: Knit.
Rows 4–19: Rep [Rows 2 & 3] 8 times—32 sts dec'd; 6 sts.
Row 20: Ccd, twice—4 sts dec'd; 2 sts.
Row 21: K2tog—1 st dec'd; 1 st.
Cut yarn and fasten off.

Figure 8: *Method D Assembly*

Corner Triangles

On RS, at each of the 4 corners labeled "CR" in Figure 8, attach H at the red triangle. Pu&k 21 sts to next corner. Work [CR].

Continue at **Borders**.

BORDERS – ALL METHODS

Top Border

On RS at the top-right corner of blanket, attach B. Pu&k 15 sts on the edge of each CR and Trp and 30 sts on the edge of each ET—225 sts.

Knit 11 rows. BO loosely.

Bottom Border

Rep as for Top, attaching B to bottom-left corner of blanket.

Right Border

On RS at bottom-right corner of blanket, attach B. Pu&k 6 sts (one per garter st ridge) on the Bottom Border, 15 sts on the edge of each CR and Trp and 30 sts on the edge of each ET, and 6 sts on Top Border—237 sts.

Knit 11 rows. BO loosely.

Left Border

Rep as for Right, attaching B to top-left corner of the Top Border.

FINISHING

Weave in ends.

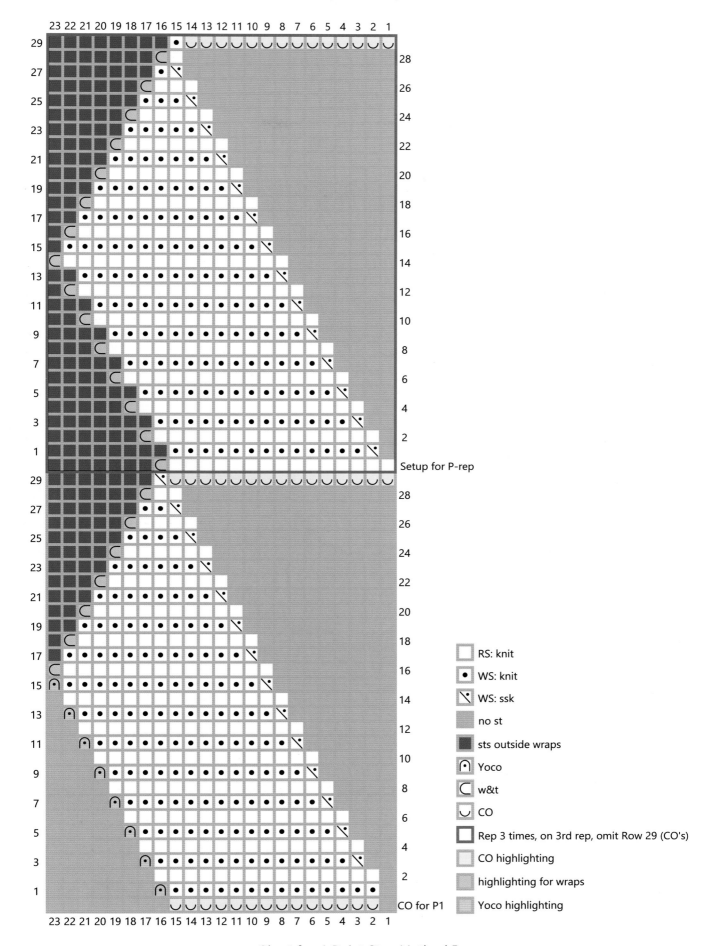

Chart for 4-Point Star, Method B

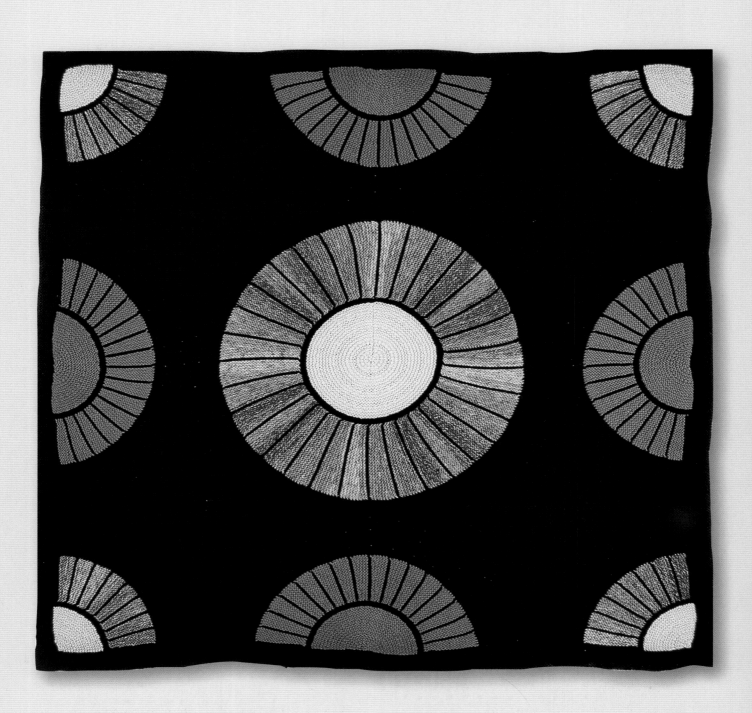

Sunburst

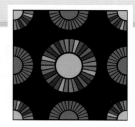

Bring rays of sunshine into your home with this blanket of multicolored suns.

- -

Techniques

Size
60 x 60"/152 x 152 cm

Yarn
Premier Yarns Muir Woods, worsted (100%
    acrylic; 170 yd./155 m; 3.5 oz./100 g):
A: 3 skeins Redwood (self-striping rust, peach,
    teal) #1074-06

Premier Yarns Everyday (100% acrylic;
    180 yd./165 m; 3.5 oz./100 g
B: 9 skeins black (black) #ED100-12
C: 1 skein soft peach (light peach) #ED100-55
D: 2 skeins peacock (teal) #ED100-31

Needles
US Size 9/5.5 mm, 16"/40 cm and 40"/100 cm
    circular needles and dpns

Notions
Stitch holder, stitch markers, tapestry needle

Gauge
15 sts and 30 rows = 4"/10 cm in garter st

Large Ray (LR)—27 sts

Rows 1 & 3 (RS): Knit.
Row 2 and all even (WS) rows to 18: Knit.
Row 5: Knit to 4 sts bef end, w&t.
Rows 7, 9, 11, 13: Knit to 5 sts bef wrap, w&t—3
    sts rem bef w&t after completing last row.
Rows 15 & 17: Knit.

Note
- This blanket is worked in blocks. The full
  Center Sun block is worked first, followed by
  small blocks with quarter and half suns. Each
  block begins with working Rays, then Center,
  then corner(s). Sts for the Center are picked
  up from the inner edges of the Rays, and sts
  for the corners are picked up from the outer
  edges. Corners use short rows to transform
  the shapes into a square. The borders are
  added by picking up sts from the edges of the
  assembled blocks.

Blanket Instructions

___

Note: *When working Rays, do not cut yarns A
and B between uses. When carrying B, at the beg
of each RS row, wrap B under A to trap B inside
the stitch at the end of the row. When switching
to B to begin ray separator, stretch outside edge
of rays to make certain B yarn is loose.*

___

FULL SUN BLOCK
See Figure 1 for shape identification and Figure 2
    for construction.

Rays
With A, CO 27 sts. *Work [LR]. Attach B without
    cutting A, and knit 2 rows for Ray Separator
    (RSP); rep from * 31 more times.
BO loosely. Leave the last st on the needle and
    do not cut B. Cut A, leaving a 20"/50 cm tail.
    With the tail of A and whip st, sew tog the CO
    and BO edges to close the circle, as shown by
    the white dashed line in Figure 1.

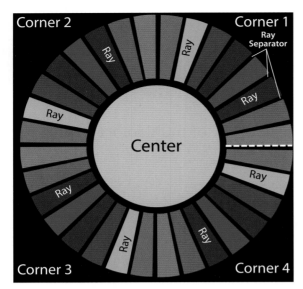

Figure 1: *Shapes of the Sun Block*

Center

On the RS, with B, working clockwise on the inside edge of the ring (red dashed line in Figure 2), and starting at the sewn seam, pu&k 1 st on each RSP, and 4 sts across the inner edge of each LR—160 sts. Join and pm for BOR—160 sts. Work [FD].

Full Disc (FD)—160 sts dec'ing to 8 sts

Worked in the round; change to dpns when necessary.

Rnd 1 and all odd rnds to 41: Purl.
Rnd 2: Knit.
Rnd 4: Cut B and attach C. *K2tog, k3; rep from * to end—32 sts dec'd; 128 sts.
Rnds 6, 8, 10: Knit.
Rnd 12: K1, *k2tog, k2; rep from * to end—32 sts dec'd; 96 sts.
Rnds 14, 16, 18, 20: Knit.
Rnd 22: *K2tog, k1; rep from * to end—32 sts dec'd; 64 sts.
Rnds 24, 26, 28, 30: Knit.
Rnd 32: *K2tog; rep from * to end—32 sts dec'd; 32 sts.
Rnds 34 & 36: Knit.
Rnds 38 & 40: Rep [Rnd 32]—24 sts dec'd; 8 sts.
Cut C, leaving a 10"/25 cm tail. Thread tail end onto tapestry needle and insert through rem sts on needle. Pull to tighten and close hole, and then tie securely.

Corners

Each corner is worked over 8 Rays + Ray Separators.

Corner 1

On RS, attach B at seam on outer edge of Full Sun. Working counterclockwise (blue dotted line in Figure 2), *pu&k 9 sts on the outer edge of LR, 2 sts on the RSP, 9 sts on LR, 1 st on RSP; rep from * 3 more times—84 sts. Work [CR].

Corner (CR)—84 sts

Row 1 (WS): Knit.
Row 2 (RS): Knit to 8 sts from end, w&t.
Row 3: Rep [Row 2]—68 sts bet wraps.
Rows 4 & 5: Knit to 4 sts bef wrap, w&t—60 sts bet wraps after completing last row.
Rows 6–25: Knit to 2 sts bef wrap, w&t—20 sts bet wraps after completing last row.
Rows 26–44: Knit to 1 st bef wrap, w&t—1 st bet wraps after completing last row.
Row 45: Knit to end.
Row 46: BO 42 sts, knit to end.
Row 47: Turn to WS, BO rem 42 sts loosely.
Cut yarn, leaving a 10"/25 cm tail for sewing.

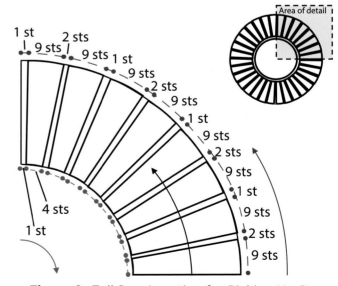

Figure 2: *Full Sun: Location for Picking Up Sts for Center and Corners*

Corners 2–4

*Turn to RS and attach yarn at next LR. Rep as for Corner 1. Rep from * 2 more times.

QUARTER SUN BLOCK

Make 4. See Figure 3 for shape identification and Figure 4 for construction.

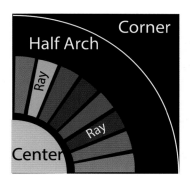

Figure 3: *Shapes for Quarter Sun*

Rays

With B, CO 17 sts. *Knit 2 rows for Ray Separator [RSP]. Attach A without cutting B; work [SR]; rep from * 7 more times. With B, knit 2 rows for final [RSP].

BO loosely. Leave the last st on the needle and do not cut B. Cut A.

Small Ray (SR)—17 sts

Row 1 (RS): Knit.
Row 2 and all even (WS) rows to 12: Knit.
Row 3: Knit to 4 sts bef end, w&t.
Rows 5 & 7: Knit to 5 sts bef wrap, w&t—3 sts rem bef w&t after knitting last row.
Rows 9 & 11: Knit.

Center

On the RS, with B, working clockwise on the inside edge of the ring (red dotted line in Figure 4), pu&k 3 sts on inner edge of each SR, and 1 st on each RSP—33 sts. Work [QD]. Cut yarn and fasten off.

Quarter Disc (QD)—33 sts dec'ing to 1 st

Rows 1 (WS)–3: Knit.
Cut B and attach C.
Rows 4 & 5: Knit.

Row 6 (RS): K1, *k2tog, k2; rep from * to end—8 sts dec'd; 25 sts.
Rows 7–15: Knit.
Row 16: K1, *k2tog, k1; rep from * to end—8 sts dec'd; 17 sts.
Rows 17–25: Knit.
Row 26: K1, *k2tog; rep from * to end—8 sts dec'd; 9 sts.
Rows 27–31: Knit.
Row 32: K1, *k2tog; rep from * to end—4 sts dec'd; 5 sts.
Row 33: Knit.
Row 34: K1, k2tog twice—2 sts dec'd; 3 sts.
Cut yarn, leaving a 10"/25 cm tail. Thread tail end onto tapestry needle and insert through rem sts on needle. Pull to tighten and tie securely.

Half Arch & Corner

On RS, attach B at right corner of outer edge of Quarter Sun. Working counterclockwise (blue dotted line in Figure 4), pu&k 1 st on each RSP except the 3rd and 7th, 2 sts on 3rd and 7th RSP, and 6 sts on each SR—59 sts. Work [HA] and then work [CR].

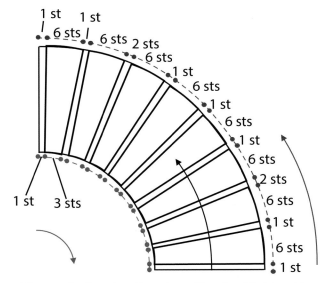

Figure 4: *Quarter Sun: Location for Picking Up Sts for Center, Half Arch, and Corner*

Half Arch (HA)—59 sts inc'ing to 84 sts

Rows 1 (WS)–5: Knit.

Row 6 (RS): K1, *bli, k7; rep from * 7 more times, bli, k2—9 sts inc'd; 68 sts.

Rows 7–15: Knit.

Row 16: K6, *bli, k8; rep from * 6 more times, bli, k6—8 sts inc'd; 76 sts.

Rows 17–23: Knit.

Row 24: K7, *bli, k9; rep from * 6 more times, bli, k6—8 sts inc'd; 84 sts.

Rows 25–28: Knit.

HALF SUN BLOCK

Make 4. See Figure 5 for shape identification and Figure 6 for construction.

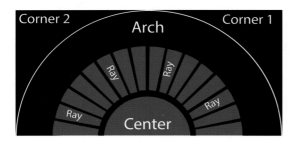

Figure 5: *Shapes for Half Sun*

Rays

With B, CO 17 sts. Knit 2 rows for RSP, attach D without cutting B. *With D work [SR], with B knit 2 rows for RSP, rep from * 15 more times. BO loosely. Leave the last st on the needle and do not cut B. Cut D.

Center

On the RS, with B, working clockwise on the inside edge of the ring (red dotted line in Figure 6), pu&k 3 sts on edge of each SR, and 1 st on each RSP—65 sts.

Work [HD].

Half Disc (HD)—65 sts dec'ing to 3 sts

Rows 1 (WS)–3: Knit.

Cut B and attach D.

Rows 4 & 5: Knit.

Row 6 (RS): K1, *k2tog, k2; rep from * to end—16 sts dec'd; 49 sts.

Rows 7–15: Knit.

Row 16: K1, *k2tog, k1; rep from * to end—16 sts dec'd; 33 sts.

Rows 17–25: Knit.

Row 26: K1, *k2tog; rep from * to end—16 sts dec'd; 17 sts.

Rows 27–31: Knit.

Row 32: K1, *k2tog; rep from * to end—8 sts dec'd; 9 sts.

Row 33: Knit.

Row 34: K1, *k2tog; rep from * to end—4 sts dec'd; 5 sts.

Row 35: Knit.

Row 36: K1, k2tog twice—2 sts dec'd; 3 sts

Cut D, leaving a 10"/25 cm tail. Thread tail end onto tapestry needle and insert through rem sts on needle. Pull to tighten and tie securely.

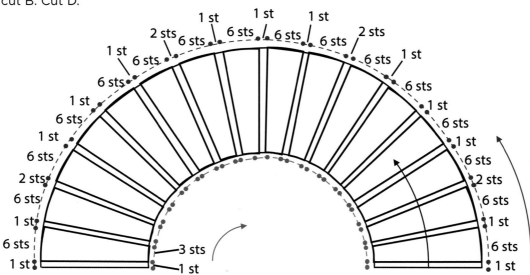

Figure 6: *Half Sun: Locations for Picking Up Sts for Center, Arch, and Corners*

Arch and Corners

Arch

On RS, attach B at right corner of outer edge of Half Sun. Working counterclockwise (blue dotted line in Figure 6), [(pu&k 1 st from RSP, 6 sts on SR) 2 times, 2 sts on next RSP, 6 sts on SR, 1 st on RSP, 6 sts on SR] 4 times, pu&k 1 st on last RSP—117 sts. Work [AR].

> **Arch (AR)—117 sts inc'ing to 168 sts**
>
> **Rows 1 (WS)–5:** Knit.
> **Row 6 (RS):** K2, *bli, k7; rep from * 15 more times, bli, k3—17 sts inc'd; 134 sts.
> **Rows 7–15:** Knit.
> **Row 16:** K3, *bli, k8; rep from * 15 more times, bli, k3—17 sts inc'd; 151 sts.
> **Rows 17–23:** Knit.
> **Row 24:** K4, *bli, k9; rep from * 15 more times, bli, k3—17 sts inc'd; 168 sts.
> **Rows 25–28:** Knit.

Corner 1

Pm after 84th st. Work left [CR] on 84 sts bef m.

Corner 2

On WS, attach B at m. Rm. Work right [CR].

ASSEMBLY

Lay out blocks as shown in Figure 7. Using long tails of B and whip st, sew tog blocks on the dotted lines. Sew strips tog along solid lines.

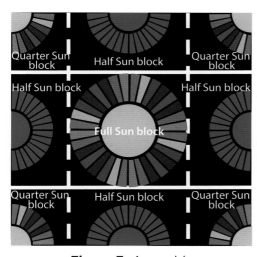

Figure 7: *Assembly*

BORDERS

Right Border

On RS, at bottom-right corner of the assembled blocks, attach B. Pu&k 52 sts on each Quarter Sun block edge and 105 sts on Half Sun block edge—209 sts. Knit 14 rows and then BO loosely.

Left Border

Rep as for Right Border, attaching yarn at the top-left corner.

Top Border

On RS, at top-right corner of the blanket, attach B. Pu&k 8 sts on the border, 52 sts on each Quarter Sun block edge, 105 sts on Half Sun block edge, and 8 sts on the 2nd border—225 sts. Knit 14 rows and then BO loosely.

Bottom Border

Rep as for Top Border, attaching yarn at the bottom-left corner.

FINISHING

Weave in ends.

Synchrony

Knit up a dynamic focal point for your home with this blanket of interlocking rings.

Techniques

Size

66.5 x 66.5"/169 x 169 cm

Yarn

Universal Deluxe Worsted Superwash (100% superwash wool; 218 yd./199 m; 3.5 oz./100 g):

A: 5 balls Twilight (navy blue) #740
B: 8 balls Dusty Blue (medium gray-blue) #718
C: 3 balls Christmas Red (bright red) #736
D: 2 balls Sangria (dark red/burgundy) #737
E: 2 balls Purplish Blue (medium purple-blue) #719
F: 1 ball Ice Rustic (light gray-blue) #772
G: 1 ball Pulp (off-white) #728

Needles

US Size 7/4.5 mm, 40"/10 cm circular needles and dpns

Notions

US Size I-9/5.5 mm crochet hook, stitch holders, stitch markers, tapestry needle

Gauge

17 sts and 34 rows = 4"/10 cm in garter st

Notes

- The blanket construction is a combination of modular knitting and sewing. Once the main design at the center of the blanket is assembled, an inner border is worked on each edge. An outer border of S-shapes is worked in strips that are sewn to the inner border. Corner pieces of the outer border are worked from picked up stiches on the edges of the strips. The edge of the blanket is finished with single crochet.
- Leave long tails when casting on or binding off shapes. These tails can be used for seaming. However, there will not be a tail available for every seam that needs to be sewn. When seaming, always choose a yarn color that matches one of the edges being seamed.

Note: *In the sample, colors A and E were reversed. Figure 1 is consistent with the written pattern.*

Figure 1: *Illustration of Pattern as Written*

Blanket Instructions

RECTANGLE

See Figure 2 for construction.

Make 8—4 each in color combinations AC (R-AC) and DE (R-DE), as shown in Figure 3. Instructions below are given for AC with DE in brackets.

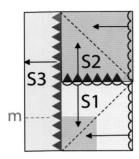

Figure 2: *Rectangle Construction*

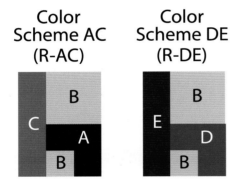

Figure 3: *Color Schemes for Rectangles*

Shape 1 (S1)

With A [D], CO 25, pm, CO 24—49 sts. Work [MS] until 25 sts rem.

Mitered Square (MS)

Row 1 (WS): Knit.

Row 2 (RS): Knit to 2 sts bef m, rm, cdd, pm, knit to end—2 sts dec'd.

Row 3: Knit.

Rep [Rows 2 & 3] for patt.

Cut A [D]. Attach B. Work [MS] until 1 st rem, ending on a Row 2. Cut yarn and fasten off.

Shape 2 (S2)

With B, CO 25 sts, pm, and starting at yellow triangle, pu&k 24 sts along the right side of the cast-on edge of S1 as shown in Figure 2 (1 st per cast-on st)—49 sts.

Work [MS] until 1 st rem, ending on a Row 2. Cut yarn and fasten off.

Shape 3 (S3)

On RS, attach C[E] at corner of S2 at the red triangle in Figure 2. Pu&k 24 sts along edge of S2 (1 per garter st ridge), and 24 sts along the edge of S1 (1 per garter st ridge)—48 sts.

Knit 23 rows. Pm before 12th st from end of row on the RS, at the color change of S1, marked by the red "m" in Figure 2. BO loosely and do not rm. Cut yarn and fasten off.

CHAIR

See Figure 4 for construction.

Make 8—4 each in color combinations AC (Ch-AC) and DE (Ch-DE), as shown in Figure 5.

Instructions below are given for Ch-AC with Ch-DE in brackets.

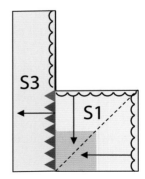

Figure 4: *Chair Construction*

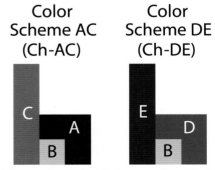

Figure 5: *Color Schemes for Chairs*

Shape 1 (S1)

Work Shape 1 (S1), as for Rectangle S1.

Shape 3 (S3)

With C[E], CO 24 sts. On RS of S1, pu&k 24 sts on edge (1 st per garter st ridge) starting at red triangle as shown in Figure 4—48 sts.

Work Shape 3 (S3) as for Rectangle.

UNITS (U1–U4)

Make 4—each Unit (U) is composed of 2 Rectangles and 2 Chairs as shown in Figure 6.

Arrange one each of R-AC, R-DE, Ch-AC, and Ch-DE as shown in Figure 6. Using long tails and whip st, sew tog along dotted lines, aligning bottom-left corners of Rectangles and Chairs with the m on edge of the adjacent S3.

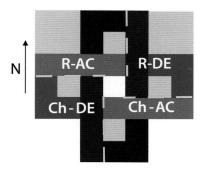

Figure 6: *Units*

Shape 4 (S4)

On RS, in the center of each U, attach B at red triangle in Figure 7. Working clockwise with dpns, *pu&k 11 sts to next corner, 1 st in corner and place on a dpn; rep from * 3 more times—48 sts.

Join in the round. Work [OS] until 8 sts rem. Rm's.

Outside-In Square (OS)

Worked in the round.

Note: *The cdd's use the last 2 sts from the current dpn and the 1st st from the following dpn; the final cdd crosses the BOR.*

Rnd 1: Purl.

Rnd 2: *Knit to last 2 sts bef end of dpn, cdd; rep from * 3 more times—8 sts dec'd.

Rnd 3: Purl.

Rep [Rnds 2 & 3] for patt.

Last Row: K2tog 4 times—4 sts.

Cut yarn, leaving a 10"/25 cm tail. Thread tail through tapestry needle and insert needle through all loops. Pull tightly and fasten securely.

SHAPE 5 (S5)

See Figure 8 for construction. S5 consists of a Cross and 4 Squares.

Cross

With A, CO 12 sts.

Rows 1 (RS)–24: Knit.

Rows 25 & 26: CO 12 sts at beg of row; knit to end—36 sts.

Rows 27–46: Knit.

Rows 47 & 48: BO 12 sts, knit to end—12 sts.

Rows 49–72: Knit.

BO loosely. Cut yarn and fasten off.

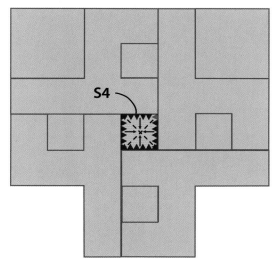

Figure 7: *Shape 4*

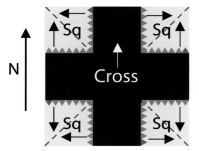

Figure 8: *Shape 5 Construction*

Squares (Sq)

On RS, in each of the four openings labeled "Sq" in Figure 8, attach F at the red triangle. Pu&k 12 sts to corner, 1 st in corner, pm, pu&k 12 sts to end of next edge—25 sts. Work [MS] until 1 st rem, ending on a Row 2. Cut yarn and fasten off.

ASSEMBLY OF U1–U4 AND S5

Arrange the four Units and S5 as shown in Figure 9, orienting shapes according to arrows. Using matching long tails and whip st, sew edges of S5 to edges of adjacent Units along dotted lines.

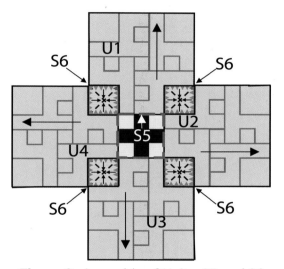

Figure 9: *Assembly of Units, S5 and S6*

Shape 6 (S6)

On RS, in each opening labeled "S6" in Figure 9, attach F at red triangle. With dpns, (pu&k 23 sts to next corner, 1 st in the corner and place on dpn) 4 times—96 sts. Work [OS] until 8 sts rem.

Next rnd: K2tog, 4 times—4 sts.

Cut yarn, leaving a 10"/25 cm tail. Thread tail onto tapestry needle and insert through all loops. Pull tightly and fasten securely.

Shape 7 (S7)

With B, CO 61 sts, pm, CO 60 sts—121 sts. Work [MS] until 49 sts rem.

Cut B, attach D. Work [MS] until 25 sts rem.

Cut D, attach B. Work [MS] until 1 st rem, ending on a Row 2. Cut yarn, leaving a long tail, and fasten off.

Assembly of S7 to Blanket Face

Lay out completed pieces as shown in Figure 10. Using matching long tails and mattress st, sew S7 shapes to adjacent shapes along yellow dotted lines.

BORDERS

Inner Borders

*On RS, attach B at right corner of one edge of blanket. Working counterclockwise, pu&k 204 sts to end of edge. See stitch counts to per edge shape on Figure 10.

Row 1 (WS): Knit.

Row 2 (RS): Kf&b, knit to last st, kf&b—2 sts inc'd; 206 sts.

Row 3: Knit.

Rows 4–15: Rep [Rows 2 & 3] 6 times—12 sts inc'd; 218 sts.

Cut B, leaving a 10"/25 cm tail. Attach G.

Rows 16–23: Rep [Rows 2 & 3] 4 times—8 sts inc'd; 226 sts.

BO loosely.

Cut yarn, leaving a 10"/25 cm tail.

Rep from * for other three edges of blanket.

Using matching long tails, and mattress st, sew corner seams tog.

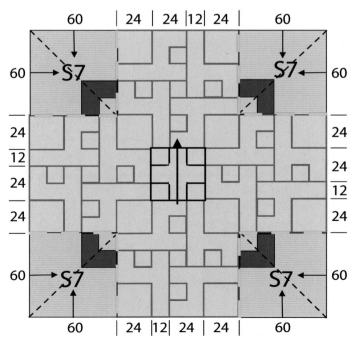

Figure 10: *Assembly of S7s to Blanket*

Outer Borders (OBs)

Make 4.

Each border is worked separately and sewn on. See Figure 11 for construction.

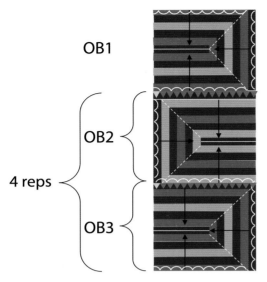

OB1

OB2

4 reps

OB3

Figure 11: *OB1, OB2, and OB3 Construction*

OB1

With A, CO 24 sts.

Rows 1 (RS)–3: Knit.

Row 4 (WS): Knit to end; pm; attach C; turn and CO 27 sts—51 sts.

Row 5: Knit to 2 sts bef m, rm, cdd, pm, knit to last 2 sts, ssk; pm; turn and CO 26 sts—74 sts.

Row 6: Knit.

Work [US].

> **U-Shape (US)** – used in Border—74 sts dec'ing to 0 sts
>
> Instructions for colors are given for OB1 & OB3, with OB2 in parentheses.
>
> ---
> ***Note:*** *Carry A bet uses and twist with working yarn at beg of each RS row. Cut and reattach C and B bet uses.*
> ---

Row 1 (RS): *Knit to 2 sts bef m, rm, cdd, pm; rep from * once more, knit to end—4 sts dec'd; 70 sts.

Row 2: Knit.

Rows 3–6: With A, rep [Rows 1 & 2] twice—8 sts dec'd; 62 sts.

Rows 7–18: Rep [Rows 3–6] 3 times, changing colors at the beg of each rep in the sequence B-A-C (C-A-B)—24 sts dec'd; 38 sts.

Rows 19–20: With A, rep [Rows 1 & 2]—4 sts dec'd; 34 sts.

Row 21: Knit to 2 sts bef 1st m, rm's, cdd twice, knit to end—4 sts dec'd; 30 sts.

Row 22: K15, turn, hold needles parallel with RS tog, and BO all sts using a 3-needle BO. Cut yarn and fasten off.

**OB2

With A, CO 25 sts, pm, pu&k 28 sts on L edge of OB1 beg at the yellow triangle—53 sts.

Row 1 (WS): Knit.

Row 2 (RS): Knit to 2 sts bef m, rm, cdd, pm, knit to end—2 sts dec'd; 51 sts.

Row 3: Knit to end; pm; turn, attach B, and CO 27 sts—78 sts.

Row 4: *Knit to 2 sts bef m, rm, cdd, pm; rep from* once more, knit to end—4 sts dec'd; 74 sts.

Row 5: Knit.

Work [US].

OB3

With A, on the right edge of OB2, pu&k 28 sts beg at the yellow triangle, pm, CO 25 sts—53 sts.

Row 1 (WS): Knit.

Row 2 (RS): Knit to 2 sts bef m, rm, cdd, pm, knit to end—2 sts dec'd; 51 sts.

Row 3: Knit to end.

Row 4: Attach C, knit to 2 sts bef m, rm, cdd, pm, knit to last 2 sts, ssk, pm, turn and CO 26 sts—74 sts.

Row 5: Knit.

Work [US].

Rep from ** 3 more times to make 3 additional sets of OB2s and OB3s.

Border Assembly

Arrange Outer Borders as shown in Figure 12. Pin and with A and whip st, sew Outer Borders to Inner Border edges along red dotted lines.

Figure 12: *Border Assembly*

Corners

On RS, in each of the corner openings labeled "CR" in Figure 12, attach A at green triangle.

Pu&k 28 sts to corner, 1 st in corner, pm, and 28 sts to next corner—57 sts.

Work [MS] following the color Stripe sequence in Figure 13 until 1 st rem, ending on a Row 2. Cut yarn and fasten off.

FINISHING

Attach B at top-right corner of blanket. With crochet hook, sc around edge of blanket, making 28 sts on each CR edge, 26 sts on each OB edge, and 2 sc's in each corner. When working on the CRs and OB2s, insert crochet hook through the garter st bump of the last st of the row. Weave in ends.

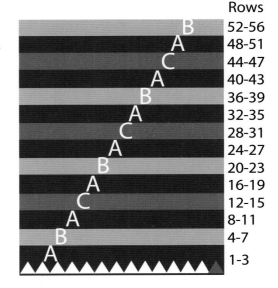

	Rows
B	52-56
A	48-51
C	44-47
A	40-43
B	36-39
A	32-35
C	28-31
A	24-27
B	20-23
A	16-19
C	12-15
A	8-11
B	4-7
A	1-3

Figure 13: *Stripe Sequence for Corners*

Tumbling

Rotating squares create the illusion of motion on this blanket worked in vibrant colors.

· ·

Technique

Size
56.5 x 56.5"/144 x 144 cm

Yarn
Cascade Yarns 220 Superwash, worsted (100% superwash wool; 220 yd./200 m; 3.5 oz./100 g):
A: 1 ball Blaze (orange) #1952
B: 1 ball Persimmon (red) #1921
C: 1 ball Christmas Green (green) #864
D: 1 ball Mint (light green) #1942
E: 1 ball Skyline Blue (medium blue) #884
F: 3 balls Banana Cream (light yellow) #1915
G: 8 balls Blue Velvet (dark blue) #813
H: 2 balls Caribbean (light blue) #847

Needles
US Size 7/4.5 mm, 40"/100 cm circular needles

Notions
Tapestry needle

Gauge
17 sts and 34 rows = 4"/10 cm in garter st

Notes
• This no-sew blanket is worked from the center out, starting with a center square. Each subsequent larger square is made by creating right triangles on each of the 4 sides of the previously worked square.
• When working stripes for Square H, carry non-working yarns up side of triangle.
• When picking up sts, pick up only on previous square and not on the corner of square made two steps previously.

Blanket Instructions

See Figure 1 for construction.

Square A
With A, CO 26 sts.
Knit 52 rows. Cut A and fasten off.

Square B
On RS, attach B. Knit 1 row, then work [Tr] until 6 sts rem, and work [Tr, Rows 1–3] once more—3 sts.
Next row: Sk2p—2 sts dec'd; 1 st.
Cut yarn and fasten off.
On RS, on each of the 3 rem sides of Square A, attach B at blue triangle and pu&k 26 sts along an edge of Square A (1 st for each garter st ridge). Work [Tr] as for 1st Triangle on Square B.

Triangle (Tr)

Row 1 (WS): Knit to last 2 sts, ssk—1 st dec'd.
Row 2 (RS): K2tog, knit to end—1 st dec'd.
Row 3: Knit to last 2 sts, ssk—1 st dec'd.
Row 4: K2tog, knit to last 2 sts, ssk—2 sts dec'd.
Rep [Rows 1–4] for patt.

Square C

On each side of Square B, working counter-clockwise, attach C at yellow triangle and pu&k 13 sts to the point where Square A intersects the edge, and 27 sts evenly to end of edge—40 sts. Work [Tr] until 5 sts rem, and then work [Tr, Rows 1 & 2] twice—4 sts dec'd; 1 st.
Cut yarn and fasten off.

Square D

On each side of Square C, working counter-clockwise, attach D at red triangle and pu&k 17 sts to the point where Square B intersects the edge, and 35 sts evenly to end of edge—52 sts. Work [Tr] until 2 sts rem, and then work [Tr, Row 1] once more—1 st.
Cut yarn and fasten off.

Square E

On each side of Square D, working counter-clockwise, attach E at red triangle and pu&k 23 sts to the point where Square C intersects the edge, and 47 sts evenly to end of edge—70 sts. Work [Tr] until 5 sts rem, and then work [Tr, Rows 1 & 2] twice—1 st.
Cut yarn and fasten off.

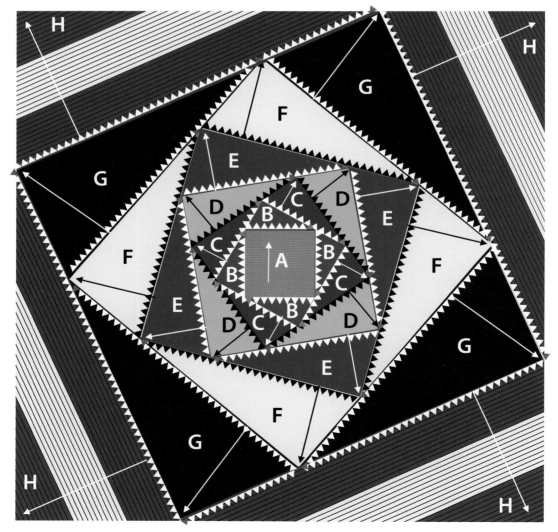

Figure 1: *Construction of Squares B–H (Each square is a set of four similarly colored triangles.)*

Square F

On each side of Square E, working counter-clockwise, attach F at red triangle and pu&k 31 sts to the point where Square D intersects the edge, and 63 sts evenly to end of edge—94 sts. Work [Tr] until 4 sts rem, and then work [Tr, Rows 1–3] once more—1 st.
Cut yarn and fasten off.

Square G

On each side of Square F, working counter-clockwise, attach G at red triangle and pu&k 42 sts to the point where Square E intersects the edge, and 84 sts evenly to end of edge—126 sts. Work [Tr] until 6 sts rem, and then work [Tr, Rows 1–3]—3 sts.
Next row: Sk2p—2 sts dec'd; 1 st.
Cut yarn and fasten off.

Square H

On each side of Square G, working counter-clockwise, attach H at red triangle and pu&k 56 sts to the point where Square F intersects the edge, and 112 sts evenly to end of edge—168 sts. Work [Tr], changing color at beg of RS rows, carrying nonworking yarn up side, as follows and shown in Figure 2.
Rows 1–43: Work 1 row with H, work 2 rows with G, [work 2 rows with H and then 2 rows with G] 10 times. Cut H—53 sts dec'd; 115 sts.
Rows 44–87: [Work 2 rows with F and then 2 rows with G] 11 times. Cut F—55 sts dec'd; 60 sts.
Rows 88–135: [Work 2 rows with B and then 2 rows with G] 12 times, working the final [Tr, Row 4] as [Tr, Row 2]—59 sts dec'd; 1 st.
Cut yarn and fasten off.

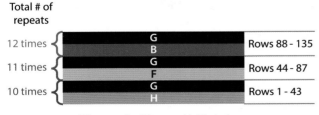

Figure 2: *Shape H Striping*

BORDERS

Left Border

On RS, attach G at top-left corner and pu&k 75 sts bet corner and the point where Square G intersects the edge, and 149 sts evenly to end of edge—224 sts.
Knit 15 rows. BO loosely and cut yarn.

Right Border

Work as for Left Border, attaching G at the bottom-right corner.

Top Border

On RS, attach G at top-right corner. Pu&k 8 sts on edge of Right Border, 75 sts bet the right corner and the point where Square G intersects the edge, 149 sts evenly to the end of the edge, and 8 sts on Left Border—240 sts.
Knit 15 rows. BO and cut yarn.

Bottom Border

Work as for Top Border, attaching G at the bottom-left corner.

FINISHING

Weave in yarn ends. Block to measurements.

Umbra

This mitered square and intarsia blanket uses shadows to create the illusion of three dimensions.

Techniques

Size
52.5 x 67"/133 x 170 cm

Yarn
Red Heart With Love, worsted (100% acrylic; 370 yd./338 m; 7 oz./198 g):
A: 1 skein Cornsilk (gold) #1207
B: 3 skeins White (white) #1001
C: 1 skein Berry Red (dark red) #1914
D: 1 skein Daffodil (yellow) #1201
E: 5 skeins Bluebell (medium blue) #1805
F: 2 skeins Minty (light aqua) #1932
G: 1 skein Bubble Gum (pink) #1704
H: 1 skein Tigerlily (tomato red) #1971
I: 1 skein Cameo (dusty pink) #1711
J: 1 skein Black (black) #1012
K: 1 skein True Blue (dark blue) #1814
L: 1 skein Iced Aqua (aqua) #1502
M: 1 skein Evergreen (spruce green) #1621

Needles
US Size 8/5 mm, 40"/100 cm circular needles, and 10"/25 cm straights

Notions
Stitch markers, bobbins, tapestry needle

Gauge
17 sts and 34 rows = 4"/10 cm in garter st

Notes
- The blanket is worked in zigzag-shaped strips that are sewn together. Strips are composed of a series of mitered squares that are picked up from the edges of previously completed squares. The mitered squares use intarsia to create the 3D effect. The border is picked up from the edges of the completed blanket face.
- Leave a 15"/38 cm tail at CO as indicated in Figures 1–4.

Tip: *Working Intarsia (used on Blocks and Half Blocks)*

Follow pattern instructions for introducing colors and transitioning between colors. When transitioning between colors, move both yarns to the WS of work. Working in garter st, this requires moving the yarns forward when working on WS rows and leaving yarns in the back when working RS rows. Twist the yarns around each other so they interlock, and then continue with the new color. Twisting yarns closes the hole that would otherwise form when transitioning between colors.

Blanket Instructions

Squares — Make 45

With each of the three color schemes S1–S3 in Figure 5, work 15 [Sq].

Square (Sq)—48 sts dec'ing to 1 st

See Figure 1 for Color Chart.

With C1, CO 24 sts. With C2, CO 24 sts—48 sts.

Row 1 (WS): With C2, knit to end of C2 sts, with C1 knit to end.

Row 2 (RS): With C1, knit to 2 sts bef end of C1 sts, ssk, with C2, k2tog, knit to end—2 sts dec'd; 46 sts.

Row 3: Rep [Row 1].

Rows 4–15: Rep [Rows 2 & 3] 6 times—12 sts dec'd; 34 sts.

Cut C1 & C2. Attach C3 at beg and C4 in center of row.

Rows 16–31: With C3 and C4, rep [Rows 2 & 3] 8 times—16 sts dec'd; 18 sts.

Cut C3 and C4. Attach C5 at beg and C6 at center of row.

Rows 32–47: With C5 and C6, rep [Rows 2 & 3] 8 times—16 sts dec'd; 2 sts.

Cut yarn and tie C5 & C6 yarns tog to fasten off.

Right Triangle (RT) — Make 3

With each of the three color schemes T1–T3 in Figure 6, work one [RT].

Right Triangle (RT)—24 sts dec'ing to 1 st

See Figure 2 for Color Chart.

With C1, CO 24 sts.

Row 1 (WS): Knit.

Row 2 (RS): K2tog, knit to end—1 st dec'd; 23 sts.

Row 3: Knit.

Rows 4–15: Rep [Rows 2 & 3] 6 times—6 sts dec'd; 17 sts.

Cut C1. Attach C2.

Rows 16–31: Rep [Rows 2 & 3] 8 times—8 sts dec'd; 9 sts.

Cut C2. Attach C3.

Rows 32–45: Rep [Rows 2 & 3] 7 times—7 sts dec'd; 2 sts.

Row 46: K2tog.

Cut yarn and fasten off.

Left Triangle (LT) — Make 3

With each of the three color schemes T4–T6 in Figure 7, work one [LT].

Left Triangle (LT)—24 sts dec'ing to 1 st

See Figure 3 for Color Chart.

With C4, CO 24 sts.

Row 1 (WS): Knit.

Row 2 (RS): Knit to 2 sts from end, ssk—1 st dec'd; 23 sts.

Row 3: Knit.

Rows 4–15: Rep [Rows 2 & 3] 6 times—6 sts dec'd; 17 sts.

Cut C4. Attach C5.

Rows 16–31: Rep [Rows 2 & 3] 8 times—8 sts dec'd; 9 sts.

Cut C5. Attach C6.

Rows 32–45: Rep [Rows 2 & 3] 7 times—7 sts dec'd; 2 sts.

Row 46: Ssk.

Cut yarn and fasten off.

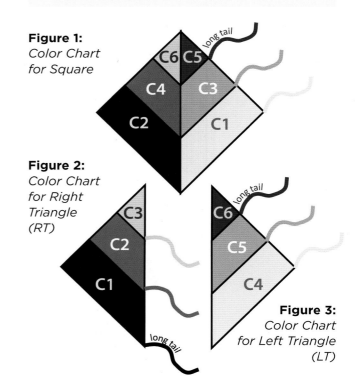

Figure 1: *Color Chart for Square*

Figure 2: *Color Chart for Right Triangle (RT)*

Figure 3: *Color Chart for Left Triangle (LT)*

STRIPS

Lay out Squares S1–S3 and Triangles T1–T6 as shown in Figure 8, orienting shapes according to arrows.

Strip 1 – Wedges

On RS, in space labeled "RW" in Figure 8, attach K to corner of first S1 at the red triangle. Pu&k 24 sts to next corner. Work [RW].

Right Wedge (RW)—24 sts dec'ing to 1 st

See Figure 4 for Color Chart.
Row 1 (WS): Knit.
Row 2 (RS): K2tog, knit to last st, kf&b.
Row 3: Knit.
Rows 4–15: Rep [Rows 2 & 3] 6 times.
Cut K. Attach E.
Row 16: K2tog, knit to last 2 sts, ssk—2 sts dec'd; 22 sts.
Row 17: Knit.
Rows 18–31: Rep [Rows 16 & 17] 7 times—14 sts dec'd; 8 sts.
Cut E. Attach L.
Row 32–37: Rep [Rows 16 & 17] 3 times—6 sts dec'd; 2 sts.
Row 38: K2tog—1 st dec'd; 1 st.
Cut yarn and fasten off.

On RS, in space labeled "LW" in Figure 8, attach E to corner of last S1 at red triangle. Pu&k 24 sts to next corner. Work [LW].

Left Wedge (LW)—24 sts dec'ing to 1 st

See Figure 4 for Color Chart.
Row 1 (WS): Knit.
Row 2 (RS): Kf&b, knit to last 2 sts, ssk.
Row 3: Knit.
Rows 4–15: Rep [Rows 2 & 3] 6 times.
Cut E. Attach F.
Row 16: K2tog, knit to last 2 sts, ssk—2 sts dec'd; 22 sts.
Row 17: Knit.
Rows 18–31: Rep [Rows 16 & 17] 7 times—14 sts dec'd; 8 sts.
Cut E. Attach L.
Row 32–37: Rep [Rows 16 & 17] 3 times—6 sts dec'd; 2 sts.
Row 38: K2tog—1 st dec'd; 1 st.
Cut yarn and fasten off.

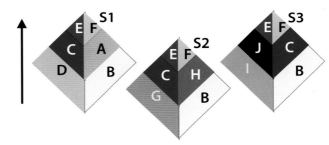

Figure 5: *Color Schemes (S1–S3) for Squares*

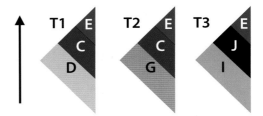

Figure 6: *Color Schemes (T1–T3) for Right Triangles (RTs)*

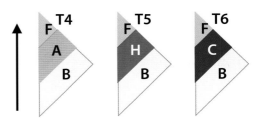

Figure 7: *Color Schemes (T4–T6) for Left Triangle (LTs)*

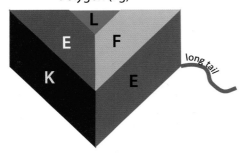

Polygon (Pg)

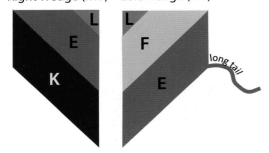

Right Wedge (RW)   Left Wedge (LW)

Figure 4: *Color Chart for Polygon (Pg) and Wedges (RW and LW)*

Strips 1 & 6 – Polygons

On RS, in each of the 15 spaces labeled "Pg" on Strips 1 & 6 in Figure 8, attach E at red triangle. Pu&k 24 sts to next corner; do not cut E. Attach K and pu&k 24 sts to next corner—48 sts. Work [Pg].

Using long CO tails, sew edges of shapes tog using whip st along the dotted white sew lines in Figure 8.

Polygon (Pg)—48 sts dec'ing to 1 st

See Figure 4 for Color Chart.

Row 1 (WS): With K, knit to last st of K, with E knit to end.

Row 2 (RS): Kf&b, knit to last 2 sts of E, ssk; with K k2tog, knit to last st, kf&b.

Row 3: Rep [Row 1].

Rows 4–15: Rep [Rows 2 & 3] 6 times.

Cut E and K. Attach F at beg and E at center of row.

Row 16: K2tog, knit to last 2 sts of F, ssk; with E k2tog, knit to last 2 sts, ssk—4 sts dec'd; 44 sts.

Row 17: Knit.

Rows 18–31: Rep [Rows 16 & 17] 7 times—28 sts dec'd; 16 sts.

Cut F & E. Attach L. Pm after 8th st.

Row 32: K2tog, knit to 2 sts bef m, ssk, k2tog, knit to last 2 sts, ssk—4 sts dec'd; 12 sts.

Row 33: Knit.

Rows 34–37: Rep [Rows 32 & 33] 2 times—8 sts dec'd; 4 sts.

Cut yarn, leaving a 10"/25 cm tail. Thread yarn through tapestry needle and insert through all sts on needle. Pull to tighten and fasten off securely.

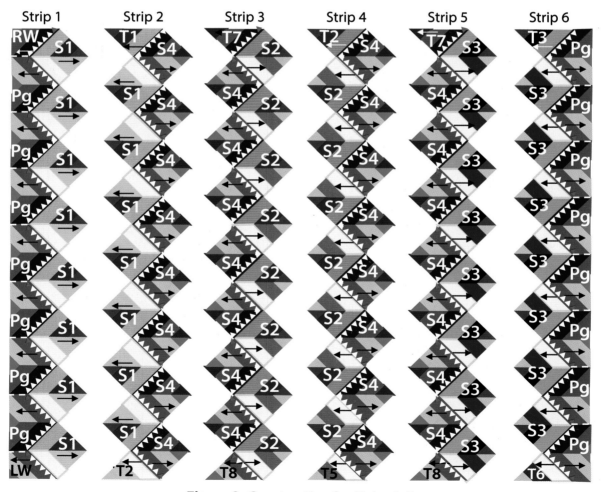

Figure 8: *Construction for Strips 1–6*

Strips 2–5 – Squares

In each of the spaces labeled "S4" on Strips 2–5 in Figure 8, attach E at red triangle. Pu&k 24 sts on edge of square to next corner; do not cut E. Attach K and pu&k 24 sts on edge of square to next corner—48 sts. Work [Sq], starting at Row 1 and using color scheme S4 in Figure 9.

Strips 3 & 5 – Triangles

In the 2 spaces labeled "T7" in Figure 8, attach K to corner of first S2 at red triangle. Pu&k 24 sts to next corner. Work [RT] using color scheme T7 in Figure 9.

In the 2 spaces labeled "T8" in Figure 8, attach E to corner of last S2 at red triangle. Pu&k 24 sts to next corner. Work [LT] using color scheme T8 in Figure 9.

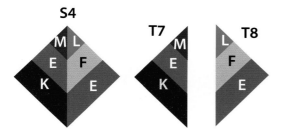

Figure 9: *Color Schemes for Strips 3 & 5 Shapes S4, T7, and T8*

ASSEMBLY

Using mattress st and long tails of matching color, sew adjacent strips tog along their zigzag edges, and aligning corners.

BORDERS

Top Border

On RS, attach B to top-right corner of blanket. Pu&k 13 sts on edge of Pg, 34 sts on each RT, and 27 sts on the edge of RW—210 sts.
Knit 13 rows. BO loosely.

Bottom Border

On RS, attach B to bottom-left corner of blanket. Pu&k 27 on LW, 34 sts on each LT, and 13 on Pg—210 sts.
Knit 13 rows. BO loosely.

Right Border

On RS, attach B to bottom-right corner of Bottom Border. Pu&k 7 sts (one per garter st ridge) on Bottom Border, 34 sts on each Pg, and 7 sts (one per garter st ridge) on Top Border—286 sts.
Knit 13 rows. BO loosely.

Left Border

On RS, attach B to top-left corner of Top Border. Work as for Right Border.

FINISHING

Weave in ends.

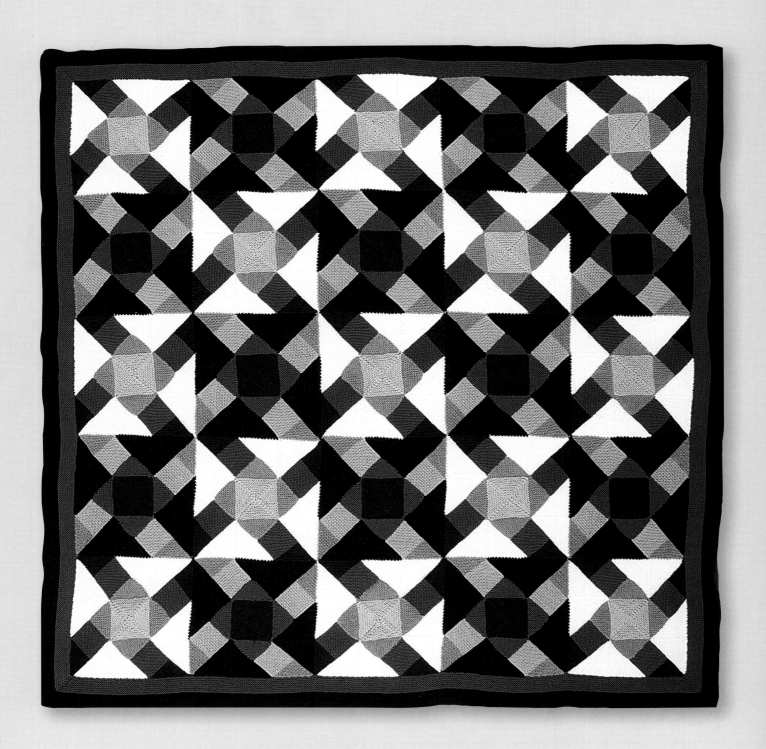

Verdant

Relax under this repeating pattern of pinwheels in soothing shades of green and blue.

Techniques

Method A: ▲ 🖊

Method B: ▲ 🖊 ♯

Size

55 x 55"/140 x 140 cm

Yarn

Lang Yarns Merino 120, light worsted (100% merino wool; 131 yd./120 m; 1.8 oz./50 g):

A: 3 balls (bright, mint green) #0174
B: 5 balls (avocado) #0297
C: 9 balls (teal) #0288
D: 4 balls (true blue) #0035
E: 7 balls (white) #0002
F: 5 balls (light lavender blue) #0021
G: 11 balls (dark navy) #0025

Needles

US Size 6/4 mm, 40"/100 cm circular needles and dpns (for Method B)

Notions

Stitch markers, tapestry needle

Gauge

23 sts and 46 rows = 4"/10 cm in garter st

Notes

- The blanket face is worked in blocks that are sewn together. There are two methods for making the Diamonds.
- Method A starts by working the center square back and forth. Stitches for the small triangles are picked up on the edges of previously completed shapes.
- Method B starts with the inner triangles and picks up stitches for the center square on the inner edges of adjacent triangles, working outside-in. Method B requires less picking up of sts and generates fewer yarn ends to weave in.
- There is a single method for making the Frame that completes each Block. The blocks are sewn together, and the borders are picked up and knit. Corner seams are sewn after the borders are worked.

Blanket Instructions

BLOCK

Make 25—13 in Color Scheme 1 (CS1) and 12 in Color Scheme 2 (CS2), following color chart in Figure 2.

A Block consists of a Diamond (worked with either Method A or Method B) and Frame.

Diamond

Method A

See Figure 3 for construction.

Square A (SA)

With yarn color specified in Figure 2, CO 19 sts. Knit 38 rows. Cut yarn. Do not BO.

Triangles (TA)

TA1

Attach yarn in color specified in Figure 2 at the red dot on the right point of TA1 in Figure 3.

Setup row (RS): Knit to end.

Work [TA]. Cut yarn and fasten off.

TA2–TA4

On each of the 3 rem edges of SA, attach yarn in color specified in Figure 2 at the red triangles in Figure 3. Pu&k 19 sts. Work [TA]. Cut yarn and fasten off.

Continue at **Frame.**

Triangle A (TA) – Method A—19 sts dec'ing to 1 st

Row 1 (WS): Knit.

Row 2 (RS): K2tog, knit to 2 sts from end, ssk—2 sts dec'd; 17 sts. Pm to identify RS.

Row 3: Knit.

Rows 4–17: Rep [Rows 2 & 3] 7 times—14 sts dec'd; 3 sts.

Row 18: Cdd—2 sts dec'd; 1 st.

Cut yarn and fasten off.

Block

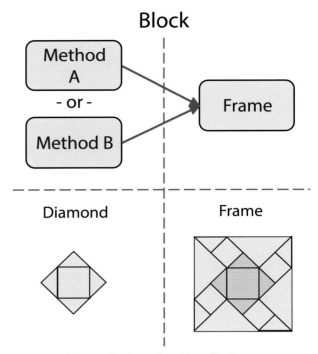

Figure 1: *Construction Options*

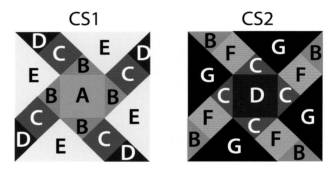

Figure 2: *Color Chart for Blocks*

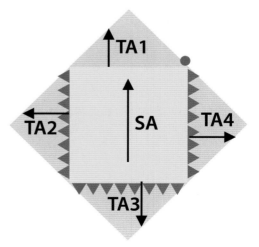

Figure 3: *Method A: Diamond Construction*

Method B

See Figure 4 for construction.

Triangles (TB)

TB1–TB4

With yarn color specified in Figure 2, CO 1 st. Work [TB] 4 times continuously. Cut yarn after TB4 and fasten off.

Triangle B (TB) – Method B—1 st inc'ing to 10 sts, dec'ing to 1 st

Row 1 (WS): Knit.
Row 2 (RS): Yoco, knit to end—1 st inc'd; 2 sts.
Rows 3–18: Rep [Rows 1 & 2] 8 times—8 sts inc'd; 10 sts.
Row 19: Knit.
Row 20: K2tog, knit to end—1 st dec'd; 9 sts.
Rows 21–36: Rep [Rows 21 & 22] 8 times—8 sts dec'd; 1 st.
Do not cut yarn.

Square B (SB)

With RS facing, arrange completed TBs as shown in Figure 4. Tie tog CO tail of TB1 to BO tail of TB4.

Attach yarn in color from Figure 2 at red triangle in Figure 4. Working clockwise, * with dpn, pu&k 17 sts evenly along long edge of first TB to next corner and 1 st in corner; rep from * 3 more times—72 sts. Work [OSB].

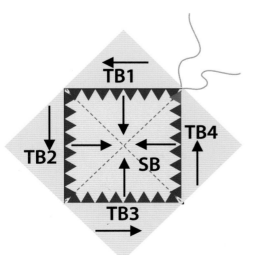

Figure 4: *Method B: Diamond Construction*

Outside-In Square (OSB) – Method B—72 sts dec'ing to 8 sts

Worked in the round.

Note: *The cdd uses the last 2 sts of one dpn and the 1st st of the next. The final cdd crosses the BOR.*

Rnd 1: Purl.
Rnd 2: *Knit to 2 sts bef end of dpn, cdd; rep from * 3 more times—8 sts dec'd; 64 sts.
Rnd 3: Purl.
Rnds 4–17: Rep [Rnds 2 & 3] 7 times—56 sts dec'd; 8 sts.
Cut yarn, leaving a 10"/25 cm tail. Thread tail through tapestry needle. Insert needle through all sts on needle. Pull tight and fasten off securely.

Continue at **Frame.**

Frame – Both Methods

See Figure 5 for construction.

Arms (AR1–AR4)

On RS, at orange triangle at the point of each
Triangle in Figure 5, attach yarn in color
specified in Figure 2. Pu&k 13 sts evenly along
edge of the Triangle to the black dot, where
the Square intersects the edge. Knit 25 rows.
Cut yarn. Attach yarn color specified in Figure
2, work [RT].

Right Triangle (RT)—13 sts dec'ing to 1 st

Rows 1 (RS) & 2 (WS): Knit.
Row 3: K2tog, knit to end—1 st dec'd; 12 sts.
Row 4: Knit.
Rows 5–26: Rep [Rows 3 & 4] 11 times—11 sts
dec'd; 1 st.
Cut yarn, leaving a 12"/30 cm tail, and
fasten off.

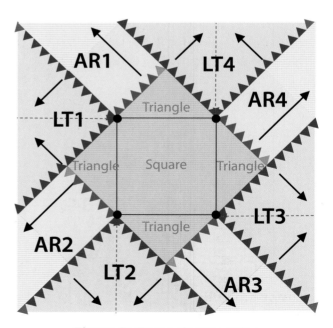

Figure 5: *Frame Construction*

Large Triangles (LT)

LT1–LT4

On RS, in each of the spaces labeled "LT" in Figure 5, attach yarn color specified in Figure 2 at the red triangle, leaving a 20"/50 cm tail. Pu&k 25 sts to next corner (black dot), 1 st on the corner of the Square, pm, and 25 sts to the next corner—51 sts. Work [LT].

Large Triangle (LT)—51 sts dec'ing to 1 st

Row 1 (WS): Knit.
Row 2 (RS): K2tog, knit to 2 sts bef m, rm, cdd, pm, knit to 2 sts bef end, ssk—4 sts dec'd; 47 sts.
Row 3: Knit.
Rows 4–23: Rep [Rows 2 & 3] 10 times—40 sts dec'd; 7 sts.
Row 24: K2tog, rm, cdd, ssk—4 sts dec'd; 3 sts.
Row 25: Cdd—2 sts dec'd; 1 st.
Cut yarn and fasten off.

ASSEMBLY

Arrange Blocks as shown in Figure 6. If Blocks were worked with Method A, orient SA so that the CO edge is at the bottom. Using long tails of LTs and RTs of matching color and whip st, sew blocks tog into 5 strips along dotted red lines, and then sew strips tog, matching block corners.

BORDERS

On RS, on each edge of the blanket, attach C and pu&k 57 sts along the edge of each Block (19 sts on the edge of RT and 38 sts along the edge of LT)—285 sts.

Row 1 (WS): Knit.
Row 2 (RS): Kf&b, knit to last st, kf&b—2 sts inc'd; 287 sts.
Row 3: Knit.
Rows 4–15: Rep [Rows 2 & 3] 6 times—12 sts inc'd; 299 sts.
Cut C, leaving a 10"/25 cm tail. Attach G.
Rows 16–31: Rep [Rows 2 & 3] 8 times—16 sts inc'd; 315 sts.
BO loosely. Cut G, leaving a 10"/25 cm tail.

FINISHING

Use long tails of Borders to sew corner seams tog with whip st. Weave in ends.

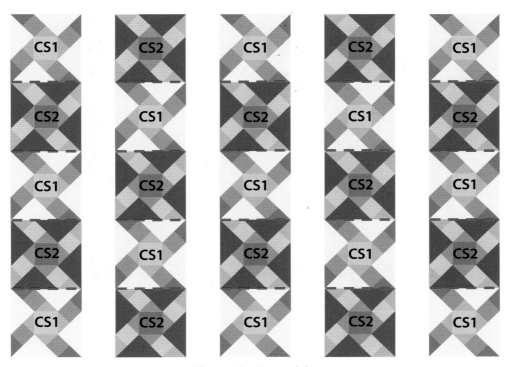

Figure 6: *Assembly*

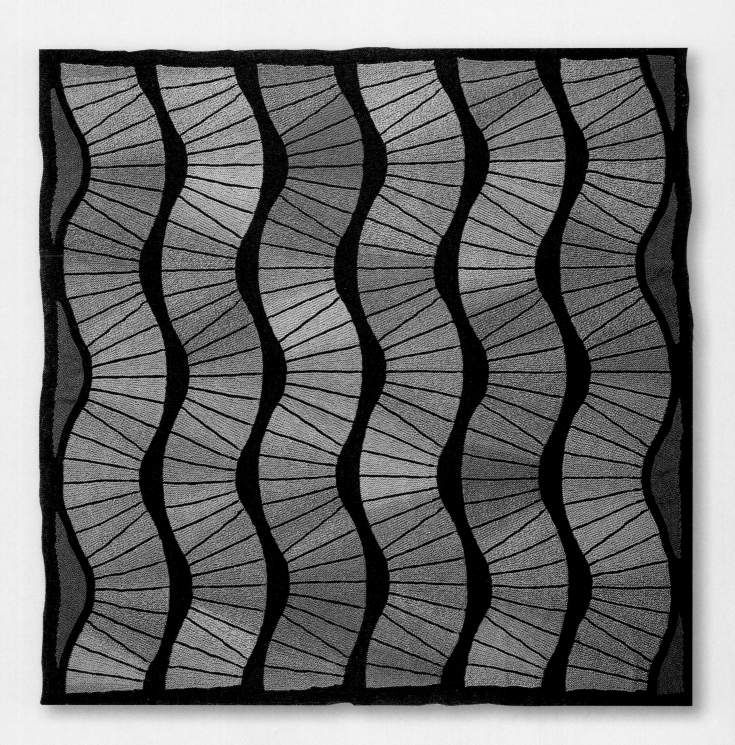

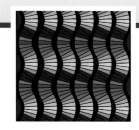

Waves

Graceful waves in gorgeous color-shifting hues make a striking piece for couch or bedroom.

Techniques

▲ ⊃ ⌢³ ⌣

Size

67 x 69"/170 x 175 cm

Yarn

Cascade Yarns 220 Superwash, worsted (100% superwash wool; 220 yd./200 m; 3.5 oz./100 g ball):

A: 8 balls Jet (black) #1913

C: 1 ball Plum Crazy (plum) #882

Cascade Yarns 220 Superwash Waves (100% superwash wool; 220 yd./200m, 3.5 oz./100 g ball):

B: 14 balls Spring (long repeating color shift of purple, blue and green) #114

Needles

2 Size US 7/4.5 mm, 40"/100 cm circular needles

Notions

Stitch holders, stitch markers, tapestry needle

Gauge

18 sts and 36 rows = 4"/10 cm in garter stitch

Notes

- This blanket is worked in strips using short rows to create the wave shape. A border is picked up on the right edge of each strip, and strips are joined using 3-needle BO. Stitches for the triangle inserts are picked up on the sides of the blanket. Borders are picked up on blanket edges.
- For wedges, carry colors A and B up the side edge bet uses; do not cut. When carrying a yarn across multiple ridges, loop the non-working yarn over the L needle from front to back at the beginning of each RS row, and then knit the first st on the L needle and the looped yarn together as for a k2tog.

Note: *The first two rows of W1 and W2 (in A) are referred to as the "separator."*

Blanket Instructions

Strips — Make 6

See Figure 1 for construction.

With A, CO 35 sts using a provisional CO.

*Work [W1] 3 times; work [W2] 6 times; work [W1] 3 times; rep from * two more times ("Rep 2" and "Rep 3" on Figure 1).

With A, knit 2 rows (the last "separator" of the strip).

BO loosely.

Wedge 1 (W1)—35 sts

Rows 1 (RS) & 2 (WS): With A, knit.

Row 3: With B, knit.

Row 4: Knit to last 5 sts, w&t.

Row 5: Knit.

Row 6: Knit to 9 sts bef wrap, w&t.

Rows 7–10: Rep [Rows 5 & 6] twice.

Rows 11–17: Knit.

Rows 18–26: Rep [Rows 4–12].

Figure 2: *Layout of Strips before Adding Borders and Joining*

Wedge 2 (W2)—35 sts

Rows 1 (RS) & 2 (WS): With A, knit.

Rows 3 & 4: With B, knit.

Row 5: Knit to last 5 sts, w&t.

Row 6: Knit.

Row 7: Knit to 9 sts bef wrap, w&t.

Rows 8–11: Rep [Rows 6 & 7] twice.

Rows 12–16: Knit.

Rows 17–26: Rep [Rows 5–14].

Lay out 6 Strips as shown in Figure 2.

ARCS AND JOIN STRIPS

See Figure 3 for construction.

Note: *When performing pu&k on strip edges, pu 12 sts on wide edge of each Wedge, 4 sts on narrow edge of each Wedge, and 1 st on each separator.*

When working Arcs at a Strip's edge, do not cut yarn until instructed.

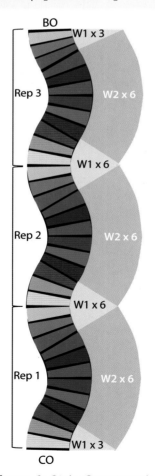

Figure 1: *Strip Construction*

Arcs—Strip 1

**On RS, attach A at red triangle at lower right corner of Strip 1. With circular needle, pu&k 1 st per garter st ridge to end at red square—325 sts. Pm after 29th (m1), 80th (m2), 137th (m3), 188th (m4), 245th (m5) and 296th (m6) sts on RS.

SH2

Work [SH2] bet red square and m6—2 sts dec'd; 323 sts.

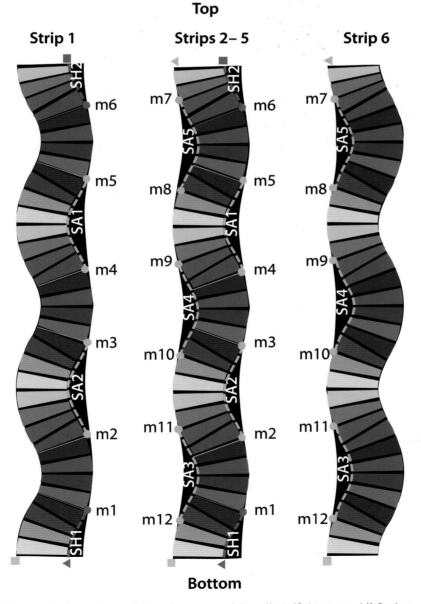

Top

Strip 1 **Strips 2– 5** **Strip 6**

Bottom

Figure 3: *Location of Small Arcs and Small Half Arcs on All Strips*

SA1

Knit to m5; work [SA] bet m5 and m4—4 sts
  dec'd; 319 sts.

Small Arc (SA)—57 dec'ing to 53 sts

Rows 1 (WS) & 2 (RS): Knit to 6 sts bef m,
  w&t—45 sts bet wraps.

Row 3: K13, k2tog, k14, k2tog, knit to 5 sts
  bef wrap, w&t—38 sts bet wraps; 2 sts
  dec'd; 55 sts.

Row 4: Knit to 5 sts bef wrap, w&t—33 sts
  bet wraps.

Rows 5 & 6: Knit to 3 sts bef wrap, w&t—27
  sts bet wraps.

Row 7: K10, k2tog, k2, k2tog, knit to 3 sts
  bef wrap, w&t—22 sts bet wraps; 2 sts
  dec'd; 53 sts.

Row 8: Rep [Row 5]—19 sts bet wraps.

Rows 9 & 10: Rep [Row 4]—9 sts bet wraps.

Row 11: K4.

SA2

Knit to m3; work [SA] bet m3 and m2—4 sts
  dec'd; 315 sts.

SH1

Knit to m1; work [SH1] bet m1 and end of row—2
  sts dec'd; 313 sts.

Knit 4 rows. Leave sts on needle. Cut yarn and
  fasten off.

Small Half Arc 1 (SH1)—29 dec'ing to 27 sts

Rows 1 (WS) and 2 (RS): Knit to 6 sts
  bef m, w&t.

Row 3: K13, k2tog, knit to end—1 st
  dec'd; 28 sts.

Row 4: Knit to 5 sts bef wrap, w&t.

Row 5: Knit.

Row 6: Knit to 3 sts bef wrap, w&t.

Row 7: K10, k2tog, knit to end—1 st
  dec'd; 27 sts.

Row 8: Rep [Row 6].

Row 9: Knit.

Rows 10 & 11: Rep [Rows 4 & 5].

Arcs—Strip 2

On RS, attach A at yellow triangle at upper left
corner of Strip 2. With 2nd circular needle,
pu&k 1 st per garter st ridge to end at yellow
square—325 sts. Pm after 26th (m7), 83rd
(m8), 134th (m9), 191st (m10), 242nd (m11) and
299th (m12) sts on RS.

SA3

Knit to m12; work [SA] bet m12 and m11—4 sts
dec'd; 321 sts.

SA4

Knit to m10; work [SA] bet m10 and m9—4 sts
dec'd; 317 sts.

SA5

Knit to m9; work [SA] bet m9 and m8, and then
knit to end—4 sts dec'd; 313 sts.
Knit 4 rows.

Joining Strips 1 & 2

Turn circular needles so that RSs of Strips are
tog, Strip 1 in front. 3-needle BO all sts. Cut
yarn and fasten off.

Arcs and Joining for Strips 3–6

Rep from ** bet Strips 2 & 3, 3 & 4, 4 & 5,
and 5 & 6.

Left Edge and Large Arcs—Strip 1

See Figure 4 for construction.
On RS, attach A at blue triangle at top-left
corner of Strip 1. Pu&k 1 st per garter st ridge
to end at blue square—325 sts. Knit 7 rows.
Pm after 13th (m1), 96th (m2), 121st (m3), 204th
(m4), 229th (m5), and 312th (m6) sts on RS.
With A, knit to m1.

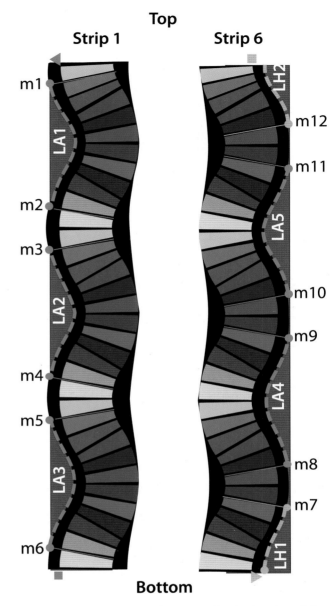

Figure 4: *Edges and Inserts for Strips 1 and 6*

LA1

Attach C and knit to m2. Turn and work [LA] bet m2 and m1. Turn to RS, cut C and with A knit to m3—13 sts dec'd; 312 sts.

LA2

Attach C and knit to m4. Turn and work [LA] bet m4 and m3. Turn to RS, cut C and with A knit to m5—13 sts dec'd; 299 sts.

LA3

Attach C and knit to m6. Turn and work [LA] bet m6 and m5. Turn to RS, cut C and with A knit to end—13 sts dec'd; 286 sts.

Large Arc (LA)—83 sts dec'ing to 70 sts

Rows 1 (WS) & 2 (RS): Knit to 3 sts bef m, w&t—77 sts bet wraps.

Rows 3–6: Knit to 3 sts bef wrap, w&t—65 sts bet wraps.

Row 7: K18, [k2tog, k4] 4 times, k2tog, knit to 3 sts bef wrap, w&t—57 sts bet wraps; 5 sts dec'd; 78 sts.

Rows 8–12: Rep [Row 3] 5 times—42 sts bet wraps.

Row 13: K9, [k2tog, k3] 4 times, k2tog, knit to 3 sts bef wrap, w&t—34 sts bet wraps; 5 sts dec'd; 73 sts.

Rows 14–18: Rep [Row 3] 5 times—19 sts bet wraps.

Row 19: K4, [k2tog, k2] 3 times, w&t—13 sts bet wraps; 3 sts dec'd; 70 sts.

Row 20: Rep [Row 3]—10 sts bet wraps.

Row 21: Knit to end.

Last Row (WS): With A, knit. Do not cut yarn; leave sts on needle. Rm's.

Right Edge, Large Arcs, and Large Half Arcs—Strip 6

On RS, attach A at yellow triangle at bottom-right corner of Strip 6. Pu&k 1 st per garter st ridge to end at yellow square—325 sts. Knit 7 rows.

Pm after 42nd (m7), 67th (m8), 150th (m9) 175th (m10), 258th (m11), and 283rd (m12) sts on RS.

Note: When working LH1 and LH2 with C, carry A up the side, twisting tog with C at edge.

LH1

On RS, attach C at yellow triangle, knit to m7. Turn and work [LH1] bet beg of row and m7. Cut C, turn to RS, and with A knit to m8—7 sts dec'd; 318 sts.

Large Half Arc 1 (LH1)—42 sts dec'ing to 35 sts

Row 1 (WS): Knit.

Row 2 (RS): Knit to last 3 sts, w&t.

Row 3: Knit.

Row 4: Knit to 3 sts bef wrap, w&t.

Rows 5 & 6: Rep [Rows 3 & 4].

Row 7: K18, [k2tog, k4] 2 times, k2tog, k1—3 sts dec'd; 39 sts.

Row 8: Rep [Row 4].

Rows 9–12: Rep [Rows 3 & 4] 2 times.

Row 13: K9, k2tog, k3, k2tog, knit to end—2 sts dec'd; 37 sts.

Row 14: Rep [Row 4].

Rows 15–18: Rep [Rows 3 & 4] 2 times.

Row 19: K4, k2tog, k2, k2tog—2 sts dec'd; 35 sts.

Row 20: Rep [Row 4].

Row 21: Knit to end.

LA4

Attach C and knit to m9. Turn and work [LA] between m9 and m8. Cut C. Turn to RS, and with A knit to m10—13 sts dec'd; 305 sts.

LA5

Attach C and knit to m11. Turn and work [LA] bet m11 and m10. Cut C. Turn to RS, and with A, knit to m12—13 sts dec'd; 292 sts.

LH2

Attach C and knit to end, turn and work [LH2] bet m12 and end. Cut C. Turn to RS and with A knit to end—7 sts dec'd; 285 sts.

Last row (WS): With A, knit to m10, bli, knit to end—1 st inc'd; 286 sts. Do not cut yarn; leave sts on needle. Rm's.

Large Half Arc 2 (LH2)—42 sts dec'ing to 35 sts

Row 1 (WS): Knit to last 3 sts, w&t.
Row 2 (RS): Knit.
Row 3: Knit to 3 sts bef wrap, w&t.
Rows 4 & 5: Rep [Rows 2 & 3].
Row 6: Knit.
Row 7: [K2tog, k4] twice, k2tog, knit to 3 sts bef wrap, w&t—3 sts dec'd; 39 sts.
Rows 8–11: Rep [Rows 2 & 3] 2 times.
Row 12: Knit.
Row 13: K5, k2tog, k3, k2tog, knit to 3 sts bef wrap, w&t—2 sts dec'd; 37 sts.
Rows 14–17: Rep [Rows 2 & 3] 2 times.
Row 18: Knit.
Row 19: K2tog, k3, k2tog, w&t—2 sts dec'd; 35 sts.
Row 20: Knit.
Row 21: Knit to end.

BORDERS

Left Border

On left edge of blanket, with A, knit 15 rows. BO loosely.

Right Border

On right edge of blanket, with A, knit 15 rows. BO loosely.

Top Border

On RS, attach A at top-right corner of blanket. Pu&k 301 sts as shown in Figure 5, along top edge of blanket. Knit 15 rows. BO loosely.

Bottom Border

On RS, attach A at bottom-left corner of blanket. Pu&k knit along arc and border edges as shown in Figure 5, and transfer from holder and knit sts from provisional CO of Waves—301 sts. Knit 15 rows. BO loosely.

FINISHING

Weave in ends.

Top Border

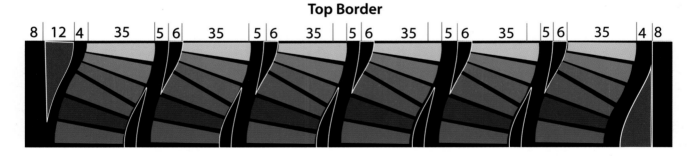

Bottom Border

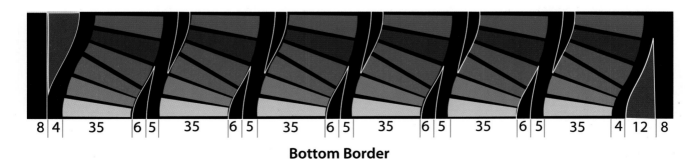

Figure 5: *Pu&k Sts along Top and Bottom Edges of Blanket*

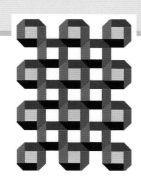

Weaverly

Shades of blues and reds intertwine to form the impression of a weaving.

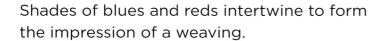

Techniques

Size
59.5 x 80.5"/151 x 204 cm

Yarn
Lion Brand Vanna's Choice, worsted (100% acrylic; 170 yd./155 m; 3.5 oz./100 g):
A: 4 skeins Silver Blue (very light gray-blue) #105
B: 3 skeins Burgundy (burgundy) #148
C: 3 skeins Scarlet (bright red) #113
D: 6 skeins Midnight Blue (deep blue) #118
E: 3 skeins Colonial Blue (medium blue) #109
F: 7 skeins White (white) #100

Needles
Two US Size 9/5.5 mm, 40"/100 cm circular needles, dpns, and straights (or shorter circulars)

Notions
Stitch holders or scrap yarn, stitch markers, tapestry needle

Gauge
14 sts and 28 rows = 4"/10 cm in garter st

Notes
- The blanket is assembled from octagons. Squares fill in the spaces between octagons. Hat shapes are picked up and worked to fill in gaps at blanket edge, and triangles fill the gaps at corners. The borders are picked up on the edges of the completed blanket.
- Since the edges of many shapes are transferred to holders and then not removed from holders until later in construction, use scrap yarn as holders rather than conventional stitch holders.

Blanket Instructions

Octagons

Make 18.

See Figure 1 for colors and Figure 2 for construction.

Square (S1)

With A, work [S1]. Cut yarn and fasten off.

Square 1 (S1)—20 sts

CO 20 sts.
Knit 40 rows.
Leave sts on needle.

Polygons (Pg1–Pg4)

Polygon 1 (Pg1)

With B, provisionally CO 16 sts, and place on R needle.
On RS, knit 20 sts of S1—36 sts.
Work [Pg]. Cut yarn and fasten off.

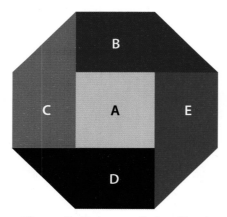

Figure 1: *Octagon Color Chart*

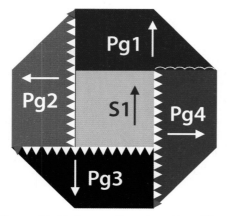

Figure 2: *Octagon Construction Chart*

Polygon (Pg)—36 sts dec'ing to 20 sts

Row 1 (WS): Knit to last 2 sts, ssk—1 st dec'd; 35 sts.
Row 2 (RS): Knit.
Rows 3–30: Rep [Rows 1 & 2] 14 times—14 sts dec'd; 21 sts.
Row 31: Rep [Row 1]—1 st dec'd; 20 sts.
Place sts on holder.

Polygons 2 & 3 (Pg2–Pg3)

Attach yarn color specified in Figure 1 at green triangle at upper left corner of last Pg in Figure 2. Pu&k 16 sts on left edge of Pg (one per garter st ridge) and 20 sts on edge of S1 (one st per ridge or CO edge)—36 sts. Work [Pg]. Cut yarn and fasten off.

Polygon 4 (Pg4)

Note: *The final Polygon (Pg4) has a perpendicular join at the left edge.*

On RS, attach color specified in Figure 2 at green triangle on corner of Pg3. Pu&k 16 sts on left edge of Pg3 (one st per garter st ridge) and 20 sts on right edge of S1 (one st per ridge)—36 sts.
Transfer 16 provisional sts of Pg1 to L needle—52 sts. Turn.
Work [Pg] over 35 picked up sts, and at the beg of each WS row, sl 1 provisional st to L needle and p2tog with the 1st [Pg] st.
Cut yarn, leaving a 25"/64 cm tail, and transfer sts to holder.

Inner Squares

Arrange the 18 completed Octagons as shown in Figure 3, oriented with Pg1 shapes at the top and Pg3 shapes at the bottom. Using long tail of each Pg4 and mattress st, sew octagons tog along yellow dotted lines.

On RS, in each of the 7 S2 Squares in Figure 3, starting at the black dot, work clockwise and transfer sts of each Octagon edge from holder to a separate dpn—80 sts. Attach F, work [OS].

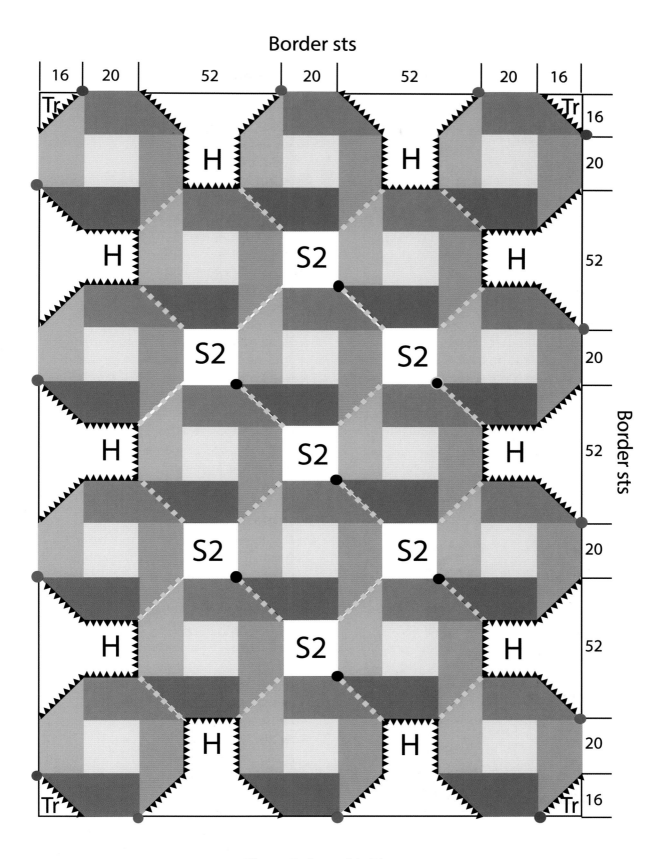

Figure 3: *Assembly Diagram*

Outside-in Square (OS)—80 sts dec'ing to 8 sts

Worked in the round on 4 dpns.
Rnd 1: Knit.
Rnd 2: Purl.
Rnd 3: K2tog, knit to 2 sts from end of dpn, ssk; rep from * 3 more times—8 sts dec'd; 72 sts.
Rnd 4: Purl.
Rnds 5–20: Rep [Rnds 3 & 4] 8 times—64 sts dec'd; 8 sts.
Cut yarn, leaving a 10"/25 cm tail. Thread tail onto tapestry needle and insert through all loops. Pull tightly and fasten off.

Hats

See Figure 3 for locations to work Hats and Figure 4 for detailed Hat construction.
On RS, in each of the 10 shapes labeled "H" in Figure 3, attach F at green dot. Pu&k 20 sts evenly to next corner, pm; *knit 20 sts from holder, pm, rep from * twice more, pu&k 20 sts evenly to next corner—100 sts. Work [Hat].

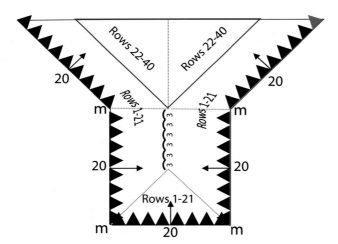

Figure 4: *Hat Construction*

Hat—100 sts dec'ing to 1 st

Row 1 (WS): Knit.
Row 2 (RS): K2tog, knit to 1 st bef 1st m, kf&b, *knit to 2 sts bef next m, ssk, k2tog, rep from * once more, knit to last m, kf&b, knit to last 2 sts, ssk—4 sts dec'd; 96 sts.
Row 3: Knit.
Rows 4–19: Rep [Rows 2 & 3] 8 times—32 sts dec'd; 64 sts.
Row 20: K2tog, knit to 1 st bef 1st m, kf&b, knit to 2 sts bef 2nd m, remove 2nd and 3rd m's, cdd, pm, cdd, knit to last m, kf&b, knit to 2 sts from end, ssk—4 sts dec'd; 60 sts.
Row 21: Knit to 2nd (now center) m. Rm all m's. Turn needles, tips together, with RS of work together. 3-needle BO 10 times, and then knit to end on WS—19 sts dec'd; 41 sts.
On RS, pm after 21st st.
Row 22: K2tog, knit to 2 sts bef m, rm, cdd, pm, knit to last 2 sts, ssk—4 sts dec'd; 37 sts.
Row 23: Knit.
Rows 24–39: Rep [Rows 22 & 23] 8 times—32 dec'd; 5 sts.
Row 40: Sl3 kwise, k2tog, pass 3 slipped sts over 1st st, one at a time—4 sts dec'd; 1 st.
Cut yarn and fasten off.

Triangles

On RS, in each of the corner triangular shapes labeled Tr in Figure 3, attach F at blue dot. Pu&k 20 sts evenly along edge. Work [Tr].

Triangle (Tr)—20 sts dec'ing to 1 st

Row 1 (WS): Knit.
Row 2 (RS): K2tog, knit to last 2 sts, ssk—2 sts dec'd; 18 sts.
Rows 3–18: Rep [Rows 1 & 2] 8 times—16 sts dec'd; 2 sts.
Row 19: Knit.
Row 20: K2tog—1 st dec'd; 1 st.
Cut yarn and fasten off.

BORDERS

Top Border

On RS, attach D at top-right corner of blanket.
Pu&k 16 sts on each Tr edge, 20 sts on each
Pg edge, and 52 sts on each Hat edge—196 sts
(see Figure 3). Knit 11 rows. BO loosely.

Bottom Border

On RS, attach D at bottom-left corner of blanket.
Rep as for Top Border.

Right Border

On RS, attach D at bottom-right corner of
Bottom Border. Pu&k 7 sts on edge of border
(1 per garter st ridge) and then 16 sts on each
Tr edge, 20 sts on each Pg edge, 52 sts on
each Hat edge, and 7 sts on border—282 sts.
Knit 11 rows. BO loosely.

Left Border

On RS, attach D at top-left corner of Top Border.
Rep as for Right Border.

FINISHING

Weave in ends.

Windfall

Imagine yourself swept up by leaves
carried in the breeze during stormy weather.

Techniques

▲ ⊃ ⤙

Size

55 x 65"/140 x 165 cm

Yarn

Berroco Modern Cotton, worsted (60% pima
  cotton/40% modal rayon; 209 yd./191 m; 3.5
  oz./100 g):
A: 4 hanks Bluffs (white) #1600
B: 4 hanks Mackeral (yellow-green) #1626
C: 4 hanks Goddard (navy blue) #1635
D: 2 hanks Wetherill (teal) #1665
E: 2 hanks Aquidneck Island (light blue) #1653
F: 1 hank Limpet (emerald green) #1657
G: 2 hanks Breakers (Kelly green) #1649
H: 2 hanks Matunuck (dark aqua) #1652
I: 2 hanks Salty Brine (light aqua) #1624

Needles

US Size 7/4.5 mm, 40"/100 cm circular needles

Notions

Tapestry needle

Gauge

16 sts and 32 rows = 4"/10 cm in garter st

Notes

- This blanket is worked in blocks. Each block
  has 7 shapes that are worked using short rows
  (tables detailing how to create these shapes
  are provided at the end of the pattern). Shapes
  1–4 are worked continuously and bound off
  after completing Shape 4. The stitches for
  Shape 5 are picked up on the curve formed
  by the left edges of Shapes 1–4 (see Figure 1),
  and Shapes 6–7 are worked continuously from
  Shape 5 to complete the block.
- The blocks are sewn together (see Figure 3);
  borders are added by picking up stitches from
  the edges of the assembled blocks.
- Blanket pieces are worked back and forth.

Blanket Instructions

BLOCKS

Make 30, one each in the color schemes in
Figure 2.

See Figure 1 for construction. A block contains
7 shapes numbered 1–7 and worked
consecutively.

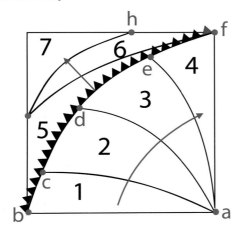

Figure 1: *Shape Identification in the Block*

Shapes 1–4

With yarn color for Shape and Block indicated
in Figure 2, CO 41 sts, leaving a 30"/75 cm tail.
Work [S1], [S2], [S3], and [S4] continuously,
changing colors as indicated. BO loosely,
leaving a 30"/76 cm tail.

Shape 5

On RS attach yarn for Shape 5 at blue triangle
at point **f** in Figure 1. Pu&k 16 sts bet **f** and **e**,
16 sts bet **e** and **d**, 19 sts bet **d** and **c**, and 9 sts
bet **c** and **b**—60 sts. Work [S5]. Cut yarn and
fasten off, leaving a 15"/38 cm tail.

Shape 6

On RS, attach yarn for Shape 6 at point **f**, leaving
a 15"/38 cm tail. Work [S6]. Cut yarn and
fasten off, leaving a 15"/38 cm tail.

Shape 7

On RS, attach yarn for Shape 7 at point **h**,
leaving a 44"/112 cm tail. Work [S7]. Cut yarn
and fasten off, leaving a 15"/38 cm tail.

ASSEMBLY

Lay out blocks as shown in Figure 3, oriented
according to arrows. Using tails of matching
color and whip st, sew blocks tog into
columns, and then sew columns together.

BORDERS

Right Border

On RS, attach B at bottom-right corner of
blanket. Pu&k 41 sts on the edge of each
block—246 sts. Knit 13 rows and then
BO loosely.

Left Border

Work as for Right Border, attaching yarn at the
top-left corner of blanket.

Top Border

On RS, attach B at top-right corner of Right
Border. Pu&k 7 sts on the border (1 per garter
st ridge), then 41 sts per block edge, and 7 sts
on 2nd border—219 sts. Knit 13 rows and then
BO loosely.

Bottom Border

Work as for Top Border, attaching yarn at the
bottom-left edge of Left Border.

FINISHING

Weave in ends.

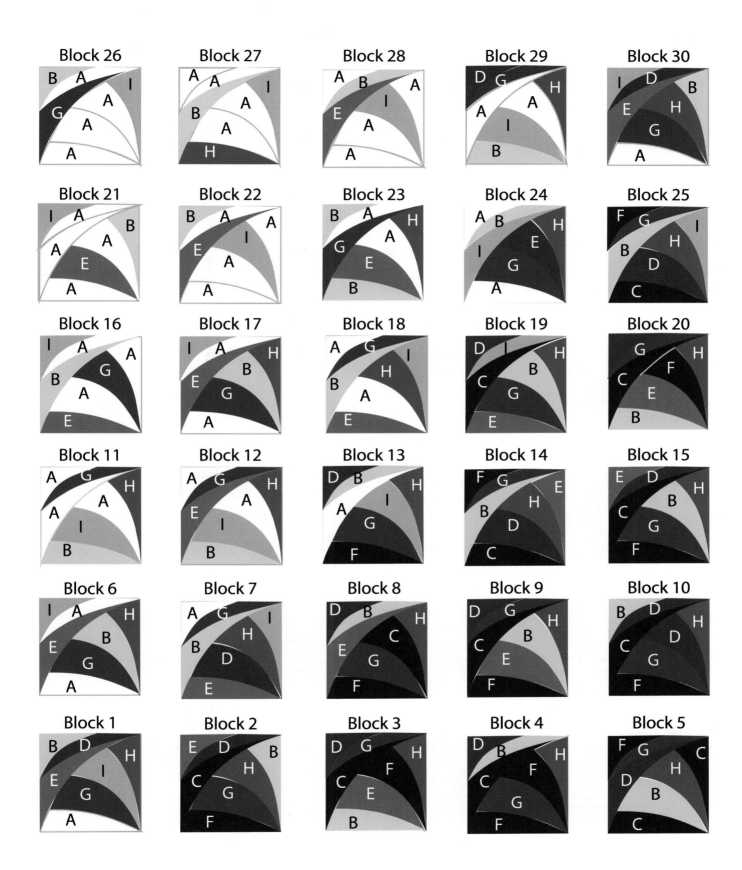

Figure 2: *Color Chart for Blocks 1–30*

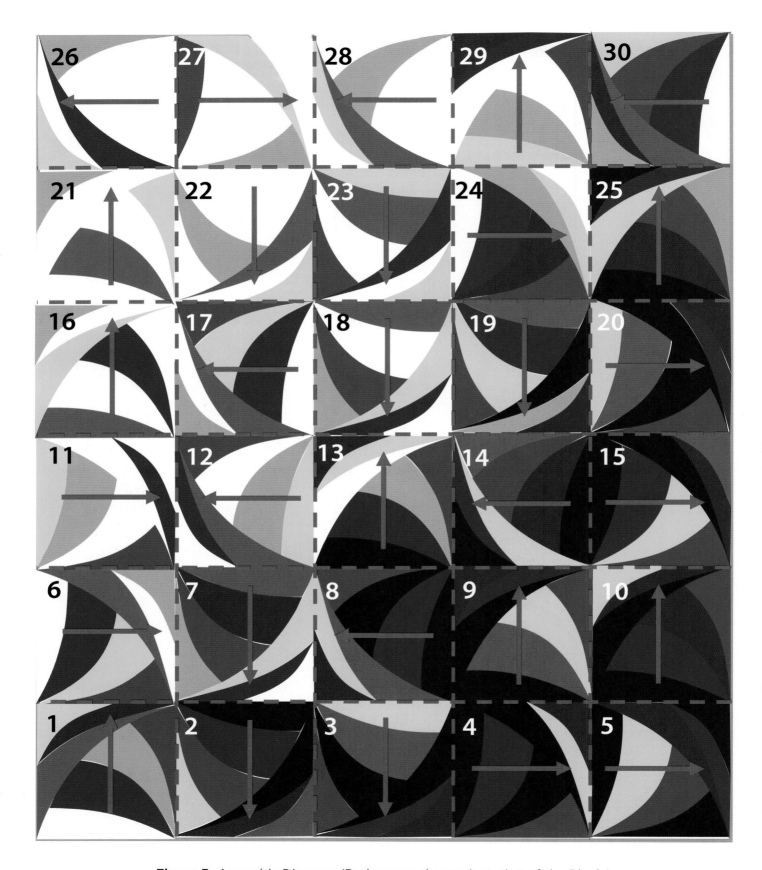

Figure 3: *Assembly Diagram (Red arrows show orientation of the Block.)*

How to Use the Tables

The detailed instructions for each Shape are given in its table. All use the following:

- If cell is **Blank**: Knit.
- If cell contains a number, **N**: Knit to [N] sts bef prev wrap, w&t.
- If cell contains **X**: Dec as specified.

The "# sts" column records the st count after completing pairs of rows where st count changes. To keep track of progress, use the cells in the "Blocks" area of the table to record completion of each RS/WS pair of rows for each of the 30 blocks.

Here is an example of how you work Shape 1. The bolded numbers are those indicated in the table, and the information in brackets reflects what is shown in the table for that row.

Shape 1 (S1)—41 sts dec'd to 38 sts

Setup row: Knit to last 3 sts, w&t.
Row 1: Knit. [Blank]
Row 2: Knit to **[2]** sts bef prev wrap, w&t. ["2" in Even column]
Row 3: Knit. [Blank]
Row 4: Knit to **[2]** sts bef prev wrap, w&t. ["2" in Even column]
Row 5: Knit to last 2 sts, k2tog—1 st dec'd; **40** sts. ["X" in Odd column]
Row 6: Knit to **[2]** sts bef prev wrap, w&t. ["2" in Even column]
Row 7: Knit. [Blank]
Row 8: Knit to **[3]** sts bef prev wrap, w&t. ["3" in Even column]
Row 9: Knit to last 2 sts, k2tog—1 st dec'd; **39** sts. ["X" in Odd column]
Row 10: Knit to **[3]** sts bef prev wrap, w&t. ["3" in Even column]
Row 11: Knit. [Blank]
Row 12: Knit to **[3]** sts bef prev wrap, w&t. ["3" in Even column]
Row 13: Knit to last 2 sts, k2tog—1 st dec'd; **38** sts. ["X" in Odd column]
Row 14: Knit to **[6]** sts bef prev wrap, w&t. ["6" in Even column]
Row 15: Knit. [Blank]
Row 16: Knit. [Blank]

Row # (RS)	Odd (RS) — X: Knit to last 2 sts, k2tog.	Even (WS) — Knit to [N] sts bef prev wrap, w&t.	Row # (WS)	# sts
Setup		Setup: Knit to last 3 sts, w&t		41
1		2	2	
3		2	4	
5	X	2	6	40
7		3	8	
9	X	3	10	39
11		3	12	
13	X	6	14	38
15			16	

Blocks—mark corresponding box to track completed rows (blocks numbered 1–30)

Shape 2 (S2)—38 sts inc'd to 41 sts, dec'd to 34 sts

Row #	Odd (RS) X: Knit to last 2 sts, k2tog.	Row #	Even (WS) Knit to [N] sts bef prev wrap, w&t.	# sts
1	(K9, bli) 3 times, knit to end—3 sts inc'd	2	Knit to last st, w&t	41
3	X	4	1	40
5		6	1	
7	X	8	1	39
9		10	1	
11		12	2	
13	X	14	1	38
15		16	1	
17		18	2	
19	X	20	2	37
21	X	22	2	36
23		24	2	
25	X	26	4	35
27	X	28	6	34
29		30		

Blocks—mark corresponding box to track completed rows (grid rows numbered 1–30, all cells blank)

Shape 3 (S3)—34 sts inc'd to 41 sts, dec'd to 32 sts

Rows	Odd (RS) X: Knit to last 2 sts, k2tog	Rows	Even (WS) Knit to [N] sts bef prev wrap, w&t.	# sts
1	K1, (k4, bli) 7 times, knit to end—7 sts inc'd.	2	Knit to last 3 sts, w&t.	41
3	X	4	1	40
5	X	6	2	39
7		8	2	
9	X	10	2	38
11	X	12	2	37
13		14	1	
15	X	16	2	36
17	X	18	1	35
19		20	2	
21	X	22	2	34
23		24	3	
25	X	26	4	33
27	X	28		32

Blocks—mark corresponding box to track completed rows (grid rows numbered 1–30, all cells blank)

Shape 4 (S4)—32 sts inc'd to 41 sts, dec'd to 35 sts

Rows	Odd (RS) X: Knit to last 2 sts, k2tog.	Rows	Even (WS) Knit to [N] sts bef prev wrap, w&t.	# sts
1	K1, (K3, bll) 9 times, knit to end—9 sts inc'd.	2	Knit to the last 4 sts, w&t.	41
3	X	4	5	40
5		6	5	
7	X	8	2	39
9		10	3	
11		12	3	
13	X	14	2	38
15		16	2	
17	X	18	2	37
19		20	1	
21		22	1	
23	X	24	1	36
25		26	1	
27	X	28	Knit to end, then BO all sts.	0

Blocks—mark corresponding box to track completed rows (grid, rows 1–30)

Shape 5 (S5)—60 sts dec'd to 42 sts

Rows	Odd (RS)	Rows	Even (WS) BO [N] sts, knit to . . .	. . . [N] sts bef prev wrap, w&t.	# sts
1	Knit.	Setup	1	5	59
3	Knit.	2	2	6	57
5	Knit.	4	2	8	55
7	Knit.	6	2	2	53
9	Knit.	8	2	3	51
11	Knit.	10	2	3	49
13	Knit.	12	2	3	47
15	Knit.	14	2	4	45
17	Knit.	16	2	3	43
		18	1	1	42

Blocks—mark corresponding box to track completed rows (grid, rows 1–30)

Shape 6 (S6)—42 sts inc'd to 46 sts, dec'd to 30 sts

Blocks—mark corresponding box to track completed rows

1	2	3	4	5	6	7	8	9	10	11	12	13	14	15	16	17	18	19	20	21	22	23	24	25	26	27	28	29	30

Rows	Odd (RS) BO [N] sts, knit to ...	... [N] sts bef prev wrap, w&t.	Rows	Even (WS)	# sts
1	(K8, bli) 4 times, knit to last st, w&t—4 sts inc'd.		2	Knit	46
3	3	2	4	Knit	43
5	3	3	6	Knit	40
7	5	3	8	Knit	35
9	5	8	10	Knit	30

Shape 7 (S7)—30 sts dec'ing to 0 sts

Blocks—mark corresponding box to track completed rows

1	2	3	4	5	6	7	8	9	10	11	12	13	14	15	16	17	18	19	20	21	22	23	24	25	26	27	28	29	30

Rows	Odd (RS) BO [N] sts, knit to end.	Rows	Even (WS) BO [N] sts, knit to end.	# sts
1	Knit 15, bli, knit to end—1 st inc'd.	2	2	29
3	2	4	2	25
5	2	6	2	21
7	2	8	1	18
9	2	10	1	15
11	2	12	1	12
13	1	14	1	10
15	2	16	2	6
17	1	18	1	4
19	1	20	1	2
21	1			0

Note: When binding off a wrapped st in Shapes 6 & 7, BO wrap and wrapped st separately: first knit and BO the wrap, and then BO the previously wrapped st.

ABBREVIATIONS

( )	a set of instructions to be repeated [Ex: (k2tog) 3 times is equivalent to: K2tog, k2tog, k2tog]; or numbers pertaining to other size or color options [Ex: Large (Small): CO 300 (250) sts, which is equivalent to CO 300 sts for Large and 250 sts for Small]
[ ]	the name of a pattern shape to be worked [Ex: Work [MS] is equivalent to: Work the pattern shape named "MS"]
beg	begin(ning)
bef	before
bet	between
bli	backward loop increase (see "Glossary")
BO	bind off
BOR	beginning of round
cc	change color
cdd	central double decrease: slip 2 sts as if to k2tog, k1, pass slipped sts over (2 sts dec'd)
CO	cast on
dec	decrease
dpns	double-pointed needles
inc	increase
k	knit
k2tog	knit 2 sts together (1 st dec'd)
k3tog	knit 3 sts together (2 sts dec'd)
kf&b	knit into the front leg of the next st, leaving it on the left needle; then knit into the back leg of the same st, and transfer the sts to the right needle (1 st inc'd)
kyok	(k1, yo, k1) into 1 st (2 sts inc'd)
kyokyok	(k1, yo, k1, yo, k1) into 1 st (4 sts inc'd)
L	left needle
m	marker

p	purl
p2tog	purl 2 together (1 st dec'd)
patt	pattern
pm	place marker
prev	previous
psso	pass slipped stitch over
p2sso	pass 2 slipped stitches over
pu	pick up
pu&k	pick up and knit [Ex: pu&k 10 sts]
pwise	purlwise
R	right needle
rem	remain(ing)
rep(s)	repeat(s)
rm	remove marker
rnd(s)	round(s)
RS	right side
sc	single crochet
sk2p	slip 1, knit 2 together, pass slipped stitch over (2 sts dec'd)
sl	slip
sl st	slip stitch (crochet)
sm	slip marker
ssk	slip 2 stitches knitwise, knit these 2 stitches together through back loops (1 st dec'd)
sssk	slip 3 stitches knitwise, knit these 3 stitches together through back loops (2 sts dec'd)
st(s)	stitch(es)
tbl	through back loop
tog	together
w&t	wrap & turn
WS	wrong side
yo	yarn over
yoco	yarn-over cast-on

GLOSSARY

backward loop increase (bli): With yarn in back, wrap yarn around left index finger, back to front, with yarn exiting to right. Insert R needle, right to left, under the front leg of the loop and slip loop off finger and onto R needle. Tighten yarn (1 st inc'd).

join-as-you-go: On RS row, work to last st, slip last st to R needle, insert R needle back to front to pick up the outside leg of the edge st of adjacent strip, slip this and slipped st to the L needle, knit these 2 sts together. Turn and work WS row as usual.

knit cast-on: Make a slipknot 6"/15 cm from end of yarn and slide loop onto L needle. *Knit st, leaving loop on L needle; slip new st on R needle back to L needle. Pull yarn to adjust tension. Rep from * to required number of sts.

mattress stitch for garter stitch: Bring together edges of pieces to be sewn, RS up. Tie yarn securely to starting point at the lower corner of the right piece. Thread tapestry needle with matching yarn color. Working on the RS, insert needle into the "bump" on the selvage edge on the left piece, and then insert the needle into the first garter st "bump" on the right edge. *Insert needle into next selvage garter st "bump" on left piece, and then insert needle into next selvage garter st "bump" on right piece; rep from * to complete the seam. Cut yarn and fasten off.

> **Note:** All needle insertions are from bottom to top of the garter st "bump" that is right on the edge of the fabric. If there are more "bumps" on one edge, pin edges together before starting and skip bumps as necessary on the piece with more bumps. After working two adjacent bumps, pull yarn to draw up some of the slack, but do not overtighten.

pick up and knit (pu&k): Attach yarn as specified by pattern. Working on the RS with a knitting needle or crochet hook of similar circumference, insert needle front to back through the edge of work and draw a yarn loop to front of work.

If working on the left or right side of a garter st piece, insert needle through the bump of the st at the edge, when possible, or the outside leg of the edge st. Change to a smaller needle or crochet hook if having difficulty inserting through bumps. If working on a CO or BO edge, insert the needle through 2 strands of yarn.

When picking up a large number of sts, divide the edge into equal length segments with markers. Divide the number of sts to be picked up by the number of segments, and assign to segments.

> **Note:** If working with a crochet hook, accumulate sts on the crochet hook's shaft, and then transfer them off the nonhook end to needle.

pinhole cast-on: To begin, wrap yarn around index finger twice, making a circle from front to back with working yarn hanging to front.

1. Using a crochet hook, insert hook into circle, bet yarn circle and finger.

2. Draw working yarn through center of circle then draw another loop through the loop on the needle, as for crochet chain st; 1st CO.

Rep steps 1 and 2 to add more sts to the crochet hook. Circle may be slipped off finger and held once a few sts have been created. When desired number of sts have been created, transfer sts one-by-one to dpns as instructed by patt. After several rounds are completed, pull tail to tighten center sts and fasten off securely.

provisional cast-on: Choose one of two methods:

Method 1—Traditional Crochet Chain: Using a crochet hook and contrasting yarn of the same weight as working yarn, make a chain with 2 times the number of sts as needed to be CO plus 1. Insert hook into the back "bump" of the 2nd chain st, draw working yarn through and transfer to needle. Rep in every 2nd back bump until the number of sts needed for the CO are on the needle. Begin knitting from these sts.

When provisionally CO sts need to become "live," undo the crochet chain from the end, 1 st at a time, and transfer sts to needle.

Method 2—Wrapping a Yarn: Use a piece of scrap yarn about 3 times the length of the edge to be cast on. With working yarn, make a slipknot in one end of the scrap yarn, and then lay scrap yarn parallel to the needle used for casting on, with the slipknotted end farthest from the needle tip. Wind the working yarn around both the needle and the scrap yarn snugly until there are the same number of winds on needle as needed for the cast on. Tie ends of the scrap yarn together. With working yarn, begin work.

Note: It may be easier to use the cable of an interchangeable needle set or a stitch holder in place of the scrap yarn.

purl backward: Do not turn work after RS row.

1. With the yarn in front, insert L needle into the front leg of the st on the R needle so the L needle is in front.

2. Wrap the yarn around the front of L needle and then bet the two needles. Pull the yarn backward to create tension.

3. Draw loop through st on R needle onto L and drop from R.

The new stitch should look like a purl stitch with yarn coming from the front leg of the stitch just created.

Rep steps 1–3 across row.

simple cast-on (aka loop cast-on): Start with a slipknot on R needle. Hold your needle in your right hand and use your fingers to keep the yarn tail out of the way. Grasp the working yarn in your left hand. Pass the working yarn around your thumb from back to front. Slip the needle tip under the loop around your thumb. Pull your thumb out of the loop and tug on the working yarn to tighten up the stitch.

single crochet for edging: Attach yarn, insert hook and draw through loop, chain 1, *insert hook through next edge st, and draw through a loop, yo and draw through both loops; rep from *.

slip stitch (crochet) for edging: Insert hook through next edge st. Bring yarn over hook from back to front. Draw the yarn through to the front and then through existing loop on the hook.

3-needle BO: Rotate R needle parallel to L needle, tips together, so that RS of work are together and WS are facing out. With a 3rd needle, BO sts 2 at a time, one from each needle as follows: Insert needle knitwise through 1st st on each of front and back needle, draw yarn through both sts, slip sts off needles onto 3rd needle. *Insert 3rd needle knitwise through next st on each of front and back needle, draw yarn through both sts, slip sts off needles (2 sts on the 3rd needle). Pass right st on R needle over left st; rep from * as specified in pattern instructions, and then return R needle to original position, turn work back to RS, sl rem st to R needle.

whip stitch for garter st fabric: Bring edges of pieces to be sewn together, RS up. Tie yarn securely to starting point on lower corner of right piece. Using tapestry needle threaded with matching yarn, *insert needle underneath next stitch leg on left piece of fabric, pull yarn through, and then insert needle underneath next stitch leg on right piece of fabric and pull yarn through. Rep from * until seam is complete.

wrap & turn (w&t) short rows: *Work to and including indicated st, slip next st pwise to R needle. Bring yarn to RS of work between needles, and then slip same st back to L needle, bring yarn to WS, wrapping st. Turn, leaving rem sts unworked, and then beg working back in the other direction. Rep from * until short rows are completed.

Note: It is not necessary to knit wraps and wrapped sts together in garter st.

yarn-over cast-on (yoco): Bring yarn over L needle and to front as for a yarn over, and then knit through the back of the yo (1 st inc'd).

ALTERNATE
BORDER METHODS

Either of these borders may be substituted for the standard garter st border specified in a pattern. Both are attached directly to the blanket and will use less yarn than the standard border.

The rate of attachment depends on the border and the edge to which it is attached. The I-cord border is attached every row and is stockinette: make 3 attachments every 4 stitches of blanket edge or 3 attachments every 2 ridges on the blanket edge. The Sawtooth border is garter st and is attached every other row: make an attachment every other stitch or every ridge. If the shapes at the edges of blanket face are diagonal, refer to the pattern to determine how many sts are pu&k on the shape's edge and use that as a guide. For the I-cord, multiply this number by 1.5 to determine the number of attachments. For the Sawtooth, use the number of pu&k for the number of attachments.

I-Cord Border

Worked clockwise around blanket edge, on WS. Using dpns the same size as used for blanket and with border color specified for blanket, CO 4 using a provisional CO. With WS of blanket facing, start with Row 1 at midpoint on one of the blanket edges.

Row 1: With yarn in back, insert L needle (containing the 4 sts) front to back through the next edge st, k2tog [1st st on needle and edge st], pull to eliminate slack yarn, knit to end, slide sts to the other tip of the needle.

Rep [Row 1] until the next blanket corner; work [Row 1] 2 times in each corner st to turn corner. Rep for other blanket edges. When reaching starting point, graft ends together.

Sawtooth Border

Worked counterclockwise on the RS of blanket.

If working CO or BO edge, pu only front loop. If working side edge, pu leg of edge st.

With RS of blanket facing and starting at midpoint of blanket edge, CO 4 sts using a provisional CO.

Row 1 (RS): Kf&b, knit to last st, [Join]—1 st inc'd; 5 sts.

Row 2 (WS): Knit.

Rows 3–10: Rep [Rows 1 & 2] 4 times—4 sts inc'd; 9 sts.

> Join: Sl last st to R needle, pu 1 st in selvage edge of blanket with L needle, sl last st on R needle back to L and k2tog last st and pu st.

Row 11: BO 5 sts loosely, knit to last st, [Join]—5 sts dec'd; 4 sts.

Row 12: Knit.

Rep [Rows 1–12] across blanket edge. Adjust attachment frequency so that a repeat is complete when the corner is reached. To turn the corner, make 6 joins (a full repeat of the pattern st) in the same corner st.

Rep border for other 3 blanket edges and on initial edge ending at starting point. Cut yarn, leaving a 10"/25 cm tail. Graft ends together.

I-cord Border (left) and Sawtooth Border (right). Yarn is Noro Silk Garden and Silk Solo provided by Knitting Fever.

SUPPLEMENTAL MATERIALS

Visit these sites for:

Pattern errata, tutorials, and additional content: http://www.theknitwit.org/geometric-knit-blankets

For questions, and to get additional materials such as charts for shapes not charted in the book, check the above website for answers and then contact the author at 30blankets@gmail.com

Please visit https://www.theknitwit.org/blog for news and updates.

 *Use this QR code to access video tutorials, charts, and additional bonus materials for this book.*

YARN SUPPLIERS

The following yarn companies have generously provided yarn for the sample blankets in this book. If a company provided yarn for more than one blanket, the number of blankets is specified after the company name.

Anzula
anzula.com
1001 N. Blackstone Ave, #101
Fresno, CA 93701

Berroco (2)
berroco.com
1 Tupperware Dr., Suite 4
N. Smithfield, RI 02896

Cascade Yarns (4)
cascadeyarns.com

Ella Rae Yarns
knittingfever.com/brand/
ella-rae/yarns
Knitting Fever Inc.
315 Bayview Ave.
Amityville, NY 11701

Erika Knight Yarns
erikaknight.co.uk

Jagger Spun Yarn
jaggerspunyarn.com
5 Water Street
Springvale, ME 04083

Knit Picks (2)
www.knitpicks.com

Lang Yarns
www.langyarns.com
Mühlehofstrasse 9
CH–6260 Reiden
Switerland

Lion Brand Yarn (2)
www.lionbrand.com
135 Kero Rd
Carlstadt, NJ 07072

Malabrigo Yarn (2)
malabrigoyarn.com
Montevideo, Uruguay

Paintbox Yarns provided by LoveCrafts
lovecrafts.com

Patons Yarn
yarnspirations.com/yarn

Plymouth Yarn
plymouthyarn.com
500 Lafayette St.
Bristol, PA 19007

Premier Yarns (2)
premieryarns.com

Red Heart Yarn (3)
yarnspirations.com

The Yarns of Rhichard Devrieze
Rhichard.com and
rhicharddevriezeyarns.com
495405 Veterans Road South
Holland Centre, Ontario
N0H 1R0, Canada

Sugarbush Yarns
sugarbushyarns.com
Listowel, Ontario, Canada

Universal Yarn
universalyarn.com
5991 Caldwell Park Drive
Harrisburg, NC 28075

Valley Yarns by Webs (2)
yarn.com/categories/
valley-yarns-knitting-yarn

ACKNOWLEDGMENTS

I am grateful to the following people who contributed so much to the book:

Vicki Egge for allowing us to take blanket photos at her lovely home.

My husband, Gerard Holzmann, for encouraging me to retire early and for his advice on book writing (not to mention doing the photography for this book!).

My brother, Wayne Smith; my editor, Candi Derr, from Stackpole Books; and my daughters, Natalie, Hannah, and Rachel Redberg and Tessa Holzmann, who helped me select the set of designs to include.

My mom, Elizabeth Smith, who patiently taught me to knit and sponsored many trips to Minnesota Fabrics during my adolescence to buy yarn for my projects.

Our dog, Ginny, who stayed by my side as I was working on this book and who eventually learned that she was not allowed to lie on the blankets while they were being measured.

Thank you to my technical editor, Natalie Delbusso, for applying her top-notch technical editing skills, making insightful suggestions, and being very responsive, and for all the little and big things she did to improve the patterns.

Sample Knitting

Thank you to the following talented individuals who knit the sample blankets for this book. The number of blankets made is included in parentheses after the names of those who made more than one blanket. The map shows the locations of the sample knitters.

Kate Agner
Julie Anderson (4)
Alan Berry
Kate Benco
Jill Fauble
Marie Franzosa
Linnette Grayum (2)

Rachel Herald
Phoebe Horton
Margaret Holzmann (4)
Erika Loftin
Ellen Lovell
Chaitanya Muralidhara
Vicki Noordhoek

Sonia Savoulian (2)
Sonya Stripe
Amy Tat
Becky Uchimura
Chantal Urrity
Lori Veteto (2)
Stacy Washington

A Map of the Sample Knitters' Locations